Studies on Asia
1965

Studies on Asia, 1965 is Volume VI in the series.

STUDIES ON ASIA, 1965

ROBERT K. SAKAI

Editor

PING-CHIA KUO
Southern Illinois University

FRANK N. TRAGER
New York University

ANDREW C. NAHM
Western Michigan University

JOHN H. BOYLE
Stanford University

JAMES SHIRLEY
Northern Illinois University

BARBARA TETERS
Iowa State University

JACKSON BAILEY
Earlham College

WILLIAM E. STESLICKE
University of Illinois

JAMES R. SOUKUP
University of Texas

HAROLD A. GOULD
University of Pittsburgh

KARL H. POTTER
University of Minnesota

WINSTON L. KING
Vanderbilt University

University of Nebraska Press
Lincoln · 1965

Publishers on the Plains

UNP

Copyright © 1965 by the University of Nebraska Press
Library of Congress catalog card number: 60–15432
All rights reserved
Manufactured in the United States of America

Contents

Introduction

With the escalation of military action in Vietnam the shadow of the People's Republic of China looms large and near. In dealing with her neighbors the Southeast Asian states, China at times adopts an attitude of reasonableness and of willingness to persuade; at other times she reveals the iron fist. Her persuasive influence in the long run must depend upon actual demonstration that the Communist way is best for underdeveloped economies. Professor Pingchia Kuo suggests that in fact the Chinese Communists have succeeded in embarking upon an industrialization program based upon the commune organizations. The achievements of mainland China, he believes, are substantial and will attract the attention of underdeveloped countries. Professor Kuo's study is his presidential address to the thirteenth annual meeting of the Midwestern Conference on Asian Affairs. Besides his popular book, *China: New Age and New Outlook*, he has contributed "Mao Tse-tung and China's 'Poor Peasants,' 1927–1957," in the 1964 issue of *Studies on Asia*.

On the military front the United States has played the leading role in checking communist expansion. The development of the American containment policy is discussed by Professor Frank N. Trager, and the present crisis in South Vietnam is viewed in the perspective of the larger cold war. Professor Trager's interpretations are noteworthy, not alone for timeliness, but also because they are the views of a veteran scholar and observer of Southeast Asian affairs. Since serving as U.S. Economic Aid Director in Burma, 1951–1953, he has made periodic visits to Southeast Asia, including one in 1964. He is a frequent lecturer for the Foreign Service Institute, Department of State, and for the various schools of the Army and Air Force. Among his extensive publications are "The Communist Challenge in Southeast Asia," in *Southeast Asia: Problems of United States Policy*, edited by William Henderson; "The Importance of Laos in Southeast Asia," *Current History* (February, 1964); "What Burma is Like," *Asia* (Spring, 1964); "Burma and China," *Journal of Southeast Asian History* (March, 1964); "Three Wars in Vietnam" (with G. K. Tanham), *Army* (May, 1964); "To Guarantee

vii

the Independence of Vietnam," *Christianity and Crisis* (November
2, 1964); and "Vietnam: Military Requirements for Victory,"
Orbis (Fall, 1964).

The severe impact of the West upon traditional Asian societies
in the nineteenth and twentieth centuries resulted in bitter factional
disputes and recourse to violent measures to attain political ends.
Such a consequence was produced when Korea was exposed to
Japanese and Western pressures. Professor Andrew Nahm closely
documents the actions of Korean "progressives" and "conservatives" and their relations with influential Chinese and
Japanese. Mr. John H. Boyle analyzes the role of the radical left
wing in Japanese politics with particular attention to its gyrating
policies toward the suffrage movement in the first quarter of this
century. The terms "left" and "right" as applied to factions within
the Kuomintang in China are discussed by Professor James Shirley.
It is his finding that the leftist label is a foreign importation which
is more misleading than appropriate when affixed to a person such
as Wang Ching-wei.

Professor Nahm is the author of a useful bibliographic study,
Japanese Penetration of Korea, 1894-1910 (Stanford University: The
Hoover Institution of War, Revolution, and Peace, 1959). Mr.
Boyle has had four years of experience in government service and
is presently studying for his Ph.D. degree at Stanford University.
The study of Wang Ching-wei and the Kuomintang left wing by
Professor Shirley is based on work at the University of California,
Berkeley, and abroad in Tokyo, Hong Kong, and Taiwan. Professor
Shirley's research was facilitated by a Ford Foundation Research
Fellowship.

Kuga Katsunan is the subject of Professor Barbara Teters' article.
Kuga she describes as a "liberal nationalist" who wished to preserve
the Japanese "national essence" by forming a constitution incorporating the principle of the separation of powers while at the
same time denying the validity for Japan of parliamentarism and
political party activities. While Kuga's early constitutional ideas
failed to materialize, another conservative institution did evolve,
not from theory, but from practice. This is the institution of *Genro*,
or "Elder Statesmen," consisting of a group of men, never clearly
defined, who exerted enormous influence in Japanese politics
especially in the first three decades of constitutional government.

Professor Jackson Bailey's careful investigation of the *Genro* is the first in a Western language, and as such, is a valuable contribution to the study of Japanese political history.

Professor Teters' work on Kuga is part of a larger study of *Nihon Shimbun* and those associated with it. She taught in a Japanese women's college in Tokyo, Seishu Joshi Daigaku, 1950–1951, and has returned to Japan for research in 1953–1955 and again in 1963. Professor Bailey has spent several years in Japan including tenure as Associate Executive of International House of Japan. He is a specialist on the last of the *Genro*. Among his writings are "Prince Saionji and the Popular Rights Movement of the 1880's," in *The Journal of Asian Studies*, Vol. 21, No. 1 (November, 1961) and "Prince Saionji and the Taisho Political Crisis, 1912–1913" in *Studies on Asia*, 1964.

Compared to the pre-World War II period when extremism and violence punctuated Japanese politics, contemporary parliamentary government in Japan has proceeded in relatively sedate fashion. Recent Japanese experience has led some observers to believe that democracy can be viable in Asia. Two studies of political pressure groups tend to support the belief that this is so in the case of Japan. The case study of the Japan Medical Association by Professor William E. Steslicke shows that the well-organized JMA does not exert an inordinate influence upon political leaders, and Professor James Soukup finds that "the Marxist assumption that business controls government and party leaders must be qualified if not discarded." Professor Steslicke's current research focus includes interest group politics and social security policy in contemporary Japan. From 1960 to 1963 as Ford Foundation Foreign Area Fellow he studied at the Universities of Kyoto and Keio. Professor Soukup is author of three articles on labor and politics in Japan found in the May, 1960 issue of *Journal of Politics* and in the January, 1960 and March/April, 1962 issues of *Orient/West*. He also has written "Comparative Studies in Political Finance: Japan," in *Journal of Politics*, November, 1963.

Traditional India, as are other areas of the world, is undergoing institutional and ideological modifications, although slowly and sometimes grudgingly. The nature of social change in India is the subject of anthropologist Harold A. Gould. By case studies he seeks to test the thesis that the extended family is dissolved by urban living and is replaced by nuclear, neolocal units. His limited samples indicate that such a mutation does not necessarily nor automatically come about. Professor Gould's findings, based in part on some three years of research in India, have been reported previously in the 1963 issue of this series.

A brief interpretation of Hindu thought and religiosity is provided by Professor Karl Potter, chairman of the department of philosophy at the University of Minnesota. He suggests that social institutions, such as the family or the castes, exist and are created to protect and preserve certain basic values and beliefs. On the other hand, Professor Winston L. King is interested in the new interpretations of saṁsāra which he detects in Theravada Buddhism, no doubt necessitated by the this-worldly emphasis of contemporary society. Professor Potter is General Editor of the forthcoming *Encyclopedia of Indian Philosophy* and is the author of several articles and two books on Indian thought, *The Padārthatattvanirūpanam of Raghunātha Siromṇi*, and *Presuppositions of India's Philosophies*. Professor King, a frequent contributor to *Studies on Asia* (1962, 1963, 1964), has written extensively on Buddhism including *Buddhism and Christianity* (1962), *In the Hope of Nibbana* (1964), and *A Thousand Lives Away* (for publication in 1965).

With the exceptions of the studies of Mr. Boyle and Professor Nahm, all of the articles in this volume were originally presented at the Midwestern Conference on Asian Affairs which met in October of 1964 at the University of Southern Illinois. It is hoped that the views expressed and the facts presented by the various authors will serve to stimulate and promote interest and scholarship in the various facets of Asian life.

Robert K. Sakai

Areas of Rising Interest in Chinese Studies*

PING-CHIA KUO

Southern Illinois University

I

Ever since the Communists came to power in China, the question of the interplay of Revolution and Tradition has been an absorbing subject for discussion among scholars. The prevailing school of thought equates the Communist revolution with extremism and China's traditional society with moderation. We are told that sooner or later the traditional moderation will exert a mellowing influence on Communism in China. Yet we have so far seen no evidence that the Communist rule is withering or weakening. In fact, Peking's control is more militant and more firmly entrenched today than ever before.

I believe that one of the most useful contributions that we can make toward a better understanding of China is a new appraisal of her traditional society. We need to recognize that the so-called traditional society means not just one thing but two different things. Communism has destroyed the Confucianist State, which was the privileged rule of the landlord-scholar-official group. This is the phase of the old order that has been swept away. But there is another, and more vital phase which we must not forget: namely, the continuing application of the teachings of Confucius.[1] The heart of Confucianism stresses man's place in society rather than the rights of the individual. It teaches that peace and order should be based on the maintenance of proper social relationships, the key to which is the observance of status and position. The Communist rule today derives its strength precisely from the implementation of these principles.

* Presidential Address delivered at the thirteenth Annual Meeting of the Midwest Conference on Asian Affairs, Carbondale, Illinois, October 23, 1964.

I

If we look at the interaction of the old and the new in this perspective, the continuity between Tradition and Revolution becomes very clear. There is the same emphasis on proper group behavior, on creative group endeavor, and on the subordination of the individual to the social order. This is the main stream of Chinese life and culture. Confucius understood it and championed it; so do the Communists. In November, 1963, a veteran British diplomat, Sir Fitzroy Hew MacLean, published a report on his visit to China in the *Saturday Evening Post*. I was deeply impressed by what he had to say. "China, to me," Sir Fitzroy wrote, "has a different feel from the other Communist countries I have been in. The Chinese have taken Communism to themselves and are making something very much their own out of it, something un-European, something particularly relevant to Asia. Chinese Communism does not seem to be an alien political system imposed from outside, but a system that the Chinese have evolved for themselves and are adapting ... to their own requirements ... and to those of their Asiatic neighbors." [2]

There is no question that moderation was a salient feature of the traditional Chinese way of life. But we must be careful not to take it out of context. Moderation was part and parcel of a paternalistic rule whose objective was to regulate the relations of man to man. Here we touch the heart of the question, that is, the Chinese type of authoritarianism. The paternalistic rule of the past and the Communist rule of today are alike in the expressions of this. [3] Chinese authoritarianism may be defined as a system of control over the life and work of the people, that neither grants liberty nor practices tyranny. It maintains that since the masses lack individual initiative, political democracy or economic laissez-faire cannot thrive on Chinese soil. It holds that the elite must lead and determine the objectives of group endeavor. At the same time, however, the Chinese type of authoritarianism keeps the use of violence to a minimum. Like the strong rulers of the past, the authorities in Peking consider forcible coercion, such as that used by Stalin in Russia, both ineffective and impermissible under Chinese conditions. [4]

In a historic speech in 1957, Mao Tse-tung said that the government indeed reserves the right to punish the enemies of the people for reaction, subversion, or any other violation of the principles of socialist construction. But aside from this, he urges persuasion and education as better instruments of government than coercion. [5] I think that here is a fertile field for scholarly investigation. The political philosophy of Mao is, in my opinion, the inescapable outcome of the sociological background of the country. We all know that the Chinese people are noted for their industriousness, for their patience, and for their great number. Because the Chinese people are industrious, the government has little need for using violence. Its greatest need is rather to plan for the people or to guide their industriousness toward desired channels of productive work. Also, because the Chinese people are patient, the government can carry out its decrees without opposition so long as they are within tolerable limits. Further, because the population is so congested and the margin of subsistence so close, the government on its part must avoid reckless measures which might jeopardize the people's incentive for production. So Mao's preferred formula is "to issue suitable orders of an obligatory nature." Here is perhaps the best example of the application of moderation within the framework of Chinese authoritarianism.[6]

Viewed in this light, the measures of the Communist regime fall into an instructive pattern. The entire nation accepts orders for hard work; yet there is little terror. Control is tight, but the methods used are not coercive. Former landlords and capitalists have been absorbed into the socialist state by a program of selective sentences to hard labor, the purpose of which is to "punish few and reform many." The public security bureaus are engaged in taking the census, maintaining registration forms, checking the people's movements, mediating neighborhood disputes, and mobilizing the masses for public welfare work. The government calls "study groups" to reason with the people, to explain the government's policies, and to inculcate the socialist way of life. It seems that once revolution is accepted in China, the effect of her tradition, far from blocking it, tends to expedite it by giving it the blessings of the national genius. Thus the government holds the initiative firmly in its changing relations with the people. The counter-offensive against the rightist intellectuals following the Hundred Flowers campaign is of course well-known. An even more significant situation has occurred more recently in the Communes. Since the summer of 1963, an end has been put to the relaxation of pressure on the peasants. Once again there are calls for reviving the Great Leap Forward and for an "economy owned by the whole people."[7]

The strategy of the leaders in Peking is to convert the people rather than to terrorize them, to encourage them to be more obedient rather than to destroy them for not being obedient enough. It is my belief that a useful reappraisal of the future of Communism in China should take these factors into primary consideration. To point our study in this direction will enable us to see how China's tradition "Sinifies" the practices of the revolution, not how it reduces the momentum of the revolution. Here lies the secret of the vitality of the new China. She has avoided the ruthless measures of the Stalinist type and replaced them with new versions of traditional statecraft, which at once meet the requirements of the land and give the revolution a sharper cutting edge. The outlook is that Communism in China will last longer without a thaw than that in Russia.[8]

II

The most momentous development in Asia today is not the confrontation of the United States and Communist China nor the ideological conflict between China and Russia. These problems belong to the realm of power politics among nations and do not directly affect the mass welfare of hundreds of millions of people. Fraught with lasting significance is the emergence of a new pattern of village economy in the 24,000 Communes in China. As we all know, the initial years of the Communes (1958–1961) were marred by administrative inexperience and natural calamities. As a result, a temporary retreat was ordered, especially in the agricultural operations which were restored to the smaller units of the producers' cooperatives. However, nothing can be farther from the truth than to say that the Commune movement has ended in failure. On the contrary, the functioning of the Communes has been greatly strengthened. Thus in September, 1962, at the Tenth Plenum of the Eighth Central Committee of the Chinese Communist Party, important decisions were taken to reaffirm and expand the collectivist principle of the Communes. And since the autumn of 1963, Communist Party publications have reopened discussions on the prospects of "transition to Communism."[9]

The real significance of the Commune movement, in my opinion, is the realization of a kind of subsidiary industrialization in the midst of agriculture. As we all know, a Commune is a hsiang-wide operation. As a unit of administration, the hsiang (or township) is centuries old and is thoroughly familiar to the people in the country. Larger than a ts'un (village) and smaller than a hsien (county), it is ideal in size to insure efficiency in controlling local industries, in undertaking the construction of irrigation works, in allocating capital investments for these projects, and in handling the purchase and distribution of rural commodities.[10] The past six years have proven that by integrating the labor force of the whole hsiang (township), a Commune can carry out large-scale construction projects without being handicapped by jealousies among the village cooperatives. Coordination of different industries is likewise better expedited by the Commune than by the producers' cooperatives. In the field of handicrafts, the larger unit of integrated labor and the control of minimal wage-payments in the Communes are conducive to mass production at low cost.[11] So while the government develops heavy industries in specific localities, a parallel drive is going on in the 24,000 Communes to promote subsidiary industries of all descriptions. This program of placing industry in the midst of agriculture certainly represents a challenging formula to awaken, mobilize, and transform China's vast underdeveloped countryside.

The greatest advantage of this program is that it helps reduce inflationary pressure. More than any other country, China (on account of her fast-growing population) needs to find a way to meet the consumer goods demands of her people without overstraining the limited capacity of her modern industrial plants. Of necessity, she cannot hope to follow the example of Western industrial nations or even of Russia. The establishment of a variety of small industries in the Communes seems to have provided the answer. Certainly a great part of the daily necessities of the rural masses is produced in their very midst. No industrial complexes have emerged to urbanize the countryside. Instead, milliards of small production units turn out goods to meet the basic needs of the population.[12] Eyewitnesses agree that except for the years of natural calamities (1959–1961), the supply of commodities has been ample and prices remarkably low.[13] Unlike the ruble, the jen-min-pi is stable. There is no need for devaluation or for replacing it with a new currency. Nor is it necessary for the government to increase note circulation or to resort to other painful measures to battle inflation.[14]

What gives added significance to the small industries trend in the Chinese villages is its relevance to a capital-poor country. Most of the projects are built in a short time with meager capital, but bring immediate (if modest) returns. Although the methods of production are unorthodox and do not measure up to modern Western standards, the telling fact is that they do meet local needs.[15] Paradoxically, products of Western specifications do not necessarily answer these needs. In any event, China's margin of growth lies precisely in these areas scorned by those using only the Western yardstick. If we are to understand China in this particular stage of her growth and if we are to grasp her impact on the rest of the world, we must not underestimate the idea of "walking on two legs"—a characteristic Maoist term meaning exploiting cheap native techniques as well as adopting the costly modern devices.[16]

Today, large numbers of low-cost furnaces and mines are in operation in the Communes. Fertilizer plants, instrument repair shops, and small machine shops are increasing in number. Self-made metallurgists (who have learned how to improve their methods at the backyard furnaces) are constructing electric furnaces which are small in size but produce high-quality steel. Handicraft shops literally cover the countryside. While each of these units has a limited production, the combined output of tens of thousands of them constitutes a powerful sustaining factor for the economy of the people. More significant still, these factories or shops are tied in with nearby towns by agreements to undertake construction work, to supply raw materials or repair parts, or to accept orders for specified finished products.[17] Thus a revolution of stupendous proportions is going on in China's villages. As the trend gains momentum, more and more nations in Asia and Africa will turn to study China's example. Of course, China's experience cannot be duplicated in every case. But there can be no doubt that this new pattern of village economy will change the economic and sociological outlook of a large part of mankind in the years ahead.

III

Our understanding of the transformation of the Chinese villages will not be complete without looking into the social revolution affecting the everyday life of the masses. In the wake of the call for increased production, there has been a new blossoming of the countryside as a result of elevating the social and cultural level of the people. This tremendous change deserves our attention because it has been brought about without depending on material increases in income. Last Christmas (1963), I received a letter from an Englishman in Swaziland, South Africa, whose task was to improve the educational and social conditions in the Bantu villages. His question was urgent and pointed: What is the secret that enabled the Chinese leaders to raise the living conditions of the masses despite their continued poverty? This correspondence was truly a revelation to me. It convinced me that systematic research in this field would be at once rewarding and imperative.

First of all, we need to evaluate all available data on the conquest of hunger and disease in the fifteen years of Communist rule. We all know that in the old days, many millions ate chaff and wild herbs, many others ate grass and bark, and many more either turned bandit or died of starvation or epidemic. Today these are things of the past. Eyewitness accounts of the Communes state that the people do not live in plenty. But with equitable food distribution, they do not have to starve; and no one is in debt.[18] The beggars or bandits of pre-Communist days are now gainfully employed; they live in huts with solid walls and under roofs that no longer leak.[19] In spite of the disastrous floods and droughts that lasted for three consecutive seasons (1959–1961), a robust recovery in the rural economy has been reported since the autumn of 1962.[20] How has it happened? What is responsible for the transformation? In April, 1964, Madame Lucie Faure, wife of the former French premier, after returning from China, wrote: "That every Chinese receive the minimum to enable him to subsist is the goal of the state, and the organization is basically efficient enough to see to it that distribution is equitable and everyone eats. Several products to be had in abundance are placed on open sale at certain seasons. In October, fruits and vegetables overflow the stands. As for clothing, all the Chinese I met had good shoes on their feet and warm clothing for winter."[21]

Next, let us take the battle against illiteracy. We all know that for many years Jimmy Yen and other education experts tried crash programs for mass education. But the Ting Hsien experiment has long been forgotten. The Communists have followed a more practical procedure. The campaign against illiteracy is carried out on the basis of mass mobilization, as an integral part of the drive for socialist transformation and socialist construction. Determined to speed up cultural progress in the villages at the same time as socializing agriculture, the Communist authorities have required everyone, young and adult alike, men and women alike, to receive some schooling in ad hoc classes, as a part of their work routine. Furthermore, a basic vocabulary (in simplified script) is taught to thousands of illiterate people in short but intensive classes. Upon completing the work, the students turn instructor to teach others the same basic vocabulary. It is officially reported that by 1970 every Chinese will have learned the most rudimentary reading and writing. Granting that the stress is on ideological indoctrination, a cultural stride on such a vast scale (changing 500 million people from illiterates to literate people in less than two decades) truly staggers one's imagination.[22]

I would also like to call your attention to the reports of recent travelers that describe the increasing modernization in China's rural areas. Formerly, schools were found only in hsien (county) capitals; now there is one school for every four or five ts'un (villages). Ninety percent of the children over seven years of age attend school. In every Commune, kindergarten-nurseries are well developed, thus enabling women to do productive work. At the same time, homes for the aged take care of old people who have no children to support them.[23] The great variety of local industries (such as slate and tile works, brick kilns, cart-and-animal transport service, fertilizer plants, carpentry shops, blast furnaces, small power plants, and telephone systems) makes it possible for the villagers to enjoy modern amenities which they never dreamt of before.[24] Telegraph and post offices, too, are available in every corner of the country. Radio broadcasting stations, shops and stores, public baths, and cinemas are found everywhere. Although the people's annual per-capita income remains extremely low (less than fifty dollars), their cost of living is kept at an unbelievable minimum. Brick apartments with terraces are in most cases rent-free. Electricity and utility charges are nominal. Medical examinations are free. Hospital beds cost twenty cents a day. Childbirth charge is three dollars. Sanitation and public hygiene, which were unknown to the peasants, are now part and parcel of their everyday living. The changes are far-reaching. New ideas spread fast. This is what I mean by elevating the social and cultural level of the people.[25] The changes not only make more intelligent citizens of the peasant masses, but they foster a better understanding between town and country and narrow the gap between the urban and rural points of view.

But most important of all, the changes demonstrate that cultural progress is possible without material increases in income. The many improvements described above were not retarded during the years of flood and drought and bad crops (1959–1961). Many things indeed cannot be achieved without capital. But there are also matters of great moment, in which capital is not the all-important factor; they are to be achieved through the successful mobilization of the spirit. In the social progress in China's vast countryside, the Communist leaders have found the key to unlock powerful forces of mass optimism and dedication.[26]

IV

There is yet another aspect in the development of Communist China which calls for careful study: namely, the winning of a genuine measure of decentralization. It is significant that as early as 1956 (only three years after the launching of the First Five-Year Plan), the Chinese Communist Party Congress made the decision that certain necessary commodities were to be produced in regional units in accordance with local supply and market conditions. Thus most of the enterprises formerly controlled by the central Ministries of Light Industry and of Food were placed under the control of the provincial authorities, while construction projects, transport projects, and small industrial projects were placed, one tier lower, under the control of the county authorities.[27]

In more recent years, along with powers of control, the local authorities have been given powers in the allocation of materials, in the management of enterprises, in making decisions for investment, and in controlling the movements of personnel. Further reflecting confidence in the loyalty of the local governments, powers have been delegated to them to float bond issues, to control the proceeds of certain taxes previously accruing to the Central Government, and to retain surplus profits obtained from the sale of their products. Under this system of "decentralized control within centralized planning," more than eighty percent of China's light industries and many of the small heavy industries have been turned over to the local authorities. As a result, the Central Government is able to concentrate on the development of the heavy industries (such as large mines, power installations, iron and steel works, heavy and precision machinery factories, oil refineries, etc.), on overall planning and coordination, and on the development of improved techniques.[28]

It may be recalled that shortly after he came to power, Khrushchev also moved to decentralize the economy of Russia. But his reorganization plan has not brought results comparable to those in China. Indeed, by cutting up the Soviet Union into a hundred economic regions and by placing each region under an economic council (sovnarkhoz), a decentralization in the execution of the central plan has been carried out. There is a notable reduction of red tape in Moscow's central bureaucracy. But what the Khrushchev plan has done for Russia is to break up the great horizontal monopolies and to replace them with a hundred regional economic councils each representing a collection of vertical monopolies. In the wake of this, new difficulties have arisen which threaten to deprive the reorganization of the true benefits of decentralization.

Specifically, there is a strong tendency for each region to strive for self-sufficiency. To quote one American economist who recently visited Russia: "The sovnarkhoz in the city of Moscow, for example, experienced difficulty in getting shipments of polyethelene from a factory in Stalingrad, which is, of course, under the jurisdiction of another sovnarkhoz. The solution of the Moscow sovnarkhoz was to allocate capital for a new polyethelene factory within its own economic region. The overwhelming factor in this decision was the supply problem in Moscow; little thought was given to the question of whether Moscow was the best location for such a plant, or whether, in terms of the entire economy, this was the best use of capital."[29]

By contrast, the Chinese program for decentralization stresses interdependence rather than independence. The Chinese slogan is: "Make the whole country into a chessboard." China's decentralized control within centralized planning is leading the country away from the autarchy of her villages. Between the Communes, fairs are organized to promote commodity exchanges. Municipalities are given jurisdiction over hinterland country to promote "mutual support" between industry and agriculture. Agreements for exchanges of products and services are entered into by neighboring provinces. There is also increasing cooperation between big state factories on one hand and rural Communes on the other—the Communes to receive technical assistance in return for doing processing or repair work for the state factories.[30]

What makes decentralization effective in China? The answers are many. Russia's sovnarkhoz program was launched twenty-eight years after the inception of the First Five-Year Plan. This was an attempt to break up the monstrosity of over-centralization (horizontal monopolies) after it was an accomplished fact. Chinese decentralization was ordered before such a monstrosity could come into being. Soviet decentralization is implemented by a specially created regional organ which in fact complicates the task. Chinese decentralization is carried out as a routine function of the regular provincial and county administrations.[31]

But the most important reason for China's success is the fact that her decentralization program has grown out of formulas and practices of proven value in the past. The Chinese Communists are clearly benefitting from experiences dating back to the 1930's. The Red bases in those years were widely scattered and unconnected. Operating as guerrillas, the Communists could not implement doctrinaire policies. Circumstances forced them to practice "dispersed industrialization" of the countryside. They improvised small munitions workshops, small coal and iron mines (crushing ore by hand), small paper, shoe, and soap factories, and factories to make simple clothes. It was manufacturing for survival. Some projects were run by the army; some by cooperatives; some by individuals. All had to yield quick returns with low investment and low construction costs. This historic ordeal, which was the unique experience of the Chinese revolution, seems to be paying dividends now in helping the Peking government to develop measures for achieving genuine decentralization.[32]

SUMMARY

To conclude, I have presented for your consideration four selected topics: (1) The nature of Chinese authoritarianism as a key to the understanding of the interaction of Revolution and

Tradition. (2) The small industries trend in the Communes as the harbinger of a new pattern of industrializing the villages without urbanizing them. (3) The social and cultural progress of the vast countryside as an achievement not contingent upon increases in income. And (4) The genuine decentralization of Chinese economy as a contrasting study alongside the sovnarkhoz program of Khrushchev.

Daily we hear all manner of generalizations about the rigid and oppressive society under the Peking regime and about the economic plight of the Chinese people. Much of this is no doubt true. But as scholars we dare not limit ourselves to a concern with ideological implications. We cannot close our minds to other aspects of a changing China which contain elements of strength. Each one of my topics touches upon a major phase in the rejuvenation of China. The social and economic changes that are slowly but surely taking hold may well have an importance reaching far beyond China's borders. The many new and underdeveloped nations are not searching for an ideology. They are looking for a workable master plan that will open the way to a solution of their own needs. They know that they will find it most readily in a country where the sociological background holds some resemblance to their own. China may well prove to be the country to point the way in this respect.

In a very real sense, the 1960's is a Development Decade for China even as it is for America. But the concepts and techniques are of necessity different. It seems to me that nothing is more important for us as scholars than to open up new paths of investigation in the direction of those differing concepts and techniques and to learn what is happening at the base of the ideological superstructure.

NOTES

1. For a fuller explanation of the need to differentiate between Confucianism and the Confucianist State, see Ping-chia Kuo, *China* (London: Oxford University Press, 1963), p. 34.

2. *Saturday Evening Post*, November 16, 1963.

3. To put it differently, Communism is moving in the traditional groove of Chinese civilization which was paternalistic and authoritarian. The most likely trend is not stopping Communism, but rather making out of it a Chinese type of authoritarianism rather than a Soviet type of authoritarianism.

4. See Guy Wint, *Common Sense about China* (London: Gollancz, 1960), pp. 31, 121; Ping-chia Kuo, *China: New Age and New Outlook* (Penguin Books, 1960), pp.

176–218; Simone de Beauvoir, *The Long March* (Cleveland: World, 1958), pp. 282–286; and Ping-chia Kuo, *China*, pp. 18–22.

5. Speech on "Correct Handling of Contradictions among the People."

6. Useful reference may be made to Chapters 6 and 7 of John Wilson Lewis (ed.), *Major Doctrines of Communist China* (New York: Norton, 1964).

7. H. Arthur Steiner has a succinct discussion of this trend in "China to the Left of Russia," *Asian Survey*, January, 1964, pp. 634–636. See also *The Red Flag* for July 10, 1963.

8. Former French Premier Edgar Faure made the following astute observation in 1958: "The Chinese state is by no means meek and mild, but it is economical to the point of miserliness of the human material at its disposal. It does not want to lose anyone who might serve it, even were it in the most menial manner. It may well be that such a system of repression, with its unforeseen changes and its penetentiary [sic] fantasies, attains a more realistic and rigorous control than the demonstrations of police force in other countries which are very much more evident and more offensive to our feelings." *The Serpent and the Tortoise* (New York: St. Martin's Press, 1958), p. 47.

9. *Asian Survey*, January, 1964, p. 635.

10. T. J. Hughes and D. E. T. Luard, *The Economic Development of Communist China, 1949–1960* (London: Oxford University Press, 1962), p. 69.

11. Alexander Eckstein wrote: ". . . it became clear by early 1958 that the collectives (officially referred to as agricultural producers' cooperatives of the advanced type) were too small in size and too large in number to serve as adequate instruments for administering and controlling vast labor projects; there were about 740,000 collectives averaging less than 200 households each. Communes, representing an amalgamation of close to 30 collectives with an average membership of about 4,930 households, proved much better suited to this purpose." See his article "On the Economic Crisis in Communist China," *Foreign Affairs*, XLII (July, 1964), 659.

12. *Ibid.*, p. 658.

13. Mervyn Jones, "Three Weeks in the Middle Kingdom," *Horizon*, VI, No. 3 (Summer 1964), 63.

14. Hughes and Luard, *The Economic Development of Communist China, 1949–1960*, pp. 55–56.

15. For a graphic description of this trend, see Edgar Snow, *The Other Side of the River: Red China Today* (New York: Random House, 1962), pp. 210–211.

16. Mervyn Jones, in "Three Weeks in the Middle Kingdom," has another phrase for this psychology—"an evenhanded dualism." See p. 60.

17. Hughes and Luard, *The Economic Development of Communist China, 1949–1960*, pp. 67 ff.; Snow, *The Other Side of the River*, p. 210; and Choh-ming Li (ed.), *Industrial Development in Communist China* (New York: Praeger, 1964), p. 22. Li wrote: "Among the basic points of the General Line put forward by the Party in May 1958 were . . . 'to develop, under centralized leadership and with overall planning, proper division of labor and coordination, centrally controlled industries simultaneously with local industries, large enterprises simultaneously with medium-sized and small enterprises,' and, as was added later, 'foreign methods' of production simultaneously with indigenous methods. . . . As a result, manufacturing

plants of all sorts sprang up all over the countryside. . . . By the autumn of 1959, some 700,000 workshops were found in operation among the 26,578 communes."

18. Mervyn Jones, in "Three Weeks in the Middle Kingdom," wrote about an early morning walk in Hankow: ". . . soon I was surrounded by about a hundred staring children. Not one was in rags; not one had running eyes, or sores on his face; not one looked skinny or underfed. There may have been hunger in the critical years of 1959 and 1960, and there may be hunger now in remote places away from the main railroad lines. But I saw no hunger in days of walking round the towns and more days of travel by slow train the length of China. The rice ration —I finally got the figures, and checked them elsewhere—is twenty kilos, or forty-four pounds, a month. The meat ration is normally one or one and a half pounds a month; most Chinese have a vegetable diet. Chickens, fish, and eggs are unrationed and always seemed to be plentiful. Prices are high in terms of wages, but not impossibly so. On a railroad platform, you could buy a whole roast duck for two yuan—$1.25 on the exchange rate, and about half a day's [Chinese] wage. I never saw a queue for food, other than a dozen people waiting to be served at the numerous little stalls that sell cakes and snacks." See p. 62.

19. David Crook, *The Manchester Guardian*, May 9, 1963.

20. Fang Chung, "All-round Improvement in China's Economy," *Peking Review*, August 23, 1963. In an interesting commentary on this article, Michael Freeberne wrote: "But the evidence suggests that Chinese progress in 1963 is something more substantial, and, furthermore, there are indications that Chinese confidence is becoming inflated in an aggressive sense. Two extremities present themselves: first, and perhaps the least likely, that this militancy will turn outwards and seek territorial aggrandizement; secondly, that this same force will turn inwards and that the energy it generates will be harnessed in some new leap forward; this latter possibility could conceivably take place before the end of the Third Five-Year Plan. This domestic upheaval is not imminent, and the launching of such a project would be dependent upon at least one more good harvest in 1964. In fact, the probable course of events is likely to lie between these extremities: a foreign policy which concedes nothing, and a stubborn, austere and unremitting internal effort." *Tijdschrift voor Econ. en Soc. Geografie*, August–September 1964, pp. 197–198.

21. Report written for France-Soir and Opera Mundi. Abbreviated version in the *Southern Illinoisan*, April 10, 1964.

22. On this subject, the U.S. Office of Education has recently issued two excellent studies: Robert D. Barendsen, *Half-Work Half-Study Schools in Communist China*; and Paul Harper, *Spare-Time Education for Workers in Communist China*. Both were published by Government Printing Office in Washington, D.C. in 1964. See also Beauvoir, *The Long March*, pp. 243–245.

23. Snow, *The Other Side of the River*, pp. 482–491; Frederick Nossal, *Dateline—Peking* (New York: Harcourt Brace & World, 1963), p. 76.

24. Snow, *The Other Side of the River*, pp. 480–481.

25. *Ibid.*, p. 541. Mr. Snow's assertions are supported by many other eye-witness accounts, most recently by that of the Canadian correspondent Richard Harrington. See his "Report from Inside Red China," *Parade*, November 29, 1964.

26. For a dramatic description of the transplanting of a mountain by means of

straw baskets and bamboo poles, see R. M. Fox, *China Diary* (London: Robert Hale, 1959), pp. 153–154. Mr. Mervyn Jones, in "Three Weeks in the Middle Kingdom," makes this interesting observation: China's "innumerable mouths—or at all events most of them—are also hands. While Soviet Russia has always had to contend with an acute labor shortage, China has labor enough and to spare. . . . If one were to walk out of the People's Central Department Store in Peking and travel westward across the Communist world, one would reach Prague before finding another store so well filled with consumer goods." See p. 63.

27. Hughes and Luard, *The Economic Development of Communist China, 1949–1960*, pp. 59–60.

28. *Ibid.*, pp. 61–63; see also Li (ed.), *Industrial Development in Communist China*, p. 24.

29. Francis M. Boddy, "Soviet Economic Growth," in Robert T. Holt and John E. Turner (eds.), *Soviet Union: Paradox and Change* (New York, Holt, 1962), pp. 83–84.

30. Hughes and Luard, *The Economic Development of Communist China, 1949–1960*, pp. 73–74.

31. In an article entitled "Centralization versus Decentralization in Mainland China and the Soviet Union," Dwight H. Perkins draws the following conclusion: ". . . there is a greater tendency in China to experiment with various forms of decentralization. In the agricultural sector, this is the result of the much lower per capita income and the comparative surplus of labor which exist in Mainland China. In industry, it is a result of the relatively greater importance and large number of small-scale industries using disparate and comparatively primitive technology. The Soviet Union, in contrast, has stuck closely to centralized controls even though this has become increasingly difficult as the economy has become more complex." *The Annals* of the American Academy of Political and Social Science, Vol. 349 (September 1963), p. 70.

32. Ping-chia Kuo, *China: New Age and New Outlook*, Chapter II.

American Foreign Policy in Southeast Asia[1]

FRANK N. TRAGER

New York University

THE GROWING AMERICAN INVOLVEMENT IN SOUTHEAST ASIA

The protection afforded the United States by the boundaries of two seas, at the same time tended to isolate this country from contact with peoples abroad. The isolation being compounded by distance, the United States was most remote from developments in the countries of the East. The knowledge we acquired was, at best, fragmentary, not very reliable, and generally gleaned from the interested accounts of the small groups of people who had particular concerns in Asia. These were mainly the early traders, who sailed to strange seas and brought back rare and marvelous spices, along with tales of Hindu potentates, exotic palaces, and rich resources; and the second group of American missionaries, often unaware of, and rarely sympathetic to, the ancient Asian cultures. The early interest of Emerson and his associates for oriental civilization and the philosophy of the East, failed to endure, and became, in the end, no more than a brief flirtation with Indian thought.

Our interest in Asia remained, for the most part, a trading and proselytizing one, until the compulsions of imperialism turned our attention to the East. The struggle for political spheres of influence and what seemed like the imminent dismemberment of China, threatened to disrupt our small eastern trade, and forced us to challenge the right of any nation to impose upon the sovereignty of another. This was subsequently expressed in the formulation of the Open Door policy in regard to China. Though we had a superficial acquaintance with another Eastern culture after the "opening" of Japan in 1853, and we had ourselves engaged in expansion in the Pacific inclusive of Hawaii and the Philippines by

1898, we were still largely ignorant of, and consequently indifferent to, the developments in the other countries of South and Southeast Asia. Having no territorial ambitions in this area, and separated from it by thousands of miles of sea and land, we remained apart while the countries of this region succumbed to the domination of the great imperialisms from the West.

There was, in fact, a generally indifferent or apathetic response to the freedom struggles in India, Burma, Indo-China, and Indonesia in the United States until the beginning of World War II. The lands beyond the Pacific were vague and unreal to insulated Americans. They appeared as a unity, indistinct from each other. The people were described racially as "Asiatics," an opprobious word, and the "yellow hordes" of Theodore Roosevelt's conception came close to being the popular picture of the peoples of Asia. That many of them belonged to the yellow race, as the Europeans, for example, belong to the white, seemed to make them all the same. That this logic was not similarly applied to the nationalities of Europe did not disturb the force of the generalization in regard to the East. That the East contained peoples of several identities who nurtured separate and vital aspirations concerning these identities, became obvious only with the Second World War, and the success of the independence movements shortly after that time. The United States, with new global responsibilities, and unprepared by its past experience to meet them, at least in the countries of Asia, became irrevocably involved in the fate of the new nations which gained independence after 1947.

At the war's end the United States government, and for the most part the American people, were committed to the necessity for an international, in contrast to isolationist, foreign policy. This time there was to be no return to the presumed security of the two oceans or to the Western hemisphere. Residual impulses toward withdrawal, toward some kind of American isolation, remained in the diversified political stream of American life, but these had become and continue to be recessive strains in the body politic. What William James once called the "rivalry of the patterns" polarized the world between the United States and the U.S.S.R. We no longer suffer from the illusion of, if we ever optimistically expected, "One World." But we know—and we know it from the days of World War II—that we are inexorably entwined in this world.

Within the first few postwar years we clearly witnessed the crumbling of old empires, the making of a new one, more dangerous and more ruthless than many of its predecessors. New states, but old nations, were to emerge from the former empires in Africa and Asia, whereas the Marxist-Leninist world of Russia, and later China, gradually engulfed hapless nations and peoples. That a polarized world of competing systems and sovereignties should develop out of the wars was and is ineluctably inherent, according to its believers, in the nature of Marxian dialectical and historical materialism. So long, therefore, as the Sino-Soviet Marxist world professes the belief in the necessary struggle of the "Two-Camps," the artifice of coexistence is merely an interim stage until the conditions necessary for a final transformation in its favor arrive. Some Americans, long before the war, had acquired a clear understanding of Soviet ideology and the uses to which it had been put by the Stalinist hierarchy. But generally the government and the people of the United States throughout the war wished and hoped or acted as if the wartime alliance might be continued into the postwar world.

The organization of the United Nations and its Charter expression of moral and quasi-legal concepts of world order became a cornerstone of United States foreign policy, acceptable to the majority of American people, because it gave expression to their hope of continuing the wartime alliance in the making of peace, and because it seemingly reflected the broad, general, benign self-image we entertain of ourselves and of our country. No better example of this expression need be cited than that of President Truman at a Navy Day celebration in New York on October 27, 1945. In this speech he restates the twelve "fundamental principles of righteousness and justice" on which "United States foreign policy is based":

(1) We seek no territorial expansion or selfish advantage. We have no plans for aggression against any other state, large or small. We have no objective which need clash with the peaceful aims of any other nation.

(2) We believe in the eventual return of sovereign rights and self-government to all peoples who have been deprived of them by force.

(3) We shall approve no territorial changes in any friendly part of the world unless they accord with the freely expressed wishes of the people concerned.

(4) We believe that all peoples who are prepared for self-government should be permitted to choose their own form of government by their own freely expressed choice, without interference from any foreign source. That is true in Europe, in Asia, in Africa, as well as in the Western Hemisphere.

(5) By the combined and cooperative action of our war Allies, we shall help the defeated enemy states establish peaceful, democratic governments of their own free choice. And we shall try to attain a world in which naziism, fascism, and military aggression cannot exist.

(6) We shall refuse to recognize any government imposed upon any nation by the force of any foreign power. In some cases it may be impossible to prevent forceful imposition of such a government. But the United States will not recognize any such government.

(7) We believe that all nations should have the freedom of the seas and equal rights to the navigation of boundary rivers and waterways and of rivers and waterways which pass through more than one country.

(8) We believe that all states which are accepted in the society of nations should have access on equal terms to the trade and the raw materials of the world.

(9) We believe that the sovereign states of the Western Hemisphere, without interference from outside the Western Hemisphere, must work together as good neighbors in the solution of their common problems.

(10) We believe that full economic collaboration between all nations, great and small, is essential to the improvement of living conditions all over the world, and to the establishment of freedom from fear and freedom from want.

(11) We shall continue to strive to promote freedom of expression and freedom of religion throughout the peace-loving areas of the world.

(12) We are convinced that the preservation of peace between nations requires a United Nations Organization composed of all the peace-loving nations of the world who are willing jointly to use force if necessary to insure peace.[2]

There is nothing notable or new in these twelve points. Together they express standard American desires for peace, security, well-being, and freedom, and opposition to armed force, coercion, and territorial aggrandizement as instruments of policy. They lean heavily on the general outline provided by President F. D. Roosevelt and Secretary Hull. Not only was the UN required "to insure peace" but President Truman underlined, as a supporting theme, the special responsibilities and hope for the maintenance of the wartime alliance. Communism was not listed along with naziism and fascism, as it came to be; and Russian collaboration, with "other peace-loving people" was a required and invited element for the future.

The difficulty, of course, is not in formulating such principles or objectives—most, if not all states indulge in the exercise—but in applying them. Events somehow get in our way. Their expression is not infrequently referred to as "Idealism" or "Moralism" in foreign policy, whereas their application and modification in terms of "interests" are similarly referred to as "Realism." Such a disjunction is philosophical nonsense, though it causes endless argument between respective proponents, and, as frequently, leads to political ambivalence even within any one group. The "Idealists" or "Moralists" temper their principles with the anticipated difficulties of policy execution; the "Realists" color their expressions of policy with objectives derived from past or future valued goals. In fact all such assertions or propositions about the principles and direction of foreign policy, whether couched in the terms used by President Truman or by others, are made in whatever reality this world has. Their application in concrete situations depends solely upon the administering will of the authorities in any state. Their success or failure in application, that is, the risks of principle, depend solely upon the capacity of a state alone or in concert with others to carry out its "will."

There is no need here to do more than to mention the broad changes which, shortly after President Truman spoke, shattered his hopes for a world of organized peace. Russia under Stalin had no intention of remaining a friendly peacetime ally. In early 1946, Stalin began to make the moves on the Soviet chessboard which led to the 1947 revival of the Comintern, now to be called the Cominform. Gone was the latest practice of the "soft" or "right" strategy which had been revived after the Nazi invasion of Russia on June 22, 1941. Stalin as a good Leninist was determined to use the occasion of war-weariness and depletion as the springboard for a communist political offensive. Non-Soviet Europe was the main target, or so it appeared. I have suggested elsewhere, that during this crucial period (1946–1949), Stalin, having pushed westward into Europe as far as he could go without further war, was primarily concerned with China; that the communist actions in Europe and South and Southeast Asia were calculated risks designed more to occupy the anti-communist world and thus afford Stalin and Mao a long awaited victory in China. Stalin's defeat at the hand of the Kuomintang in 1926–1927 was never forgotten or forgiven. He could not help but know how badly Chiang was faring in 1946 and 1947—specifically so after General Marshall returned from his "failure of a mission" and after the United States publicly withdrew on January 29, 1947, from any mediatorial role between the Chinese Communists and Chiang Kai-shek.

Whether or not this interpretation of Stalin's policies in the 1946–1949 period (major concern for communist victory in China) is correct, there is no question that Europe was in a parlous state after the war and could ill-stand any determined onslaught on her weakened economies and political structures. Hence Truman's decision to counter the Stalin offensive in *Europe* was a momentous one. The aid to Greece and Turkey, the announcement of the Marshall Plan, the specific and generalized policy of "containment" went far to give non-Soviet Europe the economic and political stimulation necessary to put its house in some (and better) order.

Containment of the Soviet world came to represent the central conception of our foreign policy. The crisis and challenge in Greece and Turkey which the Truman Doctrine, announced on March 12, 1947, sought to meet, and the implementation of the Marshall Plan through the European Recovery Plan, which followed the Secretary's speech of June 5 at Harvard University, were but the opening rounds in the execution of this policy. The Communist coup in Czechoslovakia in February, 1948, followed by the Soviet bar to Western land traffic to Berlin in June accentuated the United States determination to counter the Soviet European offensive. Peacetime conscription again proposed by Truman in March, 1948, was passed by the Congress in June along with a considerable—for those days—peacetime military budget (fourteen billion dollars) which laid the basis for military preparedness utilizing the Strategic Air Command (and the atom bomb) as the striking weapon of a proposed seventy-group air force. The North

Atlantic Treaty Organization, April, 1949, capped these actions. War with the Soviet Union was a possibility publicly discussed.[3]

THE U.S. POLICY OF AMBIVALENCE

But what of Asia? And more particularly of Southeast Asia? The United States government had attempted to base immediate postwar Asian policy—despite meaningless references to "vacuums" and absence of an Asian policy, we had an Asian policy—affirmatively on a hoped-for strong and free China, a demilitarized Japan, a series of (to be) fortified islands which we acquired as UN trusteeships but which our armed forces had in any event insisted upon controlling. This in a sense was traditional American Asian policy.

These policies interpreted in the setting of the postwar alliances and United Nations sentiment were largely incorporated in a speech given by John Carter Vincent, then Director of Far Eastern Affairs, Department of State. The Vincent speech—and it is the Department of State speaking when one of its officers makes a public address—upheld the necessity for "understanding, friendship, and collaboration between and among the four principal powers in the Pacific," China, the Soviet Union, the United States, and the United Kingdom, as the basis for this traditional Asian policy.[4] Where the United States had to make a relatively new postwar decision was in the *application* of its anti-colonial posture to the Asian colonial areas of our wartime allies. In this respect, Vincent repeated what had been generally stated in the various wartime declarations on United Nations policy with respect to dependent and colonial peoples. While affirming the principle of colonial freedom, he vaguely circumscribed it by apparently advocating the goal of "self-government."[5] The right to self-government in the vocabulary of colonial policy is not *equal* to the right of independence.

This ambivalence and uncertainty with respect to colonialism is a persistent feature of U.S. foreign policy. No matter how high sounding the declaration for freedom for dependent or colonial peoples, somehow or other "circumstances" or "interests" interfere to water down the application of the principle in the adopted course of United States action. Much of what Wendell Wilkie called the Asian "reservoir of goodwill toward the United States" has been wasted not because an absence of an Asian policy but rather because of the disparity between United States profession and practice on colonial issues. For example, Vincent in this same speech said: "In Southeast Asia a situation has developed to the liking of none of us, least of all to the British, the French, the Dutch, and I gather to the Annamese and Indonesians. With regard to the situation in French Indo-China, this government does not question French sovereignty in that area. Our attitude toward the situation in the Dutch East Indies is similar to that in regard to French Indo-China." Such a statement directly contradicts or ignores Presidential and departmental expressions of the United States wartime position with respect to a proposed trusteeship for Indo-China outside the French empire. At no time did the U.S. publicly promise to restore Dutch sovereignty as such. If secret commitments were made they, too, violated the frequent expressions for self-determination and self-government promised during the war. Certainly, Vincent's exposition of colonial policy and its application in Southeast Asia is at variance with President Truman's virtually simultaneous presentation of the "fundamental principles of righteousness and justice" on which "United States foreign policy is based."

Throughout this period (1945–1949), that is before and after the hardening of the lines between the United States and the U.S.S.R. and the fall of China, the United States, with the honorable exception of its policy toward the Philippines, was not conspicuous at any stage in living up to its anti-colonial professions of principle. Certainly out of deference to its European allies, it refrained from offering moral or material support to the nationalists of South and Southeast Asia. But if the United States had been largely unaware of the significance of prewar Asian nationalisms, it could no longer take refuge in such ignorance in the immediate postwar period when their strength and their aims were clear. As John C. Campbell sums up:

> . . . the native nationalist movements in Burma, Indo-China, and Indonesia, *already strong before the war* (italics added) made tremendous gains. Their leaders, on the defeat of Japan, were ready to strike out for independence. . . . The colonial peoples were little interested in the world ideological conflict between democracy and fascism except as it affected their own goal of national independence . . .
>
> In the early part of the war certain influential officials in the United States Government hoped for the adoption after the war of a "new

deal" for colonial peoples which would grant independence to those which were ready for it and establish international trusteeships for those which were not. In the absence of international agreement on such a program, the United States pursued a cautious policy calculated not to give offense to its allies, the European colonial powers.[6]

What Campbell calls a "cautious policy," I call a policy of ambivalence; that is, United States policy could be said to be cautious with respect to the Philippines, slowly building up the institutions of self-government, providing for a legislative timetable under the terms of which the Philippines would at a certain time (it came to be in 1946) become completely independent and sovereign. But the many United States wartime statements and the postwar actions flowing from such statements reveal the United States not as "cautious" but as simultaneously verbalizing pronouncements which appear to be in favor of the self-determination of colonial peoples and yet temporizing or withholding or withdrawing from the steps necessary to effectuate the announced policy. Political ambivalence, like psychological or personal ambivalence, consists in developing an approving self-image, replete with pleasant feelings and emotions toward items of conduct, contradicted or inhibited by unpleasant, non-approving feelings and emotions toward other aspects of the same items of conduct.

The United States acquiesced in the British armed intervention which reimposed Dutch and French sovereignty respectively on Indonesia and Indo-China, but it warned its allies ". . . not to use against the native peoples, lend-lease equipment bearing labels of its American origin."[7] It took no stand on the policies involved in the return of the British to the Indian sub-continent, Burma, and Malaya. We did, however, use our influence and aid to get Chiang's Chinese armed forces out of Burma and Indo-China.[8] It was not until after the first Dutch "police action" against Indonesia, in July, 1947, that the United States offer of "good offices" was tendered and accepted by both sides. This led to the Renville Agreement of January 17, 1948, negotiated by Dr. Frank Graham. Only when this Agreement was violated by the second Dutch "police action," December 18, 1948, did the United States take a strong stand against the Dutch, bilaterally by suspending ECA aid to Holland, and multilaterally through a most forthright denunciation of Dutch policy, given by United States delegate Philip C.

Jessup in the UN Security Council.[9] Yet the United States continued to balance its decision in favor of Indonesian independence by its concern for Dutch interests in the area, especially after the initial public disapproval of Dutch police actions had waned. The issue of "West Irian" is a prime example of United States ambivalence on a colonial question—especially since originally the claims of the Dutch and the Indonesians to this portion of the island of New Guinea could have been legitimately opposed by a UN trusteeship which might have then been applied to the whole island. Twelve years were to elapse before we devised a basis for, and offered a forum for, negotiating the solution to this festering issue.

The changeover in Britain from the Churchill to the Attlee Government in July, 1945, made this ambivalent United States policy somehow seem more tolerable; for the Attlee Government on December 4, 1945, announced its intention of abiding by Labor's promises for Indian independence. No similar declaration concerning Burma was forthcoming from Britain for another twelve months, during which time the Burmese nationalist movement led by General Aung San pressed the campaign, which eventually was successful. But nonetheless, British Labor policy toward the Indian sub-continent and Burma thus made it possible for the United States in the early postwar years to maintain its cautious or ambivalent stance in this area without suffering from excessive external criticism or twinges of violated conscience at home. The transfer of British power to Pakistan, India, Ceylon, and Burma was peacefully completed by January 4, 1948, but it was certain of completion by January, 1947. Through British Labor wisdom in accepting gracefully what I believe was inevitable anyway, the free world scored one of its great victories. If the reservoir of Asian good will toward the United States did not thereby directly benefit, at least considerable English waters were added to its storage.

These events coincided with growing tension between the West and the Soviet Union. U.S. policies in Europe, in contrast to those in Asia, were clear and vigorously executed. The collapse of the wartime alliance during late 1946 and early 1947 was precipitated by the Stalinist political offensive in Europe and Asia, to which the United States responded with the policy of containment.[10]

There is no doubt but that containment in Europe and the Middle East was pursued vigorously and effectively by the United States, culminating in effect in the North Atlantic Treaty Organization (NATO) signed April 4, 1949. But if containment was a sound policy in Europe and the Middle East, as I believe it was—short of the "war" that was talked about in the spring of 1948 (see above, Note 3)—why was it not a sound policy for Asia? U.S. large-scale, but not absolute, withdrawal from China obviously resigned that country to the growing military success of the Chinese Communists who had established contiguous borders and supply lines with Soviet Asia. The Wedemeyer report [11] dated September 19, 1947, had if anything strengthened the opinion that the grave situation in China threatened strategic and political interests. Everyone agreed that a victory for the Chinese Communists would be a defeat for the United States. Yet the great debate on China which took place in the United States after 1947, posed the issue as a disjunction: either for or against the Communists; for or against Chiang Kai-shek and the Kuomintang. Though I do not propose to enter the "China tangle," it seemed to me then and now that disjunctions may be logical, but not necessarily political, constructs. The terms of the debate and the debaters obscured the real issues and blocked a proper search for alternatives to the Chinese Communists. The difficulty was compounded by the apparent failure to assess correctly the potential danger of an aggressive Chinese Communist regime in control of mainland China. Protected on the north and west by Soviet power, it was predictable that the twin objectives of such a regime would be concerned with its eastern flank where it faced U.S. power in occupied Japan and Okinawa, and with South and Southeast Asia. Here were important sources of minerals, rubber, and rice for China's growing population and production. And, here as the self-proclaimed inheritors and dispensers of Chinese tradition, the Chinese Communists would especially seek to establish a sphere of influence. The *Nanyang*, Burma, Thailand, and the then Indo-China area, had long been regarded not only as a "spillway" for Chinese population and civilization but also as an area where ancient, and as in the case of Burma, frequently dubious claims of suzerainty might be reasserted. Only the *immediate* choice of tactics to be pursued by the Chinese Communists was open to speculation. But that they would vary or combine standard and well-known international Communist strategy and tactics was also predictable. Meanwhile the Communists succeeded in advancing their power throughout 1947 and 1948. They were not contained either by the Kuomintang or by diminishing American involvements in Asia.

Obviously, containment as a policy was not applied to mainland China. British—not U.S.—policy made it possible for four newly independent nations in South Asia now to join in the concert of free nations. This left in Southeast Asia, apart from British Malaya, which had been offered a choice but put aside its decision, the problems of the French in Indo-China and the Dutch in Indonesia. Apparently, as indicated above, the effrontery of the second Dutch police action and the effective criticism voiced by the Soviet bloc in the UN finally decided United States policy makers to move in the direction of recognizing and supporting Indonesian independence. This belated action in late 1948 and early 1949 came after, not before, the Indonesian Nationalists in power suppressed an attempt at an armed Communist rebellion (Madiun) in September, 1948.

Throughout the long devastating years from the postwar return of the French in Indo-China to Dien Bien Phu in 1954, the United States supported with incredible consistency the imperialist aims of France in Indo-China. If corruption, mismanagement, failure to win popular support, rejection of necessary reform, indifference to the plight of the overwhelmingly rural masses, dictatorship under the facade of parliamentarianism were among the potent reasons for turning away from Chiang Kai-shek, then U.S. support for French imperialist policy in Indo-China was all the more unwise, for all these factors plus the additional one of white foreigners imposing alien rule were present in the French debacle in Indo-China. If the advent of a Communist regime was regarded by the administration as a tragic, but perhaps inescapable, consequence of Kuomintang inner rot, a view which I have here rejected, then steps could have been taken at the end of World War II, and certainly before 1954, to bring about a genuine transfer of power in the states of Indo-China which would have had a chance of saving more from the Communists than south of the 17th parallel— if, indeed, that will be saved! No amount of rationalization about the need for France in NATO, or in the unborn European Defense Community, or in the stillborn Western European Union serves to explain why the United States continued to support France's last-ditch Asian colonial venture long after we had become the happy beneficiary of the British decision in South and Southeast Asia and after the United States had belatedly decided that the Dutch should be relieved of most of their self-imposed white man's burden in Indonesia. Support of the French in Indo-China can be made to fit into the policy of containment of Asian Communists only by dubious assumption that the French in Indo-China were the sole alternative to a Communist take-over. If such an assumption had been made, time and circumstance—difficult as it has been— since 1954 have demonstrated its falsity. For there were and are genuine anti-communist nationalists in Indo-China who gave their lives to fight against French and Communist imperialism.

But perhaps we should examine United States relations to Asia and Asian events free from what then should be regarded as the "European" policy of Communist containment once the decision about the withdrawal from underwriting a Chiang victory in China had been taken. This does not mean that the United States was any the less concerned with the dangerous east and west thrust of Soviet imperialism and Communist infiltration, subversion, and revolution. Rather it means that the United States would no longer anchor its Asian policy to the wartime goal of building up a strong, democratic China. What were the alternatives to this? Until further disclosure of classified material, it would appear that pending the final outcome of China, the fearfully awaited victory of Mao Tse-tung over Chiang Kai-shek, a six-fold interim policy for Asia was in the making even before Secretary of State Acheson delivered his National Press Club speech on the "Crisis in Asia—An Examination of United States Policy." [12] First, Japan would replace China as the basic American Asian ally. [13] Second, American strategic security would be anchored to a line of island defenses running from the Aleutians through Japan, Okinawa, and the Philippines. [14] Third, the United Kingdom would have primary defensive responsibility for the Asian Commonwealths, remaining British-Asian colonies, and Burma. Fourth, belated acceptance of Indonesian independence and recognition, both of which were on the way, while *faute de mieux* there was acceptance of France as having paramountcy in Indo-China. Fifth, non-involvement in such Asian regional efforts as (a) the Nehru-sponsored Asian Relations Conference at Delhi (1947); (b) the abortive Southeast Asian League

(1947–1948), Bangkok, which grew out of the Delhi Conference and had received some impetus from the Burmese; and (c) the second, primarily Indonesian-concerned, Asian Conference at New Delhi (1949) and related phenomena. The exception to this was our interest in the UN agencies concerned with Asia. Finally collective security pacts were considered premature and were therefore to be avoided.[15]

Whatever future this six-fold interim policy may have had, it obviously came in for critical re-examination and modification as the full force of the Communist thrusts in Asia were experienced. It is to these I now turn.

The Growing Communist Penetration in Southeast Asia

I do not wish to suggest that until the collapse of China in 1949 the U.S. ignored the problem of communism in Asia. Quite the contrary. Our postwar efforts and experience in China are rooted in an attempt both unsuccessful, and, from my point of view, errorful, to deal with this problem. Our magnificent responses to the same problem in Europe—already referred to—represent then and now a decisive victory. There we responded to what I have called the hardening of the Stalinist line after the spring of 1946 with alacrity and with the means to stop the forward thrust of Moscow after its initial war and postwar gains. Our responses to the Communist challenge in Asia were initially based on the faulty assumption that if a united-front government between Mao and Chiang were established a viable China could result therefrom, and that in such a process the non-Communist forces would survive and perhaps thrive. This was not to be. In the rest of Asia we were, *until 1950*, content for the most part to accept a secondary posture to the (former) Metropolitan powers. In the case of the French in Indo-China, we persisted in this stance until the first Geneva Conference of 1954 signalled the loss of Vietnam above the 17th parallel. The future of Laos is now tied to the agreements of the Second Geneva Conference (1961–1962), the results of which already indicate the probability of further loss.

Communist activity in Asia in general, and in Southeast Asia in particular, begins, approximately, with the Second Comintern meeting in Petrograd and Moscow in 1920 when Lenin advised a "turn to the East." From that time forward, whatever the shifts in Communist policies, Communist action was designed to free the "oppressed peoples" from the imperial powers and from those who —in communist jargon—did the bidding of the imperialists. These are always designated as "lackeys," "feudalists," "big landowners," and "big bourgeoisie"—no matter how patriotic and how nationalist (i.e. anti-colonialist) some of them in fact were and are. Ho Chi Minh—among others in Asia—is one of Lenin's leading surviving associates from those early Comintern days.[16]

Close students—and others—of communism in Asia have been and are properly attentive to the alternations and variations in Communist ideology, strategy, and tactics. Most recently the public debates within the international Communist movement, especially between Moscow and Peking have aroused considerable interest. The author of the fullest study on this subject finds that there are "three general schools of thought" with respect to Sino-Soviet relations and the world Communist movement. He characterizes these as: (1) those who hold "that conflict between Russia and China, to the extent that it exists, is of little consequence" because the two powers "have a single overriding aim in common—the conquest of the non-Communist world"; (2) those who hold "that a break between the Soviet Union and China is inevitable . . . [their] interests . . . are essentially and ultimately incompatible"; and (3) those who hold that "there are serious differences of interest and outlook" but that "the overriding common aims of both, their joint commitment to an international revolutionary process . . . which they believe is historically inevitable and which they believe it is their duty to aid, their shared determination to establish communism throughout the world, set limits on conflict between the two."[17]

This current debate—before and since the elimination of Khrushchev from Soviet leadership—on Sino-Soviet conflict is not a mere hair-splitting exercise—though it could become that if one is so inclined. It is a crucial debate in the sense that if one identifies himself with the second general school, his policy with respect to Moscow and to Peking will vary substantially from advocates of the other interpretations. It may lead to an acceptance of "agreements" or "understandings," as for example the June, 1961 (Kennedy) one with Khrushchev which seriously, and I believe adversely, affected U.S. policy in Laos. Zagoria and others who share Zagoria's views tend to illustrate their first school with some "strawmen." There is little difference between the first and third school. Both are agreed *on the conclusive character of the overriding common aims of the Sino-Soviet axis*—and this is the quintessentially important point. They vary only on less important matters, such as their estimates of how "serious" the debate really is; how long it may last (e.g., what happens after Mao?), how many times if not continuously in their history Soviet and other communist parties have demonstrated this capacity for fratricidal and literally murderous factionalism. Only degrees of sophistication and historical competence in teasing out and evaluating the propositions of the Sino-Soviet debate separates its members. On the other hand, the second school which expects an "inevitable break" because of the "incompatible" national and other interests between the Chinese and the Russians does represent another and opposing viewpoint.

For the purposes of this paper, whatever the detail of the debate, the Russians and the Chinese have separately and together re-affirmed allegiance to Marxist-Leninist orthodoxy. That is, they have reaffirmed their adherence to the classical Leninist-Stalinist version of the "two-camp" division of the world: the "old world" system of imperialism, capitalism, colonialism, and fascism versus their "new world" or "socialist system." The complete triumph of the latter is expected. "Objective conditions" provide opportunities of supporting "just wars"—wars of "national liberation."

Since I reject the view of the second school as most probably incorrect, I shall present the main points of Communist penetration in Asia in terms either of Moscow or Peking or both operating in alternation or in concert. For with respect to their overriding aim, that is to drive the U.S. out of Asia, to neutralize what remains there as an initial or parallel move, and then to communize it, the Moscow-Peking axis currently displays itself as if it were dancing a political minuet. What difference has it made to the Royal Laotian Government, to the Republic of Vietnam, to SEATO, to the United States, if the Russians supplied the Communist forces (Pathet Lao, Viet Minh, and Viet Cong) by means of an airlift to Tchepone, the key town on the Ho Chi Minh Trail (the corridor down the eastern border areas of Laos), a town just south and west of the 17th parallel dividing North and South Vietnam? And to vary slightly this rhetorical question, what difference has it made to these same regimes if the Chinese continuously supply the Pathet Lao, Viet Minh, and Viet Cong by means of contiguous border and water routes to Hanoi? In both instances Communist forces were and are using Communist material and skill to defeat what remains of freedom in Laos, to subvert Vietnam, and to endanger the north and eastern borders of Thailand and northern borders of Cambodia.[18]

Between the wars the Communist movement found the means and the manpower to make inroads in Asia. Broadly speaking, it fed on agrarian unrest, domestic petty warlordism, and on the discontent of the "downtrodden" urban masses. It flourished, generally in proportion as it espoused a nationalist, anti-imperialist line. In China and Indo-China, particularly in Vietnam, it built lasting communist parties trained in orthodox Leninist fashion. During World War II the Communist parties largely "supported" the Allies after the Nazi invasion of Russia. In so doing, their leaders became recognized as "national" figures by the Allies and became the recipients of military materiel ostensibly to be used to fight the Japanese. Typical examples of this might be cited in terms of the Hukbalahap,[19] the Tagalog language name for the Philippine Communists, and the Malayan Communist party. Later these Communist parties and others, as in Burma and Vietnam, were able to use this materiel in launching their postwar rebellions.

Though the citation of dates arbitrarily structures the genetic reality of historical developments, it is both convenient and not inaccurate to say that when Stalin on February 9, 1946, made an "election" speech rededicating Soviet energies to the policy of world revolution, he then initiated a new series of events which propelled Communist penetration into Asia. This movement was furthered by the organization of the Cominform in September–October, 1947—the reincarnation of the earlier Comintern—and by the simultaneous organization or rejuvenation of a number of Communist instrumentalities and Front groups which served as the sluices for Communist activity in Southern Asia. Among these were the World Federation of Democratic Youth, the International Union of Students, the Youth Conference of Southeast Asia (sometimes called the Conference of the Youth and Students of Southeast Asia), the Conference of Communist and Workers' Parties within the

British Commonwealth, the World Federation of Trade Unions, the Prague International Youth Conference, and others.

All the meetings and conferences held in 1947–1948 were subject to the new line expounded at the Cominform meeting by Andrei Zhdanov. It called for a fight against the imperialists by the "emancipationist anti-imperialist forces . . . based on the U.S.S.R. and the new democracies." It called for military force where necessary to get rid of the "ruling classes of the metropolitan countries . . . who . . . can no longer govern the colonies on the old lines."

The decisions of the Cominform were carried around the world by Communist couriers and other Communist channels cited above, making an appearance in Asia at a series of meetings in Bombay in November–December, 1947, and in Calcutta in February–March, 1948.[20] The Cominform had determined to increase the tempo of its activities in South and Southeast Asia. Emissaries and nationals of the various parties in attendance at "Calcutta" returned to their respective countries. And then, as if on signal, Communist uprisings began in Burma in March, 1948; in Malaya in June, 1948; and in Indonesia in September, 1948. Previously launched uprisings were now intensified in Indo-China, the Philippines, India, and Malaya-Singapore with guidance from the French, American, and English-Australian Communist parties.

Nehru in India and Sukarno and Hatta in Indonesia were successful in quickly suppressing the rebellions with force. The Philippines had to wait for Ramon Magsaysay. First as defense minister in 1950 and later as president—until his tragic death in 1957—he carried out a counter-insurgency plan which in time deprived the Huks of any genuine platform. British armed forces, gradually gaining support of the Malay community against the predominantly Chinese membership of the Malayan Communist Party, took a decade to liquidate that rebellion. The Burmese government with little outside aid is still wrestling with the remnants of the Communist rebellion. (However, Burma has also had to face dissident and insurrectionary ethnic groups.) Thailand and Cambodia thus far have escaped open insurrection. North Vietnam slipped behind the Communist curtain in 1954, while South Vietnam now with stepped-up military assistance from the U.S. has been fighting the Viet Cong (the Communists) since 1955.

Obviously Communist activity in Asia has been continuous, especially since the revival of the Cominform. Whether the leadership and materiel were provided by Moscow, or after 1949 by Peking or by both, are interesting questions but politically and otherwise irrelevant to the fact of Communist subversion, infiltration, insurrection, and warfare. Though the Communist line in Asia always made some doctrinal distinctions between the imperialists (the enemy) and the non-communist anti-imperialists and nationalists (the occasional friends of the Communist Party-led urban and rural masses), Communist action has always been directed, in varying strategy and tactics, against both the "imperialists" and these anti-imperialist nationalists. The Communist rebellions of 1948 which continued as long as possible in South and Southeast Asia were, except in Indo-China and Malaya, directed against newly independent, anti-colonial, nationalist regimes.

Two extraordinary facts emerge from this period of intense Communist activity in South and Southeast Asia. First, their rebellions were not successful in the newly independent countries. The indigenes in these countries, *without* any large scale Western support, fought to preserve their independence and succeeded. Nor were the rebellions successful in the case of Malaya; there in time British policy, after a false start, found a key to Malaya's independence, and its military effort enlisted cooperation from the Malay nationalist elite. When British arms could supply protection to the rural inhabitants, both Malayan and Chinese, the Communist rebellion was defeated.

The second fact is that in Indo-China the reverse of the Malayan situation occurred. There the French were unwilling to support genuine anti-communist nationalists—many of whom were liquidated by Ho Chi Minh's Communist Party while the French were "negotiating" with him. Some six weeks after the Chinese Communists took Peking (January 23, 1949), the French hastily renegotiated the conditions, whereby the puppet emperor Bao Dai returned to Vietnam as Chief of State. But he, under the constraints of the French, was politically and morally incapable of arousing and sustaining national belief in Vietnamese freedom. And so, in time, Ho and Giap won the North, symbolically at Dien Bien Phu on May 6, 1954.

The United States contributed a considerable, though minority, portion of the estimated eight billion dollar cost of this French misadventure. Before its final denouement, in early 1954, Vice-President Nixon and Secretary of State Dulles publicly attempted to arouse American public opinion for American military intervention in support of the French. But their "trial balloons" were quickly burst.[21] They had not only started too late, they were also proposing to back the wrong horse. And certainly the memory of the recent costly war in Korea with its inconclusive ending was too fresh in American memory to undertake another unpromising situation.

On June 19, 1954, Ngo Dinh Diem became premier of the South Vietnam government, and on July 21 the Geneva Agreements were signed (the U.S. did not sign; we issued a separate declaration taking note of the terms), formally ending the Indo-Chinese war. Under these Agreements Vietnam was divided into the recognized Communist regime north of the 17th parallel and the Republic of Vietnam south of that line. The agreements called for the cessation of hostilities in, and the continued recognition of the independent kingdoms of, Cambodia and Laos. But they also recognized the Communist Pathet Lao presence in the two provinces adjoining the province of Luang Prabang, namely Phong Saly on the north and Sam Neua on the northeast, both bordering on the Democratic Republic of Vietnam (DRVN), the Communist state.[22]

Herein remained the source of the continuing crisis in Laos.[23] For these two provinces of Laos have been used as forward bases by the Communists to train and to infiltrate Pathet Lao and Viet Minh cadres. Phong Saly and Sam Neua became the Pathet Lao "Yenan" for further insurgency, not only against the kingdom of Laos but also against the Republic of Vietnam. This area, contiguous to and supplied from the DRVN, is the northern anchor of what has become the Ho Chi Minh Trail running down the eastern borders of Laos and Cambodia into Vietnam.

Stalin's death in March, 1953, and the Geneva Conference in 1954 represent a convenient landmark for a summation of the Communist advances in Asia since 1946–1947. They had won mainland China and had taken Tibet. They maintained the partition of Korea at the 38th parallel. (The Geneva Conference also ended the negotiations provided for in the Korean Armistice Agreement which looked toward a peace treaty based on free elections throughout Korea. There is, of course, no peace treaty, and no elections have been held or are presently contemplated.) They had won North Vietnam above the 17th parallel and had an internationally recognized toe-hold in two provinces in Laos. So much, by the force of arms.

Now, a new turn was in the making. Again to use a date, though there is some evidence that Stalin before his death was already pointing to yet another shift, Chou En-lai at the end of April, 1954, began a series of successive meetings with Asian premiers Nehru, U Nu, and Ho Chi Minh. Out of these came the so-called "Five Principles" of peaceful coexistence (the *Panchshila*), and, in a not unrelated fashion, the Bandung, Indonesia Conference which, among other things, endorsed these principles. For the next few years the Communists were to use the "soft" or "right" line in order to press for new gains. Ho Chi Minh, however, warned the Free World via a broadcast heard from the Peking radio, July 22, 1954, that "we must devote all possible efforts during the peace to obtain the unification ... of the nation ... We shall struggle infallibly ... the struggle will be long and difficult ... to conquer victory." [24]

THE U.S. RESPONSE TO THE COMMUNIST PENETRATION, 1950–1954

The effort made by Secretary Dulles to secure united action, that is, armed intervention, to prevent the loss in Indo-China, was a belated move to counter the Communist advances just cited. But it was not the first such move; it came as a logical development, as we shall see, from the events following the fall of China in October, 1949. Once the Truman Administration had come to the conclusion that it could not affect the course of events in mainland China after the failure of the Marshall and Wedemeyer missions (1946–1947), it elected to play a "wait and see" role in that quarter. Subsequently, certainly until 1949, the above-referred-to six-fold interim policy in Asia appears to have been operative. That it was inadequate seems to be evident; that it may be partially, but only partially, explained by our heavy involvement in countering effectively the Communist advances in Europe seems to me to be also evident. We could not serve, or more precisely we did not see ourselves serving, as the global gladiator in defense of freedom. Nor were our actual and potential allies geared for the collective struggle. It is question-able even today whether some of them in Western Europe have as yet made the necessary decisions! Whatever the explanation, the full victory of the Chinese Communists and the June, 1950, Com-munist aggression in Korea mark the end of this less than satisfying period and its Asian policies.

Secretary of State Acheson's speech before the National Press Club on January 12, 1950, is the watershed for the former interim policy. In this "defensive perimeter" speech U.S. military, political, and economic policy was drawn *off* mainland East Asia. South Asia would be helped, Acheson said, but the major "responsibility is not ours." Our European allies—whether or not they deserved the praise, as England then did, and as the others (France and Holland) then did not—were applauded for making progress with the colonial and ex-colonial areas. Essentially the speech was a masterful lawyer's statement, but also an evasive one. It was an apology for a past policy already in transition.

From the viewpoint of formulating and executing a strong U.S. policy toward Southeast Asia, late 1949 may well be regarded as the beginning of an *annus mirabilis*. Stung by the criticism at home because of the administration's policy toward China, and galvanized by the complete victory of the Communists in China, the Department of State initiated a series of moves which led to a long-needed over-hauling and expression of administration policy in and for free Asia. The most significant, though not always consistently executed, aspect of this change was the unexpressed, but nonetheless clearcut, decision to replace our Western allies as the primary power with respect to free Asia. Our allies for one reason or another could not sustain their past roles. It is useful and pertinent to look at these moves:

(1) On August 5, 1949, the Department released its unprece-dented study, *United States Relations with China with Special Reference to the Period 1944–1949*. Secretary Acheson's preface "closed the book" on Nationalist China. "We must face the situation as it exists." The fact was the failure of the Kuomintang to hold China—a failure "which this country tried to influence but could not."

(2) On August 15 the State Department *Bulletin* (Vol. 21, pp. 236–237) announced that a committee composed of Philip C. Jessup, Raymond B. Fosdick, and Everett Case (later John Leighton Stuart was added to this committee) had been appointed to study

and make recommendations concerning Asian policy. The committee did not publish any report, but its general views were presented by Raymond B. Fosdick in a *New York Times Magazine* article, February 12, 1950.

(3) On December 15, 1949, Philip C. Jessup was designated as an ambassador-at-large to go to Asia in order to review the situation, take part in the conference of American diplomats in Bangkok in February (see 6 below), and make recommendations on his return, March 15, 1950.[25]

(4) On January 12, 1950, Secretary Acheson delivered his already referred to "defensive perimeter"—"Crisis in Asia"—speech (*Bulletin*, Vol. 22, pp. 111–118), which he repeated several times during the next few months, notably at the San Francisco Commonwealth Club, March 15, 1950. The Secretary of State seems to have been one of the last to voice the changes then in preparation.

(5) On January 31, 1950, Assistant Secretary of State George C. McGhee addressed the New York Far East-America Council of Commerce and Industry on "United States Economic Relations with South Asia" (*Bulletin*, Vol. 22, pp. 334 ff.).

(6) On February 15, 1950, the Department announced the conclusion of its "Regional Conference of U.S. Envoys in Bangkok" which had been called to consider "the affirmative steps which could be taken by the United States to carry out its announced policies of extending friendly support to the states in Asia which may desire such assistance" (*Bulletin*, Vol. 22, p. 502). The support would be both military and economic for those states resisting Communist aggression.

(7) On February 23, 1950, the Department announced that a mission headed by R. Allan Griffin (who later became ECA Southeast Asia Director) would visit Saigon, Singapore, Rangoon, Bangkok, and Djakarta "to prepare the way for the most expeditious and efficient use of whatever technical assistance funds may become available for that area." (*Bulletin*, Vol. 22, p. 411; see also p. 791 for Griffin's return in May, recommending a sixty million dollar economic and technical assistance program, the funds of which would come from the unexpended balance of China aid funds.) Earlier, on January 19, Assistant Secretary McGhee had announced U.S. support for the newly launched Colombo Plan.

(8) On March 21, 1950, General MacArthur announced a SCAP-Japan and Burma trade agreement—"the first formal trade agreement" between these two countries—for the exchange of forty-nine million dollars worth of goods during calendar 1950 (*Bulletin*, Vol. 22, p. 525).

(9) On March 27, 1950, Ambassador to India Loy W. Henderson delivered an important address on "Objectives of U.S. Policies Toward Asia" before the Indian Council of World Affairs, New Delhi (*Bulletin*, Vol. 22, pp. 562–567).

(10) On the same day Deputy Undersecretary Dean Rusk, with a strong interest in Asian affairs, "was transferred to head the Bureau of Far Eastern Affairs." This occurred at a time when George F. Kennan, "the third ranking officer in the Department," secured his leave for Princeton's Institute of Advanced Studies (announced by Secretary Acheson later, April 22, 1950). Mr. Kennan's departure from the Department gave an added impetus to Asian interests. I think it can be demonstrated that his major diplomatic concerns furthered the Europe-centered orientation which had so largely dominated the viewpoint of the Department in the previous years.

After 4:00 a.m. on June 25, 1950—an event which according to one spokesman of the Department had not been anticipated—the Asian interest became even more accentuated. There is no question that the administration had determined several years before the final event that it could not stop the Communists in China; there is equally no question that within hours of the event the administration determined that it would contest by arms this further evidence of Communist aggression in Korea. The final onrushing debacle in mainland China and the response to it by sincere, as well as malevolent, forces at home precipitated this need for an accentuated Asian policy. The Korean War gave additional urgency and character to the formulation and execution of this policy. As John Foster Dulles, then a consultant to Secretary Acheson, said, "the Korean attack opened a new chapter in history. No one knows how that chapter will end. . . ."[26] Over and over again the administration gave expression to Asian policies directly arising out of the Korean War. It also kept in view its concern for policies in Asia not immediately connected with Korea. I shall close the list of the *annus mirabilis* with two policy statements, both by Dean Rusk:

(11) "Fundamentals of Far Eastern Policy," speech before the American Veterans of World War II, September 9, 1950, and "Security Problems in the Far East," speech of November 15, 1950, before a National Conference on Foreign Policy.[27]

Inspection of any or all of the foregoing entries reveals both the shape and content of the new policy. Though this is nowhere explicitly stated, it would appear that our new posture in Asia had been concerted with that of our major Western allies. The United Kingdom had convened a ministerial Commonwealth conference at Colombo, Ceylon, in January, 1950, which paralleled U.S. actions. This led to the organization of the Colombo Plan for Asia[28] to which we gave some kind of commitment. And following the January 29, 1950, French National Assembly ratification of the recognition of Vietnam, Cambodia, and Laos as independent states within the French Union, the United States and the United Kingdom extended recognition to these states on February 7.

Thus it was clear at the beginning of 1950 that in the first instance we would by choice and by agreement assume a more active role in the area of former British responsibility (South Asia, Burma), and toward the Republic of the United States of Indonesia, and that we had made basic if questionable decisions with respect to what had been French Indo-China. Secretary Acheson had announced that the United States accepted the "necessity of assuming the military defense of Japan" and that the defensive perimeter of the Pacific defined as "the Aleutians to Japan and then ... to the Ryukyus ... must and will be held."[29]

The essentials of this new policy before the outbreak of the Korean War can perhaps best be examined in the presentation of the "Objectives of U.S. Policies Toward Asia" by Ambassador Loy W. Henderson at New Delhi.[30] After a careful introduction which referred to the character of the United States, the early remoteness from but interest in Asia, and the nature of U.S. global responsibilities, Ambassador Henderson turned to his two main themes: the "handicaps," including "elements of mistrust" in U.S.-Asian relations, and the specific U.S. "policies toward Far Eastern countries." He found and bravely catalogued the difficulties (handicaps and mistrust) as:

(1) deficiency of knowledge and understanding, on the part of large sections of the American people, of the points of view and the particular

problems of various peoples of Asia [which] sometimes results in lack of action, when action should be taken, or in the wrong kind of action. ... (2) insufficiency of human and natural resources in the United States in the face of the world-wide demand. ... (3) a high degree of sensitivity at any action on the part of foreigners which might even remotely be construed as an effort to influence the conduct of their (Asian) internal affairs or of their relations with other countries. This sensitivity in some instances is so acute that the United States hesitates to take or suggest certain measures which might be helpful for fear that such action may do more harm than good ... (4) people in Asia who are sincerely convinced that efforts ... to extend technical or financial aid are prompted not by a desire for a peaceful, orderly progressive world but by some kind of economic imperialism. ... (5) people who really believe that actions taken by the United States through the UN or through other channels ... are motivated by great power politics and selfish considerations. ... (6) influential [Asian] groups who apparently do understand and appreciate the objectives of the United States with regard to Asia but who shrink from close cooperation with the United States lest such cooperation create hostility toward them on the part of powerful forces of the world [the Sino-Soviet bloc but not named]. ... (7) the existence ... of national, religious, race, class, and other animosities also renders difficult efforts to bring about a prosperous, peaceful, free and progressive Asia.

After completing this impressive and still relevant delineation of the difficulties, he then enumerated specific policies, beginning with the reaffirmation of the absence of any U.S. territorial ambition and of any desire to obtain special political or economic position in Asia. In turn he rapidly covered Japan, the Philippines, Indonesia, Vietnam and the other two Associated States, Burma, China, and India. He reiterated our security interests in Japan and the Philippines and our intentions and agreements respectively with these countries. He outlined practical considerations (e.g., mistreatment of American consular and business representatives) in contrast to the (Communist) nature of its political leadership as the basis for U.S. non-recognition of the Peking regime. He defended the atomic and hydrogen bomb policy of the United States. And in referring to each country he specified U.S. willingness to give "appropriate assistance" to further its progress in the direction of economic stability, political independence or self-government, and territorial integrity.

The unexpected Korean War further clarified, deepened, and extended the objectives of U.S. policies toward Asia. It is indeed questionable whether the administration would have had the opportunity of carrying out its objectives if the Korean War had not occurred. The first half of 1950 witnessed the height of Senator Joseph R. McCarthy's vicious, irresponsible attacks on the State Department. The bipartisan foreign policy approach associated with the names of Senator Arthur S. Vandenberg and consultant John Foster Dulles was under increasing handicaps from within the Republican Party.[31] Congress was in no mood to give the President the funds required for his $42.2 billion budget based on an estimated $5.1 billion deficit. Seldom in the twentieth century had a Secretary of State been so much the target of opposition forces as was Dean Acheson during this period. National and international confidence in his concept of a "defensive perimeter" supported by "situations of strength" was not widely exhibited. However, Communist aggression in Korea changed most, if not all, of this. It permitted the administration to go forward with the process of developing and executing the Asian policy-in-the-making from late 1949.

One of the most striking expressions of policy toward Free Asia during this *annus mirabilis*, which remained basically unchanged until the disaster of the French at Dien Bien Phu in 1954, was voiced by Dean Rusk, then Assistant Secretary for Far Eastern Policy, on September 9, 1950, in his "Fundamentals of Far Eastern Policy." The "Fundamentals" were sharply and clearly set forth. We entertain, said Rusk, "hopes for Asia and the world," hopes of "freedom, equal partnership, security, peaceful process, material well-being, cultural exchange and good neighbors," which are "policies not facts." In describing obstacles within the United States to achieving these objectives, he noted that "we have much to learn and unlearn . . . we are inclined to forget that we have relations with other people, not control over them." We err, he observed, in proposing solutions to them "which often [have] nothing to do with their situation in fact, nor with their cultural traditions, their moral codes, their capabilities or their needs." Most important, Rusk felt, "is our example. . . . what about the Asians (and other races) in our communities . . . The peoples of Asia are sitting as a great jury and are passing judgement upon our way of life; there is no place for us to hide from our own performance."

Rusk then outlined an eleven point "program for action" in order to get on with our objective and to overcome the principal obstacles. These were freshly and vigorously stated; and by September, 1950, they had been frequently heard: We can help Asians and governments, "we cannot take over"; we have no desire for privilege. We shall support the national aspirations of the peoples of Asia to be free, to determine their own institutions. We shall act vigorously and loyally as a member of the UN to deal with aggression, to carry out UN resolutions in favor of a free and united Korea. We shall seek a peaceful settlement of the Formosa problem by international action while sustaining the historic ties of friendship between the American and Chinese peoples. We shall strongly support the full and equal participation of the nations of Asia in the family of nations. We shall move toward a Japanese peace settlement. We shall support applications for membership in the UN of Ceylon, Indonesia, Nepal, Korea. We shall view with sympathy and interest Asian security or welfare regional efforts. We shall work with our friends in Asia to strengthen their own institutions—that means military assistance to Indo-China and the Philippines and to others in Southeast Asia whose security is being threatened.[32] It means economic and technical assistance following the investigations of the R. Allen Griffin Mission, the Daniel Bell Mission (Philippines); it means support for Point Four and UN aid programs for Asia. We should expand our information and exchange programs.

The Rusk, Henderson, and other statements of 1949–1950 constituted a sufficiently broad and forward-looking range of Asian policy. One could point out that the policy in these statements retained the now typical, grave inconsistency or ambivalence: the oft-repeated reference to supporting the national aspirations of the peoples of Asia to be free and our simultaneous support for the French in Indo-China.[33] It also seemingly defended certain illusions such as Secretary Acheson's view: "We still believe that the Chinese are going to be Chinese before they are going to be Communists. We believe that the people of Indo-China will see this menace which is coming towards them."[34] But no one could deny that here was a reasoned and reasonable, full U.S. Asian policy on which action was expected. In the final analysis, the test of the policy was its application to Asia in general, and to specific Asian countries. Then, as now, the presence and threat of Communist China, on or off stage, helped to stimulate the formulation and execution of Asian policy in the United States.

Thus, in response to this threat, and with extraordinary rapidity, first under the Truman Administration and then continued by the Eisenhower Administration, the United States proceeded to negotiate a series of bilateral and multilateral "mutual defense" treaties culminating in the Manila Pact and Treaty of September, 1954. It was this which created the Southeast Asia Treaty Organization, SEATO. It is important to note these treaties, for every one is still "on the books," and some of them (e.g., Japan, 1960) have been renewed, or otherwise re-emphasized (e.g., our agreement with Thailand, March 1962) under SEATO. They are, in chronological order:

The Mutual Defense Treaty with the Philippines, August 30, 1951.
The Security Treaty with Australia and New Zealand (ANZUS), September 1, 1951.
The Peace Treaty and Security Treaty with Japan, September 8, 1951.
Mutual Defense Treaty with Korea, October 1, 1953.
Mutual Defense Treaty with Republic of China, September 2, 1954.
The Manila Pact and Southeast Asia Collective Defense Treaty with Australia, France, New Zealand, Pakistan, Philippines, Thailand, and the United Kingdom, September 8, 1954.[35]

The promotion of stability with freedom and justice, improvement in the conditions of living, and security against aggressive communism were and are the bases for all these instruments—including the economic aid agreements—of policy. That is, beginning with 1950, and especially after the outbreak of the Korean War on June 25, 1950, we had determined to no longer wait and see, to no longer play a secondary role in an area of major importance, other than in the fatal exception of French Indo-China. The unexpected and unprepared for Korean War deepened and extended these commitments.

In short, between 1950 and 1954 the United States had redefined its policies and instituted programs consonant with its new treaty obligations. In addition to those security treaties mentioned above, we negotiated aid and other types of agreements with every country of Free Asia. It appeared as if we had determined to brook no further advance of international Communism in that area.

Containment—to use that somewhat difficult word—was at long last to be applied to Asia as it had already been applied in Europe. In effect our bilateral security treaty arrangements with Korea, Japan, Republic of China, and the Philippines; our multilateral security arrangements and accompanying protocols with Pakistan, Philippines, Thailand, Australia and New Zealand, and Laos, Cambodia, and Vietnam; and our aid agreements with the neutralists in Asia signified our determination to redraw the "defensive perimeter" roughly at the Himalayas, the 17th parallel, the 38th parallel, and the China Seas. During the remainder of this decade we, on occasion, as in the case of Quemoy and Matsu, were called upon to demonstrate our determination to hold this line. And, at least on one major occasion during the contest in Laos, the United States and its SEATO allies issued a preventive warning which momentarily dampened hostilities in that quarter.[36]

I do not mean to suggest that all was clear or easy sailing in this post-Korean, post-Geneva 1954 environment. There were, as there always are, genuine problems which demanded careful consideration and application of policy. Those familiar with the international situations in East Asia, Southeast Asia, and South Asia can pick from memory and from the news files the particular problems which loomed in any one year. But on the whole, with the exception of the threat to the off-shore islands, still held by the Republic of China, there was no issue which seemed to require the mobilization of American and allied military power to back American and allied policy—other than the deepening crisis in mainland Southeast Asia. And it is to this that I now turn.

THE CRISIS IN MAINLAND SOUTHEAST ASIA: THE CHOICES BEFORE US

Some recent facts are worth noting before proceeding to the main issue. We have helped to settle the vexing question of West Irian which paved the way for the still primitive restoration of Dutch-Indonesian relations. This means that with the minor exception of a portion of the island of Timor, Western imperialism has disappeared in Southeast Asia. In terms of policy this fact should be used vigorously to counter the strident and false propaganda charges made by some Southeast Asians and all Communists. However, its unlamented departure did not add any insurance to the peace of Southeast Asia. Though Malaya has proceeded with its determination to make "Malaysia" work, it is saddening to note that both our ally the Philippines, and our "friend" Indonesia continue to fish in the troubled waters of the North Borneo territories. All the meetings since June, 1963, including the prestige intervention of both the UN and the then attorney general, Kennedy, have failed to dissuade Sukarno from his militant "confrontation" with Malaysia. The 1962 rebellion in Brunei, which has not yet joined Malaysia, obviously designed by the Indonesians to accomplish that end, appears to be under control. But subversion and guerrilla activity continue in Sarawak and North Borneo, while Singapore is in danger from the Communist-infiltrated, if not led, Barisan Sosialis party, the major opposition to the Peoples Action Party Government. The United Kingdom and other Commonwealth members have come to the support of Malaysia as a member of the Commonwealth. Indonesia's spurious claims and guerrilla-type aggression won little support—outside of Communist countries—in the UN from which she has now separated. Burma carefully nurtures her neutralist, non-aligned posture, while Cambodia, using the same words to describe policy, is enjoying the luxury of pulling at Uncle Sam's beard and of seeking all kinds of candy-bribes for "good behavior" from her new-found friends in Peking and Paris. Thailand has cause to be worried about infiltration and disorder in her vulnerable provinces abutting on Laos, and to be concerned while her ally the United States fully determines its policy in Laos and Vietnam.

Additional facts and factors could be cited to demonstrate that at this time Southeast Asia is experiencing a rising temperature of instability, which automatically conspires to put it high on any conceivable Sino-Soviet target list. Initial U.S. disengagement in Laos following the Geneva Agreements of 1962, and political deterioration in Vietnam after the November 1963 coup against Ngo Dinh Diem contributed to the crisis. What the United States determines to do for its friends and allies on mainland Southeast Asia will shape the security of these countries. The main issue in 1965 is the same as it was in January, 1950, when Acheson described the crisis in Asia: Where *is* the perimeter of the defense against Communist imperialist aggression? Will it be once again withdrawn from the mainland of Asia? Or, will the still free countries of Southeast Asia—among others—be given the means and the continuing support to remain free?

From 1950 onward there has been little doubt that the United States has resolved to maintain a position of strength and direct interest in Asia. It has sought to create and ensure a defensive shield of anti-Communist power to prevent any further large-scale aggression from Communist China. It has exerted its efforts to assist in building up viable economies and stable political institutions which, it hopes, will be democratic but in any event able to nullify both external and internal Communist efforts to dominate or subvert these countries. In certain instances it has trained and equipped local defense and police forces capable of dealing with border incidents, guerrilla actions, and local insurrections. Behind these there has stood the capacity to use conventional and nuclear weapons from Pacific Ocean and related bases as an ultimate deterrent to overt Communist aggression.

However, throughout this period the United States has tended ". . . to treat foreign relations as a series of crises, of moves and countermoves in the cold war, in which . . . [it] attempted to combine firmness in holding the line against Communist expansion with measures to build up defensive strength in the free world." [37] But a crisis-approach has not supplied the answers to the main issue noted above. Our disengagement in Laos after Geneva 1962 proved by 1963 to be an invitation to further aggression from and loss to the Pathet Lao-Viet Minh complex in Laos. As a consequence, on invitation from the Lao premier we have become re-engaged in Laos.

Our task in this Southeast Asia area is to identify our interests if any and to identify what we mean when we say, if we continue to say it, that the security of the United States is involved in the defense of Southeast Asia. That we said it during the Truman, Eisenhower, Kennedy, and Johnson administrations is a matter of record. "Interests" and "security," however, are words or concepts which we bandy about rather lightly and freely, and we frequently do not take the pains to define them. Let us therefore look at the problem of interests and security more closely.

Lest there be any doubt on this subject, at least with respect to present U.S. policy, let me refer to one of the many statements of the Secretary of State on the question of objectives or interests. Secretary Rusk says in *Five Goals of U.S. Foreign Policy* (Department of State Publication 7432, October, 1962), "We ought to deter or to defeat aggression at any level, whether of nuclear attack or limited war or subversion and guerrilla tactics—that is, 'security through strength.'" He has repeated this theme on numerous occasions: for instance, in a careful address at Valparaiso University on April 25, 1964, in which he insisted that the "security of the United States—and of the free world as a whole—is deeply involved in the Western Pacific. . . . Southeast Asia also is vital to our security;"[38] and again before the Senate Foreign Relations Committee on March 9, 1965, when he said that "we are pledged to meet challenges—whether direct attack or subversion—which threaten our security or the security of those who want to be free . . ." (*New York Times*, March 10, 1965).

That there are limited war and subversion and guerrilla tactics now occurring in mainland Southeast Asia, none could deny. If the Secretary's language means what it appears to mean, then, according to his conception of U.S. goals, we are or ought to be involved in the defense of Southeast Asia because our interests are there and because its defense involves in some way or another our security. But, on the other hand, if one reads the *Report* of Senator Mike Mansfield and his Presidential Study Mission colleagues on *Vietnam and Southeast Asia*,[39] one may be driven to conclusions on policy which lead in an opposite direction to that implied by Secretary Rusk's statement of goals. The content of this *Report* appears to me to be factual, yet its conclusion and its interpretation of the facts seem to represent a sad indication of a tendency to withdraw from Southeast Asia, a tendency to say that our interests are not in Southeast Asia, a tendency to extend the disengagement tried in Laos. More recently Senator Wayne Morse has charged that the United States is a "provocateur of military conflict in Southeast Asia," that we have violated the UN Charter and that we should withdraw from Vietnam.[40] The only appropriate response to this charge is "nonsense." But the voices for withdrawal mount.[41]

In the light of such actual or potential differences between leading members of the same political party apparatus, what then *are* our interests in the area?

If China had not become communist, if the Soviets had not moved to the East as they have regularly since 1920, then I would say that our interests in Southeast Asia, especially after we legislated for the independence of the Philippines, were minimal. We would still have our ancient historical interests in the "Spice Islands," and the ordinary trading and commercial interests of one nation with another, more, rather than less, friendly wherever possible. However, these do not constitute overwhelming U.S. economic or political interests in Southeast Asia. We would wish its 225 million people well. Now especially that they have attained their independence, we would hope that in time and in accordance with their respective rich cultures they would build viable political and democratic states, and that they would move out of the more or less mono-cultural economies of their past and move toward more fruitful and effective economies as they developed their resources. In all this we would help in terms of our capabilities and their requests.

But 1949 changed this low-key picture. From January, 1950 on we too turned to the East. In one policy statement and action after another, we have said in no unmistakable language, and we have signed treaties and agreements sanctioning our words, that we will *do* what Mr. Rusk said we would do in the above-quoted statements. These are comparable with the ones he made when he became Assistant Secretary of State for the Far East in 1950. Then and now we have said that we will seek to deter aggression in the area in whatever form it arises, and that we will do so because we have recognized the nature of the enemy who seeks to destroy the freedom of others. We wish to deter him from further encroachment and aggression in Southeast Asia, and elsewhere. *That* is our interest in Southeast Asia. All other interests flow from and around this primary one.

We may have lost sight of this primary objective. For if we were to continue to disengage ourselves in Southeast Asia as Senators Mansfield, Morse, and others, and De Gaulle propose, there is little doubt, it appears to me, that the Sino-Soviet Bloc would continue its move further into the *Nanyang*—the move to the South Seas. It will do so because Southeast Asia is a desirable and desired target area. It is an area which the Bloc needs for political, as well as economic and demographic, purposes. It has at times pursued this objective by the current method of revolution as in Laos and Vietnam. And it has also used the current method of the "carrot and the stick," of aid and trade, selecting specific target countries such as Burma, Cambodia, and Indonesia, to each of which the Bloc has presently made sizeable commitments—Indonesia up to $1.1 billion, including significant military aid; Cambodia about $75 million; Burma about $103 million. (Total Bloc aid to Asia, 1954–1963, amounts to $2.5 billion.) These are not small sums in Southeast Asia.

The Kennedy and Johnson Administrations inherited the Southeast Asian policies of its two predecessors. The basic guidelines have not been changed. They also inherited the growing crisis in mainland Southeast Asia. The seeds of that crisis were left implanted in Laos in the two provinces already named (Phong Saly and Sam Neua), and in the continuing determination of the Communists to take over South Vietnam by any and all means. But the cause of the crisis is the determination of the communist world to use the occasion(s) of the weaknesses of the non-communist world to advance its objectives. Since the end of Geneva 1954 and the beginning of SEATO, Communist forces in Southeast Asia have carried on a continuous above- *and* underground campaign against Vietnam and against the Royal Laotian Government.[42] The Communists' campaigns have been aided by inabilities among the leaders of these two countries, by their failures to win and hold the support of the people, and by other indigenous factors. But the Communists have also been aided by indecision and irresoluteness among Western leaders to apply policies which they so solemnly adopted. And, they have also been aided by the failure of the neutralists publicly to recognize and to condemn or otherwise act on Communists' machinations.

In Khrushchev's view—despite the Chinese Communist charge of "revisionism"—endlessly repeated in a variety of Communist jargon, we are to be "kicked out" of Laos and Vietnam "like the French." He and the comrades are equally clear about the future. "Sooner or later the red flag will fly over the whole world" (the *New York Times*, May 19, 1962). It is noteworthy that Khrushchev coupled the Laotian and Vietnamese situations, for though both countries regained their independence as a consequence of the demise of French imperialism in Indo-China, he described us as the partners or protectors of those whom he calls "the feudal lords," that is, the "class enemy." Hence, of course, the Communists in and out of these countries are cooperating in a fight for "national liberation "—a just war by Communist definition! The Geneva 1962 agreements in no way deflected these efforts. The successors to Khrushchev are not likely to change these views which he so pithily expressed.[43]

What difference does it really make to us if it is Communist China or Communist Russia or both which achieves paramountcy in the area? Would our security be any the less affected? Would our interests be any the less imperiled?

I can find only negative answers to these questions. It makes no difference whether it is China or Russia, separately or together, that wins victories in Southeast Asia. Our interests and our security would be imperiled to the extent that a Communist takeover in mainland Southeast Asia would strategically divide the Indian Ocean from the Pacific Ocean. Mainland Southeast Asia in Communist hands could interdict free flow between the Indian and the Pacific Oceans and would give Communist China an outlet which she sorely needs and one which traditional China has always sought by conquest. If Southeast Asia were to go, piecemeal, behind the curtain—iron or bamboo—then our physical position in the Western Pacific Ocean would be jeopardized, our Pacific and Indian Ocean allies (South Korea, Japan, Taiwan, the Philippines, Australia, New Zealand, Thailand, and Pakistan)—and our friends—would be in danger, and our free access to the Persian and Aden Gulfs, as well as to the East coast of Africa could be, to say the least, made difficult. Our direct interests and security have become involved in Southeast Asia as never before in our history.

Perhaps a more significant question should be asked: How long should we tolerate "wars of national liberation"—that is, planned Communist insurgency? And this question is directly related to the final one: What becomes of our commitment, endlessly repeated since 1950, "to help those peoples and nations of Asia who are determined to be free to maintain their freedom and security"? (Secretary Rusk, "Policy, Persistence and Patience," cited.) To paraphrase the words of Cicero to Cataline: How long will our patience endure the abuse of such wars?

It is at this point that we have been given what appears to be four choices by Secretary of Defense Robert S. McNamara, confirmed in effect by Secretary of State Dean Rusk.[44] These are "withdrawal," "neutralization" or "negotiation," concentration "on helping the

South Vietnamese win the battle in their own country," and "initiation of military actions outside South Vietnam, particularly against North Vietnam, in order to supplement the counter-insurgency program in South Vietnam."

A full analysis easily reduces these options to variations on two themes. The first is in fact what Senators Mansfield and, even more, Morse recommend, namely, withdrawal. For any negotiation leading to so-called neutralization is at this stage tantamount to U.S. withdrawal from Vietnam. And withdrawal, based on previous experiences with negotiations at Geneva in 1954 and 1962, permits and encourages Communist forms of subversion and "underground" warfare. The second option embraces in two stages McNamara's third and fourth options. This is engagement in some to-be-defined sense. Until February 7, 1965, we were apparently content to sacrifice Vietnamese and American lives *on an exclusively defensive war fought on South Vietnam's soil.* This strategic and tactical military anomaly could not remain constant. It had to yield to the clamor for neutralization and withdrawal or be "escalated"—in current jargon—*so as to punish the aggressor, the Communist North, on his soil.*

At this writing (early March, 1965) it is not yet clear how far the present Administration has determined to pursue this course of engagement. What is clear is that, for the first time since 1954, the Communist North begins to experience in the southern one-third of its terrain the military punishment it has been inflicting for a decade on South Vietnam and Laos. If the implications of such a military policy were to call for the *destruction* of the Communist regime in North Vietnam, then the risks of optimum escalation—that is, bringing Communist China into open warfare—are real. However, if such a policy was designed, as I argued some years back, "to maintain the current defensive perimeter" of South Vietnam, then I believe that these risks are both necessary and minimal.[45]

How long will we tolerate externally inspired, led, and fed Communist "wars of national liberation"? The answer to this question ought, it seems to me, to be clear. That is: we ought to do more to make understandable and acceptable at home and abroad the notion that Communist "wars of national liberation" will not be tolerated by us and, specifically, that we have a present commitment in mainland Southeast Asia. We probably cannot afford in fulfillment of this commitment to consume even the three years, suggested at one time by Admiral Harry Felt's optimistic estimate of the situation, because Americans will either get tired or enraged by their continuing casualties in the area. If we are going to try to hold Southeast Asia because it is our purpose to deny it to the enemy so as to give it the chance of finding its own way in freedom, then in terms of interests and security we are faced with an immediate need to move forward on Southeast Asian policy decisions in South Vietnam.[46] These decisions require of us a combined military-political-economic investment in South Vietnam as a full partner, under a joint or combined military command, capable of two major military tasks, simultaneously supported by a civilian political-economic reconstruction effort designed to give stability to the Republic of Vietnam. The military tasks relate to (1) threatening, penetrating, undermining, and attacking North Vietnam so as to compel its Communist regime to cease and desist in and withdraw from its war against the South; and (2) securing the borders of the RVN and gradually, by a "clear and hold" campaign, establishing law and order throughout the land. The civilian tasks relate to assisting a Vietnamese constituency (1) to establish and maintain a government; and (2) assisting that government in the manifold tasks of reconstruction and development in such a way as to provide elementary livelihood, security, and welfare for the majority of the citizens. In the simplest terms I can devise this means giving to the South Vietnamese cultivator—be he lowlander or montagnard—a change from almost a quarter of a century of continuous warfare to two or three peaceful crop-years with one legitimate, protective, and concerned government. Such a boon would have the possibility of winning the "hearts and minds" of men without whose loyalty no regime is worth the candle.

If this were to be done, the United States would be well on the road to fulfilling its international, moral, and political commitments to the people of Southeast Asia who wish to enjoy their *own* freedom —as we do ours.

NOTES

1. Material in the first two sections of this paper, presented at the Midwest Conference on Asian Affairs, Southern Illinois University, October 1959, is based on my forthcoming study, *Burma's Independence*.

2. Harry S. Truman, "Restatement of Foreign Policy of the United States," Department of State *Bulletin*, Vol. 13 (October 28, 1945), pp. 653–656.

3. John C. Campbell, *The United States in World Affairs, 1948–1949* (New York: Harper, 1949), p. 6.

4. John Carter Vincent, "The Post-War Period in the Far East," Department of State *Bulletin*, Vol. 13 (October 21, 1945), p. 644. Note that this speech closely paralleled in substance and in time President Truman's Navy Day speech cited above.

5. Vincent essentially did not go beyond the "right of presently dependent Asiatic [*sic*] peoples to self-government" and preparations for this with timetables. (This is a narrow construction of the 1943 United States "Declaration by the U.N. on National Independence.") However, later in the year, Ralph Bunche, speaking for the Department, offered a curious and politically untenable definition of "self-government" as "independence." Department of State *Bulletin*, Vol. 13, p. 1039.

6. John C. Campbell, *The United States in World Affairs, 1945–1947* (New York: Harper, 1947), p. 300.

7. *Ibid.*, p. 301. (There were no penalties attached to removing labels.) The warning was issued by Secretary of State Byrnes on October 24, 1945. In December 1945, the United States urged "all parties to resume conversations (in Indonesia) and to seek a peaceful solution in harmony with the U.N. Charter."

8. The Department of State *Bulletin*, Vol. 13, pp. 261, 338, had announced that the United States and Thailand had resumed diplomatic relations following a Thai statement on August 19, 1945, "declaring null and void the declaration of war, January 25, 1942, against the United States" and describing, briefly, the Free Thai Resistance movement against the Japanese. However, on January 16, 1946, the United States announced its refusal to recognize Thailand's occupation of Indo-Chinese territory, and in November, Thailand and France signed an agreement in Washington in which Thailand ceded back the disputed territory while withdrawing her UN Security Council complaint against the incursion of French troops.

9. For a concise and useful account, see William Henderson, *Pacific Settlement of Disputes: The Indonesian Question, 1946–1949* (New York: The Woodrow Wilson Foundation, 1954).

10. See X (George Kennan), "The Sources of Soviet Conduct," *Foreign Affairs*, Vol. 25 (July 1947), pp. 566–582.

11. Department of State, *United States Relations with China, . . . 1944–1949* (Washington, D.C.: Dept. of State, 1949), pp. 764–814.

12. This is the "Defensive Perimeter" speech, January 12, 1950, after the fall of China. The Department of State *Bulletin* Vol. 22 (January 23, 1950), pp. 111–118. It should be remembered that this speech was given while a review of, and new perspectives for, American Asian policy were in the process of formulation by a State Department committee. Philip C. Jessup, Raymond B. Fosdick, President Everett Case of Colgate, and our last ambassador to China, J. L. Stuart, were consultants to this committee. Its appointment had been announced in the Department of State *Bulletin*, Vol. 21 (August 15, 1949), pp. 236–237.

13. "By the end of 1948 . . . it was agreed among American policy makers that

the struggle between the Soviet Union and the United States had reduced the importance of the effort to change Japanese society, and that it was of greater significance to rebuild Japan as a useful base for American power and to reduce the strain on American resources. . . . The United States consequently encouraged the development of a Japanese army—the national police reserve, trained and equipped by the American Army—despite the anti-war provision of the American-drafted Japanese Constitution." William Reitzel, M. A. Kaplan, C. G. Coblenz, *United States Foreign Policy, 1945–1955* (Washington, D.C.: The Brookings Institution, 1956), pp. 173–174. It is interesting to note that in this closely written 535-page book, South and Southeast Asian policy is treated rather sketchily on pp. 222–229; 312–318, and *in passim*.

14. Interview with General Douglas MacArthur, *New York Times*, March 2, 1949. Quoted in Campbell, *The United States in World Affairs, 1948–1949*, p. 303.

15. On May 18, 1949, Secretary of State Acheson endorsed a statement by Nehru "to the effect that a Pacific Defense Pact would be premature until 'present internal conflicts in Asia' were resolved." Quoted in Richard P. Stebbins, *The United States in World Affairs, 1949* (New York: Harper, 1950), p. 61. NATO had already been signed (April 4, 1949).

16. I do not propose to detail here the history of the Communist movement in Southeast Asia. See Frank N. Trager *et al.*, *Marxism in Southeast Asia, A Study of Four Countries* (Stanford: University Press, 1959). See also, F. N. Trager, "The Communist Challenge in Southeast Asia," *Southeast Asia: Problems of United States Policy*, ed. William Henderson (Cambridge: M.I.T. Press, 1963), Ch. 6. I shall, however, attempt to sketch in the main points of reference so that the reader can approach today's problems with at least a supporting background.

17. Donald S. Zagoria, *The Sino-Soviet Conflict 1956–1961* (Princeton: University Press, 1962), pp. 3–6. Zagoria had been closer to the second school in his earlier writings on this subject. He now classes himself within the third school, close to those who hold to the idea of "break" but a break which "need not make less serious the challenge presented by the Communist world."

18. The Department of State has issued two important "White Papers" which amply document this. See, *A Threat to Peace*, Publication 7309 (Washington, D.C., 1961), Parts I, II; and *Aggression From the North*, Publication 7839 (Washington, D.C., February 1965).

19. This is an abbreviation for *Huk-Bong Bayan Laban Sa Hapon*, the People's Anti-Japanese Army (later, the *Hukbong Magpalayang Bayan* or the Peoples' Liberation Army). See, J. H. Brimmell's *Communism in South-East Asia* (New York: Oxford University Press, 1959), pp. 194–219, especially, for wartime roles of the Malayan and Philippine Communist parties.

20. I have frequently referred to their presence at this time in Asia as "the Calcutta story" and have treated it in some detail in Trager, *et al.*, *Marxism in Southeast Asia*, pp. 263–273.

21. See the useful collection, Allan B. Cole (ed.), *Conflict in Indo-China and International Repercussions, A Documentary History, 1945–1955* (Ithaca: Cornell University Press, 1956), pp. 172–174, which contains the Dulles-Nixon references. Secretary Dulles proposed, but failed to get, "united action" for an Allied military intervention based presumably on a French commitment for "real independence"

for the Indo-Chinese states. See also, Richard P. Stebbins, *The United States in World Affairs, 1954* (New York: Harper, 1956), pp. 221–225. This failure to secure "united action" in 1954 is a prototype of the similar failure to achieve united action for Laos at the March 27–29, 1961, SEATO meeting.

22. See, Donald Lancaster, *The Emancipation of French Indo-China* (New York: Oxford University Press, 1961), esp. Chs. XVI–XVIII. The official documents of the 1954 Geneva Agreements have been frequently published. See *Documents relating to . . . Korea and Indo-China at the Geneva Conference, April 27–June 15, 1954,* Cmd. 9186, and *Further Documents . . . Geneva Conference, June 16–July 21, 1954,* Cmd. 9329 (London: HMSO, 1954).

23. For the continuation of these events, see Frank N. Trager, "Laos and the Defense of Southeast Asia," *Orbis*, VII (Fall 1963), 550–582.

24. Richard P. Stebbins, *The United States in World Affairs, 1954,* p. 256. There is nothing, I repeat, nothing enigmatic or mysterious about Communist policy for all who care to *read*.

25. See, Philip C. Jessup, "Report to the American People on the Far East," Department of State *Bulletin*, Vol. 22 (April 24, 1950), pp. 627–630. This was delivered as an address over the ABC network on April 13, 1950.

26. John Foster Dulles, an address, San Francisco Commonwealth Club, July 31, 1950, Department of State *Bulletin*, Vol. 23, pp. 207 ff. I have omitted from the forgoing list of policy statements on Asia, President Truman's inaugural "Point Four" address of January 20, 1949, and its Act for International Development incorporated in the June 5, 1950, Foreign Assistance Act, because these did not become especially important for South and Southeast Asia until fiscal years 1952 and 1953, respectively.

27. Department of State *Bulletin*, Vol. 23, pp. 465–468; and pp. 889–894.

28. British Commonwealth Consultative Committee, *The Colombo Plan for Cooperative Economic Development in South and Southeast Asia* (London, 1950), Cmd. 8080. Burma, Thailand, the Associated States of Indo-China, and Indonesia were also present for the first meeting. The United States expressed "complete sympathy" for the effort and together with the International Bank for Reconstruction and Development was expected to furnish funds for the execution of projects which fell within the £838 million required from external sources in order to complete the projected six-year program. U.S. funds would be presumably counted as a consequence of U.S. bilateral aid agreements in the area.

29. Acheson speech, "Crisis in Asia," Department of State *Bulletin*, Vol. 22, pp. 115–116. In his Commonwealth Club address of March 15, 1950 (Department of State *Bulletin*, Vol. 22 [March 27, 1950]), the Secretary of State went at least one step further. He suggested, without further clarification, that the United States would support free peoples resisting subversion by armed minorities or outside pressure.

30. Department of State *Bulletin*, Vol. 22, pp. 562–567.

31. For a personalized, valuable, and brief account of this episode, see John Foster Dulles, *War or Peace* (New York: Macmillan, 1953), pp. 120–137, 178–184. See also his chapter on "Policies in Asia" in which he claims that these policies did not have the benefit of "bipartisanship with respect to Far Eastern policies. So far there has been none, and none has been sought." (p. 232.)

32. In the later speech of November 15 Rusk gingerly led up to the question of a Security Pact for Southeast Asia but stopped at the point of giving it "thought." Department of State *Bulletin*, Vol. 23, p. 893. This seems to foreshadow the Manila Pact of 1954. In a speech one year later, November 6, 1951, he indicated that "initial steps" had been taken toward such a pact and expressed hopes for "further cooperation." Department of State *Bulletin*, Vol. 25 (November 19, 1951), pp. 821 ff. Earlier in 1949, the Congress "over the Administration's objections" had written into the Mutual Defense Assistance Act (PL 329, 81st Congress), a declaration supporting a joint or regional security organization for the free countries of the Far East. This may have influenced the State Department.

33. Dean Rusk appears to have recognized the inconsistency. In a speech, "The Underlying Principles of Far Eastern Policy" (Seattle: World Affairs Council, November 6, 1951), he said, "Many Americans have been troubled in the past about the issue of colonialism in Indo-China. We believe that the question is well on the way to solution . . . it is not surprising that doubts remain in Indo-China and among other countries of Asia." Department of State *Bulletin*, Vol. 25 (November 19, 1951), pp. 821 ff. However, he did not say what kind of solution was on the way.

34. "Foreign Policies Toward Asia," Department of State *Bulletin*, Vol. 23 (September 18, 1950), p. 464.

35. These documents and explanatory texts are conveniently gathered in *American Foreign Policy 1950–1955* (2 vols.; Washington, D.C.: U.S. Government Printing Office, 1957), Vol. I, Part V.

36. On September 26, 1959, SEATO announced that "in the event of its becoming necessary to defend the integrity of Laos against intervention, SEATO has made preparations so as to be able to act promptly within the framework of the Manila Treaty." Quoted in Pote Sarasin, *Report of SEATO 1959–60* (Bangkok: Post Publishing Co., April 1960), p. 3. The warning was issued at the time of the "revival of Communist (Pathet Lao) insurgency . . . supported by the Communist regime in North Vietnam." Here SEATO was "acting" under Article IV, Section 2 of the Treaty, and in connection with a Lao government entirely sympathetic to its purposes. When subsequently in 1960 another government was installed at Vientiane following a military coup (Prince Souvanna Phouma and Captain Kong Le) SEATO as such was silent though the event brought satisfaction to the Sino-Soviet bloc and encouragement to the "Communist (Pathet Lao) insurgents." When this government was displaced by Lao forces friendly to the West, and when its security was threatened by the Sino-Soviet bloc and the "Communist (Pathet Lao) insurgents," SEATO was publicly and hopelessly divided in its counsels, to the obvious satisfaction of its Communist opponents.

37. "Basic Aims of United States Foreign Policy," a study prepared by the Council on Foreign Relations for the Senate Committee on Foreign Relations, *United States Foreign Policy* (Committee Print No. 7, 86th Cong., 1st sess.; Washington: Government Printing Office, 1959), p. 8.

38. "The Situation in the Western Pacific" (Washington, D.C.: Dept. of State, n.d. 1964), p. 1. See also, "Policy, Persistence and Patience," Publication 7809 (Washington, D.C.: Dept. of State, January 1964).

39. *Vietnam and Southeast Asia, Report* (Washington, D.C.: Government Printing Office, 1963). The *Report* endorsed the view that U.S. aid should be diminished in South Vietnam, and that consideration should be given to President De Gaulle's suggestion calling for the neutralization of South Vietnam. See also Senator Mansfield's related statement as quoted in the *New York Times*, February 20, 1964.

40. Wayne Morse, "The U.S. Must Withdraw", *Christianity and Crisis* (November 2, 1964).

41. Advocates for "negotiations" usually recognize that the ensuing "neutralization" of Vietnam and Laos necessarily implies the withdrawal of the United States. But they take comfort in the supposition that the Communist forces will then also withdraw. See for example "The News of the Week in Review," *New York Times*, February 28, 1965, for a rather full view of this situation and debate on it.

42. See Frank N. Trager, "'Never Negotiate Freedom': The Case of Laos and Vietnam," *Asian Survey*, I (January 1962), 3–11.

43. Soviet Military Chief Marshal R. Y. Malinovsky repeated such views while voicing criticism of Khrushchev's "subjectivism and hasty decisions." *New York Times*, February 23, 1964.

44. See speech by Secretary McNamara, March 26, 1964, at the James Forrestal Memorial Awards Dinner (release; Washington, D.C.: Department of Defense, March 26, 1964); and Secretary Rusk's News Conference, *New York Times*, September 14, 1964. See also, Secretary McNamara's review of Southeast Asia as the "most acute" area of Communist expansion and of which "South Vietnam is the keystone." House Armed Services Committee on . . . 1966 Defense Budget, *Statement* (Washington, D.C.: Armed Services Committee, February 18, 1965), pp. 10–14.

45. See Frank N. Trager, "The Far East," *National Security, Political Military and Economic Strategies in the Decade Ahead*, eds. D. M. Abshire and R. V. Allen (New York: Praeger, 1963), pp. 327–363; 432–442. My thesis was that the way to defend "Saigon" is to penetrate, undermine, threaten, and if necessary attack "Hanoi" . . . "at his bases on his terrain."

46. I have described elsewhere the specific requirements for this policy. See Frank N. Trager, "To Guarantee the Independence of Vietnam," *Christianity and Crisis* (November 2, 1964), pp. 213–215; and "Vietnam: The Military Requirements for Victory," *Orbis*, VIII (Fall 1964), 563–583.

Reaction and Response to the Opening of Korea, 1876–1884

ANDREW C. NAHM

Western Michigan University

The end of Korea's policy of isolation and subsequent developments stimulated political ferment among the contending factions in Seoul. The contest for political power was particularly intense and bitter between men who were conservative and pro-Chinese and those who were progressive and anti-Chinese. The latter advocated reform for the modernization of the ancient kingdom of Korea. The politics of reaction and response, while setting the pattern of conflict between political groups in Korea, marked the beginning of active participation by foreign powers in Korea's domestic affairs. Meanwhile, the movement launched by the Progressives signaled the rise of modern nationalism in Korea.

This paper deals with: (1) the initial reaction of the anti-foreign groups to the opening of Korea; and (2) the clash between the conservative party called *Sadaedang* and the reform party called *Kaehwadang* which brought about the bloody events of December of 1884.

ANTI-FOREIGN REACTION

Different types of reaction developed immediately after the conclusion of the Kanghwa Treaty of February 26, 1876, between Korea and Japan and the commercial agreements signed between them. The uncompromising, anti-foreign sentiment was voiced by conservative intellectuals who were genuinely concerned with the preservation of Korea's traditional ethics and values. The politically oriented anti-foreign (both anti-Western and anti-Chinese) movement was promoted by the Regent Taewŏngun, who was the father of King Kojong (1851–1919). The third type was the response which developed among the more progressive elements in and outside the Court of Kojong. The interaction between these groups created in Seoul a sensitive and explosive political situation, which was further aggravated by the Treaty of Amity and Commerce between Korea and the United States (often called the Chemulp'o or Shufeldt Treaty) of May 22, 1882.

Long before the conclusion of these treaties, the tradition-bound Confucian scholars had advocated and implemented an anti-foreign policy which was directed against the "Western Learning" movement and the Catholicism that had come into Korea.[1] In spite of repressive legal measures against them, the progressive scholars' interest in Western thought, science, and religion continued to increase, and the number of Catholic converts multiplied. The increasing frequency of the visits of foreign vessels to Korean waters and the Western demands for commercial intercourse fostered even more anti-foreign sentiment in Korea. To halt the spread of foreign influence, Taewŏngun ordered the massacre of the French Catholic missionaries and Korean converts in March, 1866, and when the American schooner *General Sherman* violated Korean territory in the summer of that year, Koreans burned the ship and killed its crew. At the same time, Taewŏngun strengthened Korea's coastal defense against Western intruders and possible invasions by French and American troops; and when American aggression did come, in the latter part of the spring of 1871, Taewŏngun ordered his troops to repel the "barbarians," and he warned the people about the evils of the Westerners by erecting a stone monument in the Chongno Square in Seoul.[2] At the same time, he decreed that those who advocated peace with the "Western barbarians" would be considered traitors, and would suffer appropriate punishment. However, a combination of factors forced Taewŏngun to quit his post as regent in 1873, leaving him powerless to prevent the renewal of diplomatic and commercial relations between Korea and Japan. He could only despise the Westerners who arrived in Korea and wait for an opportunity to put his reactionary program into operation.

The Korean-Japanese treaty revived the anti-foreign movement, and a critical opinion of the government policy developed in some quarters, particularly among orthodox Confucian intellectuals such as Yi Man-son, Kim P'yŏng-muk, Ch'oe In-hyŏn, and others who regarded the ideals and the system of China's ancient sage kings (Yao, Shun, and Yü) as the Golden Rule, and preached that the teachings of Confucius were the foundation of the moral and ethical system of the people. They were convinced that the "barbarian customs" were lecherous and sensual and therefore extremely harmful to ancient values, and that alien interests and influence would certainly weaken the moral and ethical foundation of the kingdom. Their policy may be described as "repel evils and rectify the conditions of the people." Their attitude was reactionary and conservative toward domestic matters and both anti-Western and anti-Japanese on foreign policy.[3] Therefore, they opposed the rise of Western thought and religion in Korea, and they agitated for the prevention of Japanese influence there.

Scholars such as Kim P'yŏng-muk were thoroughly convinced that once foreigners were permitted to enter Korea, inevitably alien thought and practices would corrupt the people. So violently opposed to the opening of Korea was Kim that he, along with Yi Man-son and Hong Chae-hak, submitted memorials to the king protesting the policy of dealing with foreign powers. They even demanded that Kim Hong-jip, the king's envoy to Japan in 1880, be put to death because he had advised the king to import Western civilization and establish close ties with Japan, a policy which had accomplished extensive modernization in a short period of time.[4] The memorial submitted by Kim P'yŏng-muk, author of the book entitled *Ch'ŏkyang taei* ("The Principles of Anti-Westernism"), contained so many harsh and disrespectful elements that he was sent into exile in the summer of 1881.[5] However, Kim and others continued to fight for the lost cause and maintained their uncompromising intellectual conservatism to the end.

The opposition of intellectual conservatism to the introduction of Western civilization and the establishment of diplomatic relations with Japan and other powers was a futile battle against the currents of modern times. No matter what the values of the Confucian system may have been, the political corruption and economic stagnation that had lasted for many centuries under the autocratic government administered by the Confucian literati weakened the very foundation upon which that system was built. The people had lost confidence, both in those values, and in those who advocated them. Moreover, Korea was in no position to reject the wishes and demands of the Japanese nor those of the European powers.

The anti-foreign movement in Korea was closely related to the anti-government, and particularly anti-Min (Queen Min and her supporters), sentiment. The politically motivated anti-foreign policy was promoted by Taewŏngun, who became a bitter enemy of Queen Min after his retirement in 1873. Thus he welcomed the crisis which developed in Seoul in the summer of 1882, two months after the conclusion of the Korean-American treaty of 1882. The event which precipitated this crisis dates back to October, 1881, when secret police discovered a conspiracy led by Yi Chae-sŏn, an illegitimate son of Taewŏngun, against Queen Min and her clan. Mass arrests were made, the conspirators were sentenced to death, and many military officers who had joined the plot were imprisoned. This first attempt to overthrow the Min power by those who were against the opening of Korea created a chain reaction in the summer of 1882. The military uprising of July, 1882, known in Korean history as *Imo kunnan*, began as a local riot in Seoul staged by soldiers who had not been paid for almost a year and who were opposed to the modern military training program of the government.[6] The rioting soldiers, while registering their grievances, stormed the Ch'andŏk Palace and other government buildings in Seoul and killed many members of the Min party.

Taewŏngun quickly took advantage of this situation to regain power so that he might fulfil his goals, which were to crush the Min power, and to carry out his anti-foreign policy. After taking command of the insurrectionists, Taewŏngun was able to force Queen Min to flee from her palace, and he also murdered many pro-Min and pro-Chinese officials. Meanwhile, the insurrectionists, after killing a Japanese military instructor, threatened to harm the lives and damage the property of the Japanese. The mob joined the soldiers and forced several Japanese, including Minister Hanabusa Yoshitake, to flee to Inch'ŏn, and then to Japan.[7] But, Taewŏngun failed to retain his position, as the Chinese intervened.

Grand Secretary of the Ch'ing government and Viceroy of Chihli, Li Hung-chang, who was in charge of foreign affairs for the government in Peking, received news of the insurrection in Seoul, and immediately dispatched Commander Wu Ch'ang-ch'ing and two other generals to the peninsula with some 5,000 troops.[8] Arriving in Seoul, the Chinese quickly restored order, kidnaped and transported Taewŏngun to China where he was imprisoned until October, 1885, and returned Queen Min to power in Seoul. A treaty was signed between Korea and Japan on August 30, 1882, settling personal and property damages inflicted upon the Japanese during the insurrection.[9]

Korea had been a vassal state to China since the Manchu conquest in 1637.[10] Traditionally, however, the Ch'ing government refrained from interfering in Korea's domestic affairs as long as Korea continued to recognize China's suzerainty and remained obedient to her wishes, and as long as no other powers challenged China's political and economic positions in Korea. However, an antipathy developed among some Koreans toward Chinese domination, and Korea's gradual involvement in international complications created a new situation for the Chinese government.

The Chinese had been suspicious of Taewŏngun's intentions, as well as of Japan's, in Korea for some time. China's apprehension concerning Japanese intentions was a logical reaction to the new situation that had developed in her vassal state; in the first place, Japan, by recognizing Korea's sovereignty and independence in the treaty of 1876, and by concluding commercial agreements with Korea, challenged China's claims to suzerain rights and commercial privileges in Korea.

As yet, Japan had not developed a territorial appetite for Korea; but she was determined to achieve three objectives there: (1) the destruction of China's claims in Korea and the end of Chinese control there; (2) increased political influence and the furtherance of Japan's economic interests; and (3) the prevention of Korea's becoming a threat to the security of Japan.[11] In order to accomplish the second and third objectives, the Japanese government, prior to 1894, endeavored to achieve the first goal without going to war with China.

As China sank deeply into political and economic crisis following the Opium and Arrow wars, and especially after the T'ai-p'ing Rebellion, the leaders of the Ch'ing government became irrational, and an extreme sense of insecurity and frustration prevailed among them. As a result, extremists in Peking, such as Chang P'ei-lun and

T'eng Ch'en-hsiu, advocated positive action against Japan while "she was weak," as well as the suppression of anti-Chinese sentiment in Korea.[12] Even Li Hung-chang, who was much more realistic and cautious than the others, felt that increased Japanese interests and influence in Korea constituted a menace to the security of China and to her position in Korea, and should not be tolerated.[13] Hence, Li, by taking advantage of the Korean situation in the summer of 1882, carried out his policy to whip Korea back into the Chinese orbit and reassert China's claims there. Subsequently, trade regulations between Korea and China were revised (in October, 1882, and again in March, 1883), with the incorporation of new features which ensured for the Chinese a special position in Korea.[14] In December, 1882, the Korean government was reorganized and patterned after that of the Ch'ing. Two Chinese were made counselors, and Ch'en Shu-t'ang, another Chinese, was made the Chinese Commissioner for Commercial Relations in Korea. Li Hung-chang installed a Chinese agent, Paul G. von Möllendorff, a former German consul at Tientsin, as vice-president of the Korean foreign office and inspector-general of Maritime Customs for the Korean government; General Wu Ch'ang-ch'ing and Commander Yüan Shih-k'ai supervised Korean military affairs; and an ardently pro-Chinese Korean, Cho Nyŏng-ha, was appointed president of the foreign office.

Chinese influence in Korea grew stronger after Li Hung-chang established direct control over Korea through his agents, and the Korean reform movement which had arisen was thereby paralyzed. As a result, Korea became even weaker and more defenseless, a ready victim for foreign aggression. The dry-rot of Chinese conservatism and reactionary policy pervaded everywhere. Naturally, the re-establishment of Chinese domination over Korea strengthened the political position held by Queen Min and her supporters, but at the same time, it stimulated the growth of anti-Chinese sentiment.

SADAEDANG VS KAEHWADANG: KAPSIN CHŎNGBYŎN

The reassertion of Chinese suzerainty and strict control in Korea also aroused nationalistic sentiment, and this spirit was fostered by a group of young aristocrats in Seoul. The rise of this group caused the pro-Chinese conservatives to become even more reactionary;

consequently, conflict between the two antagonistic groups in Seoul became intense, and the struggle for power between them brought about the violent event known as *Kapsin chŏngbyŏn* (the "Political Incident of the Year Kapsin") on December 4–6, 1884.

The leaders of the conservative *Sadaedang* (the "Great-Power-Serving-Party") were Queen Min (King Kojong's wife), her young nephew Prince Min Yŏng-ik, and their adviser Paul G. von Möllendorff. Queen Min was the guardian of the interests of the Min clan and its allies, and the real power behind the throne occupied by the unhappy King Kojong. Her actions were motivated by selfish interests, and whatever she did was the result "of expediency and partisan animosity rather than intellectual conviction."[15] The Queen was determined to maintain the *status quo*, not only in regard to the balance of power between her party and others, but also in terms of the relationship *vis-à-vis* China. Although she was uneducated and superstitious, the Queen was capable of perceiving the possibility of strengthening her own position and protecting her clan's interests by allowing limited, slow changes in Korea, and her political skill and knavery surpassed that of the other members of the Min party.[16]

Prince Min was a "young man of pleasing manners and gracious address," but he demonstrated no trace of progressivism, and his policy, like that of his aunt, was based on selfish, partisan interests. Although he was aware of the necessity of change in Korea, his awareness was overshadowed by his concern for his family interests. He had been exposed to the "light" when he visited the United States and Europe as a member of King Kojong's first mission to the West in 1883–1884, and his belief in reform had been somewhat strengthened during his visit. But as he confessed to the American minister General Lucius Foote, he "returned into the dark" when he returned to Seoul.[17] When he saw the Progressives and the king preparing for the "vigorous infusion of Western civilization" into Korea, Prince Min became a determined enemy of the progressive movement and its advocates.[18]

Behind the reactionary forces in Korea was the German adviser von Möllendorff, the watchdog of Li Hung-chang and faithful servant of Queen Min. He considered the Progressives as "scoundrels" who would bring "terrible mischief to the country," and he was "fully aware of the Japanese aims to destroy Chinese influence in Korea" which he was sent to protect.[19] He was loyal to China, and he had evinced strong resentment when his policies were challenged by the young Korean Progressives.[20]

The young nationalists, who had become aware of Korea's backwardness, advocated political, economic, and social reform. Their supreme objective was the immediate achievement of complete and permanent independence for Korea, for they were certain that as long as China maintained her domination over Korea, and as long as the Min party and the Chinese jointly blocked Korea's progressive reform movement, Korea was sure to suffer disastrous consequences. Therefore, men who shared similar ideas and convictions gradually rallied around Kim Ok-kyun, a young official in the government who was the epitome of anti-Chinese reform spirit in Korea.

Kim Ok-kyun (1851–1894), son of a Confucian scholar, studied Confucian classics at the school in Kannung which was established by Yi I, one of the most outstanding scholars in Korea, who is better known as Master Yulgok.[21] After completing his basic studies in Kannung, Kim went to Seoul where he attended the national Confucian Academy. There he became associated with sons of some of the powerful families in Korea. He was a bright, intelligent, and ambitious student, and Kim's future as a dynamic leader seemed predestined. At the age of twenty-two he passed the metropolitan examination in *munkkwa* (Division of Classics) with the highest literary distinction of *chang'wŏn*. After serving in various capacities in the government, he was made Deputy Transmitter of Royal Edicts in the Office of Transmitters, an office which enabled him to establish a personal relationship with the king.[22] Thereafter, he rose to prominence and was appointed Counsellor of the Board of Punishment before his thirtieth birthday.

In Seoul, Kim foresaw the impending crises at home and abroad, and as a conscientious and patriotic official was keenly aware of the dangerous situation arising. He felt strongly the need for reforms in Korea, and his basic conviction was further strengthened by his acquaintance with such scholars as Yu Tae-ch'i and Monk Yi Tong-in. Moreover, through reports submitted by the king's emissaries such as Kim Ki-su, Kim Hong-jip, and Ŏ Yun-jung who had visited Japan and elsewhere, he became aware of conditions in other lands.

Kim Ok-kyun's conversion to a progressive and nationalistic philosophy occurred when he met, and eventually became a disciple of, Fukuzawa Yukichi, the champion of liberalism and progressivism in Japan.[23] Kim's visit to Japan in 1881 enabled him to become acquainted with new ideas and systems. What he saw in Japan not only astonished, but also inspired, him. Affected by Fukuzawa's progressive philosophy, and impressed with achievements made by the new leaders in Japan, Kim came to the conclusion that nationalism and progressivism, alone, could reconstruct and improve the conditions of his people and country. He felt the pressure of time keenly, and became seriously concerned with the impact of foreign intrusion, especially that of China.

During his sojourn in Tokyo, Kim established personal relationships with such outstanding Japanese leaders as Itō Hirobumi, Inoue Kaoru, Gotō Shōjirō, Itagaki Taisuke, and Fukuzawa Yukichi; they, in return, came to regard him as a potential modern leader for Korea. Moreover, his "marked intelligence and attractive manners" left a very favorable impression among the European diplomats in Tokyo.[24] He was concerned with the welfare of his people and the destiny of his country, and he demonstrated his hatred for injustice, backwardness, and outmoded conventions of the past. At every opportunity, he preached the doctrine of progress, and he considered it his duty to lead his young friends toward the goal of the amalgamation of Western ideas with the best of his own tradition.[25]

Kim deepened his relationships with the Japanese leaders when he went to Japan in September, 1882, as a member of the goodwill mission sent by King Kojong following the conclusion of the treaty between Korea and Japan. The mission was headed by Pak Yŏng-hyo, son-in-law of the late king; Kim Ok-kyun was his adviser. At this time the Progressives hurriedly produced a Korean national flag (the present-day Republic of Korea flag), instead of using the old flag that symbolized Korea's vassalage to China. The mission was cordially received, and friendly relations between the two countries were restored. The mission was also able to secure a loan of 170,000 yen from the Specie Bank in Japan to finance reform programs in Korea.

Upon returning to Seoul, fully converted to nationalism and progressivism, young Kim and his friends banded together for the national cause, and they won the king's support for their reform program. Thus, a political group known as *Kaehwadang* (the "Progressive Party") emerged.[26] The main objectives of the Progressive Party were: (1) to open Korea to Western civilization; (2) to establish a modern government; and (3) to achieve complete and permanent independence from China.[27] Because of their goals and activities the Progressives stood diametrically opposed to Queen Min's party.

Despite the conservatives' opposition, the king and the Progressives were able to carry out certain reform measures;[28] but they demanded more reforms, and wanted a speedier implementation of their modernization program than the Chinese and Korean conservatives would allow. Antagonism between the two parties mounted steadily, and the personal relationship between Prince Min and von Möllendorff on the one hand, and Kim and his comrades on the other, grew gradually worse. Prince Min became convinced that so long as the Progressives schemed to eliminate Chinese control and to destroy the Min monopoly of power, there could be no room for either compromise with, or tolerance for, such a movement. Since neither was possible between the two antagonistic groups, each conspired to destroy the other. In 1883, these rapidly deteriorating relations prompted the reactionaries to launch an all-out effort to stamp out progressivism and crush the reform movement. Pak Yŏng-hyo, who had carried out numerous reforms as mayor of Seoul, was transferred to the governorship of a province, and the first modern press, *Hansŏng sunbo*, which was the voice of the Progressive Party, was forced to discontinue operation.[29]

In view of the worsening political situation and the increasing intensity of animosity between the two political groups in Seoul, moderates such as Kim Hong-jip, Ŏ Yun-jung, and others attempted to bring about a reconciliation between the two hostile camps by introducing a gradual political reform program, and by preaching the need for national defense. At the same time, they proposed international cooperation between Korea, China, and Japan for mutual survival, emphasizing the dangers arising from the encroachment by imperialistic Western powers.[30] They also endeavored to find neutral ground upon which Korea, without antagonizing China, could achieve her independence and modernization. However, their efforts were unsuccessful.

The Progressives felt the growing danger of a plot to annihilate them, as the Chinese in Seoul became more arrogant and Korean conservatives grew more reactionary. Their realization of such a possibility led them to become more emotional and radical, and to seek more and immediate aid from the Japanese, who frequently displayed their anti-Chinese sentiment while showing their willingness to help the Korean Progressives to achieve their goals. King Kojong and the Progressives also sought American cooperation through Minister Foote who believed that the influence of the United States should become a permanent factor in the progress of Korea. However, the Korean Progressives, particularly Kim Ok-kyun, felt that they understood the Japanese better than they did the Americans, and they thought that their neighbor seemed to be more willing to help them. But on a trip to Japan in the fall of 1883, Kim discovered, to his dismay, that the Meiji leaders were not only reluctant to commit Japan in Korea's domestic affairs, but were also suppressing a pro-Korean movement in Japan. The disheartened Kim then attempted to solicit American or French aid, but with no success.[31] He returned to Seoul empty-handed, and as of the spring of 1884, it seemed to the Progressives that all hope was lost, and that Korea had no choice but to remain a vassal state to China and suffer national humiliation.

The sudden intensification of the Franco-Chinese conflict over Annam in the fall of 1884 created an entirely new situation, not only for China, but also for the Progressives and their opponents in Korea.[32] The Japanese minister Takezoe Shin'ichirō, who, until his return from Tokyo to Seoul in October, 1884, had maintained a cool, if not suspicious, attitude toward the Progressives, now demonstrated his sympathy and willingness to help the national cause of the reform party.[33] Not only Takezoe, but also other Japanese who were in Seoul, actively encouraged Kim and his friends to take bold steps to accomplish their goals.[34] As a result, the Progressives, in cooperation with the Japanese, laid plans for a *coup d'état.*

Sensing the approaching crisis, the American Minister Foote and British Consul Aston in Seoul cautioned the Progressives to be moderate in their movement, and they advised Kim not to rely too heavily on the Japanese. Even Yüan Shih-k'ai sensed the brewing storm in Seoul and sent a confidential message to Li Hung-chang on November 11, saying that the king and many of his supporters were planning to seize an opportunity to shake off Chinese control in order to achieve full independence and modernization. "I fear," he wrote, "that in three years' time the result of this policy will become evident."[35]

In spite of the warnings given by the American and British representatives, the crisis approached rapidly, sooner even than Yüan had expected, as the Progressives completed their plans for the coup. King Kojong, too, was convinced that he would have no better opportunity to win his kingdom's independence and to liberate himself from the Min domination.[36] The "great event" occurred on the eve of December 4, 1884.[37] Prince Min was mortally wounded, and many pro-Chinese ministers and generals of the army were put to death by the revolutionaries,[38] but no harm was done to the Queen. The reform government was established during the night, and the King gave his approval. The Japanese soldiers commanded by Capt. Murakami Masamori were called into the palace to protect the King and his newly-born government.[39]

The policies which the ephemeral revolutionary government proclaimed on December 5 expressed strong nationalism and a certain degree of progressivism. It was declared, among other things, that:[40]

(1) The Chinese government must free Taewŏngun and allow him to return to Korea.

(2) The practice of sending tributes to China must be abolished.

(3) Factionalism must be abolished, and equality among the people must be established.

(4) Men of talent must be employed in the government, regardless of their birth or social origin.

(5) The taxation system must be revised, and the welfare of the people must be promoted.

(6) The Office of Eunuchs must be abolished.

(7) A modern police system must be established to prevent crime.

(8) Political prisoners and those who were sent into exile injustly must be freed.

(9) Corrupt officials must be punished.

(10) The Bureau of Trade, which benefited the Chinese, must be abolished.

(11) The national financial administration must be in the hands of the Board of Revenue, and all other offices which handled finance must be abolished.

(12) Conferences of Ministers and Councillors must meet at the Assembly Hall, and all government decrees and regulations must be made public.

(13) All political offices and agencies other than the Six Boards (Ministeries) must be abolished.

Thus, the so-called "Kim Ok-kyun's *samil ch'ŏnha*" began.[41]

Outside the palace, rumors spread among the citizenry that the King and the Queen had been murdered by the Japanese. Counter-revolutionary forces were organized by Yüan Shih-k'ai and Korean reactionaries, and the Chinese and Korean soldiers attacked the palace on the afternoon of December 6. The handful of Japanese and Korean defenders could not match the overwhelming odds and the stillborn reform government was crushed. The King was taken into custody by the counterrevolutionaries, but some Progressives who survived the ordeal managed to escape to the Japanese legation with the Japanese, and then to Japan via Inch'ŏn.[42] The Min party was restored to power, and a Korean-Japanese protocol of January 9, 1885, settled several issues which had developed as a result of the abortive coup.[43] The Tientsin Treaty of April 18, 1885, signed by Li Hung-chang and Itō Hirobumi, removed temporarily the danger of war between China and Japan over Korea.[44]

CONCLUSION

Korea proved to be "the sick man of the Far East" toward the end of the nineteenth century, and Japan played a role similar to that of Great Britain in the Middle East. Unlike the British, however, the Japanese displayed no desire to go to war with China for the sake of the sick man during the latter's early confrontation with China. While Japanese policy makers believed that Korea's independence and her modernization would be desirable for the security of Japan, their primary interest in Korea lay in promoting their own political influence and economic interests, the latter seeming much more vital. They pursued a safe and sane policy, and attempted to gain maximum profit with minimum risk. Only a handful of Japanese "liberals" (who were against the oligarchical control) and their agents in Korea agitated for aggressive action in behalf of the Korean reform advocates.

An ideology known in Korea as *sadae jui* or *mohwa sasang*[45] dominated the minds of the leaders in general, particularly those of the Min clan. So strong was the influence of *mohwa sasang* on Korean aristocrats (*yangban* in Korean), that they copied things Chinese blindly and regarded non-Chinese thought and practices as "barbarous and evil." Politically, the conservatives were subservient to China, and the absence of any spirit of intellectual and political independence on the part of the government inevitably undermined national or racial self-consciousness among the people of Korea as a whole. Thus, when Confucian intellectuals such as Kim P'yŏng-muk spoke of safeguarding the cultural tradition and ethical values of Korea, they meant the preservation of Chinese thought and institutions.

The Progressives espoused nationalism and progressivism, but their nationalism was romantic in nature, and their reform ideas were superficial and lacked deep conviction. Although their vocabulary included such words as liberty, equality, justice, and progress, they were under the influence of traditional political elitism. Far from promoting the concept of popular sovereignty, they even failed to take into consideration the importance of popular support. Their dreams of transforming Korea into a modern nation proved to be only fantasy, for neither they nor Korea were ready to duplicate the pattern that had changed Japan from a feudal nation into a modern empire.

The young reform advocates, although sincere and dedicated, were naïve, impatient, and inexperienced, both in their thinking and in practical politics. The romantic idealism of the progressives—no matter how inspiring, logical, and just in itself—proved to be ineffectual in the realm of practical affairs. They failed to take into consideration the political and geographical importance of Korea to China, while overestimating the goodwill of the Japanese. Moreover, they were ignorant of, or overlooked significant differences in historical experience and stages of economic and social development between Korea and Japan: Japan had never been subjected to Chinese domination, whereas Korea had been a vassal state to the Yüan, the Ming, and the Ch'ing dynasties for many centuries; furthermore, the economic and social changes that had taken place in Japan since 1600 had not occurred in Korea.

There can be little doubt that the Progressives understood progressivism only in its narrower sense, precluding democratic concepts and practices in the affairs of the nation. This was so primarily because, as their counterparts in Japan had demonstrated, a Western type of liberalism has a difficult time growing and flourishing in the cultural soil of Asia. In more ways than one, the Korean Progressives resembled the European romantic nationalists of the 1840's and 1850's. The philosophy of *kaehwa* ("progress and enlightenment") in nineteenth-century Korea, as in China and Japan, meant only the abolition of ancient laws and systems, but not of the objectionable practices and traditions of the past. Notwithstanding all these obstacles, the Progressives did give birth to Korea's spirit of independence and to the reform movement.

One can only speculate as to what might have been the results of the Progressive revolution in 1884 had China not intervened. It is certain, however, that the Progressives would have faced enormous problems in their attempts to create a modern nation. Had Korea won complete independence from China, it is questionable whether she would have been able to maintain that sovereignty and independence in the face of growing Japanese imperialism and Russian expansionism. Furthermore, economic and social progress would have been extremely slow and difficult.

One thing is clear, however; whatever possibilities may have existed for the realization of national independence, social reform, and economic development in Korea, Chinese intervention in Korea not only jeopardized any hopes of the Koreans for freedom from external domination and frustrated their aspirations for national regeneration and cultural progress, but it also intensified conflict between China and Japan in the succeeding decade.

NOTES

1. *Sŏhak* or the "Western Learning" movement began in Korea at the beginning of the seventeenth century, and flourished during the following century. Catholicism came to Korea at the end of the eighteenth century via China. For details, see Hyŏn Sang-yun, *Chosŏn yuhak sa* ("History of Korean Confucianism") (Seoul: Minjung sogwan, 1954), pp. 433–445; Gregory Henderson, "Chŏng Ta-san, A Study in Korea's Intellectual History," *The Journal of Asian Studies*, XVI, 3 (May 1957), 377–386; Oda Seigo, "Ri-chō no hōtō o ryakujo shite Tenshukyō hakugai ni oyobu" ("Factionalism in Yi Korea and the persecution of Catholicism"), *Seikyū Sakusō*, IV (September 1930), 1026; Yamaguchi Masayuki, "Kinsei Chōsen ni okeru Seigaku shisō no tōzen to sono hatten" ("Introduction and development of Western Learning in recent Korea"), *Oda sensei sōju kinen Chōsen ronshū* (Keijo: Ōsakayagō shoten, 1934), pp. 1004–1040.

2. *Chōsen shi*, comp. Chōsen Sōtokufu (35 vols.; Keijo: Chōsenshi Hensankai, 1932–1940) Vol. VI, Part 4, p. 247. (Hereafter cited as CS.) The warning read: "Western barbarians invaded our land. If we do not fight, then we must appease them. When appeasement is made, it then leads us to the selling of our country. [Therefore], let our sons and their sons be on guard."

3. Hyŏn, *Chosŏn yuhak sa*, p. 444.   4. *Ibid.*, p. 446.

5. *Ibid.*, p. 447; CS, Vol. VI, Part 4, pp. 572, 576–580. For Kim P'yŏng-muk's biography, see *Chōsen jimmei jisho* ("Biographical dictionary of Koreans"), ed. Chōsen Sōtokufu. (Keijo: Chūsuiin, 1937), p. 881.

6. For details, see Tanaka Naokichi, "Nissen kankei no ichi dammen: Keijō Ningo no hen" ("An aspect of Japanese-Korean relations: the Imo Incident in Seoul"), *Meiji gaikō shi kenkyū* ("Studies on diplomatic relations of the Meiji period"), ed. Nihon Kokusai Seiji Gakkai (Tokyo: 1957); *Nihon gaikō monjo*, edited and compiled by the Japan Foreign Office (1936—), XV, 216–226. (Hereafter cited as GM.) Reports, personal memoirs, and newspaper articles on the case are collected in Miyatake Gaikotsu, *Ningo Keirin jihen* ("The Imo Incident in Korea") (Tokyo: Tokyo Teikoku Daigaku, 1932).

7. Minister Hanabusa left Inch'ŏn aboard the British ship *Flying Fish* on July 26. He returned to Inch'ŏn on August 12 and negotiated for a treaty. GM, XV, 231.

8. Generals Ma Chien-chung and Yüan Shih-k'ai went to Korea while Ting Ju-ch'ang took his fleet to Inch'ŏn.

9. During the anti-Japanese mob demonstration, the Japanese legation building was burned down. Korea was forced to pay 500,000 yen of indemnity to Japan in this treaty. GM, XV, 200–204; Tabohashi Kiyoshi, *Kindai Nissen kankei no kenkyū* ("Study of recent Japanese-Korean relations") (2 vols.; Keijo: Chōsen Sōtokufu. Chūsuiin, 1940), I, 759–784.

10. Korea became again a vassal to the Manchu empire in 1637, as she had been to the Yüan and the Ming dynasties earlier.

11. Iwakura Kō Kyūseki Hozonkai (ed.), *Iwakura kō jikki* ("The authentic records of Prince Iwakura Kowashi") (3 vols.; Tokyo, 1927), III, 897–899; Itō Hirobumi, *Hisho ruisan: Chōsen kōshō shiryō*, ed. Hiratsuka Atsushi *et al.* (26 vols.; Tokyo: Hisho Ruisan Kankokai, 1934–1936), I, 251–253. (Hereafter cited as HR: CKS.) Japanese newspapers such as *Chōya*, *Akatsuki*, and *Yūbin Hōchi Shimbun* advocated these policies. *Jiji Shimpō*, which was established by Fukuzawa Yukichi, was particularly concerned with the Korean question. See Ishikawa Mikiaki's article of September 1, 1897, in *Jiji Shimpō*, dealing with its editorial of August 13, 1883. Ishikawa Mikiaki, *Fukuzawa Yukichi den* ("Biography of Fukuzawa Yukichi") (4 vols.; Tokyo: Iwanami shoten, 1932), III, 270–275.

12. Wang Yun-sheng, *Liu-shih-nien lai chung-kuo yü jih-pen* ("China and Japan during past sixty years") (7 vols.; Tientsin: Ta-kungpao, 1934), trans. by Nagano Isao and Hatano Kan'ichi into Japanese as *Nisshi gaikō rokujūnen shi* ("Sixty Years' history of Sino-Japanese relations") (4 vols.; Tokyo: Kensetsusha, 1933–1936), I, 175, 176, 258–261, 267–269. Hereafter cited as Wang, *Nisshi gaikō*.

13. Li Hung-chang, *Memoirs*, trans. R. C. Robert and W. F. Minnix (Boston: Houghton Mifflin Co., 1913), p. 249; *Ch'ou-pan I-su shih-mo: T'ung-chi ch'ao* (100 chüan; Peiping: The Palace Museum, 1930), Bk. 82, p. 31b. (Hereafter cited as

IWSM: TC.); Li Hung-chang, *Li wen-chung kung han-kao*, comp. Wu Ju-lun (34 chüan; Paoting: Lien-chi Shu-she, 1902) Bk. 1, pp. 45b–49b. (Hereafter cited as LWCK:HK.)

14. CS, VI; 4, pp. 651–652, 703–704; Wang, *Nisshi gaikō*, I, 290–295.

15. Carl F. Bartz, Jr., "The Korean Seclusion Policy, 1860–1876" (Ph.D. dissertation, University of California, 1952), p. 16. One writer described her as "a strong and formidable character, brilliant and magnetic . . . brainiest woman of the entire Orient," who was "an uncompromising conservative, a fearless leader, and the power behind the throne." Mary V. T. Lawrence, *A Diplomat's Helpmate: how Rose F. Foote, Wife of the First United States Minister and Envoy Extraordinary to Korea, Served Her Country in the Far East* (San Francisco: H. S. Crocker Co., 1918), pp. 12–25; Annie E. Bunker, "My First Visit to Her Majesty the Queen," *Korean Repository* (Seoul: Korea), II, 374, 426; Lilias H. Underwood, *Underwood of Korea* (New York: Felming H. Revell Co., 1918), p. 87 ff.

16. Lawrence, *Diplomat's Helpmate*, pp. 12–13.

17. No. 62, Foote to Frelinghuysen, April 8, 1884 and No. 83, Foote to Frelinghuysen, June 17, 1884.

18. No. 128, Foote to Frelinghuysen, December 17, 1884.

19. R. von Möllendorff, *P. G. von Möllendorff* (Leipzig: Otto Harrassowitz, 1930), p. 77.

20. *Ibid.*, pp. 97, 98.

21. *Kin Kyoku-kin den*, ed. Kokin Kinenkai (2 vols.? Tokyo: Keiō Shuppansha, 1944), I, 40–44. (Only one volume was published.) (Hereafter cited as KKD.) For Kim's biographical data, see Matsumoto Masazumi, *Kin Kyoku-kin shōden* ("Detailed biography of Kim Ok-kyun") (Tokyo: Kōseidō, 1894); Kerimsa (ed.), *Chosŏn wiinjŏn* ("Biographies of eminent Koreans") (Seoul: 1948), chapter on Kim Ok-kyun.

22. KKD, I, 46.

23. For his relationship with Fukuzawa Yukichi, see Ishikawa, *Fukuzawa*, III, 285–289; KKD, I, 130–143; Watanabe Shujirō, *Tōhō Kankei* ("Affairs of the eastern nations") (Hamamatsu: Hokokai, 1894), pp. 124–186. See also Kim Ok-kyun's *Kapsin illok* ("The Kapsin diary") whose Japanese text is found in Watanabe, *Tōhō Kankei*, pp. 124–186, and the Chinese text is found in HR: CKS, I, 430–467.

24. *Jiji Shimpō* (Tokyo), September 11, 1882; Joseph H. Longford, *The Story of Korea* (London: T. Fisher Unwin, 1911), p. 329.

25. KKD, I, 147–149; Ishikawa, *Fukuzawa*, III, 285; Tabohashi, *Kindai Nissen kankei*, I, 899.

26. *Kaehwa* means progress and enlightenment. The party was also called *Tongniptang* (the "Independence Party") or *Ilbondang* (the "Japanese Party"). Outstanding members of the Progressive Party were Kim Ok-kyun, Pak Yŏng-hyo, brother-in-law of King Kojong and son-in-law of the late King, Hong Yŏng-sik, the former prime minister's son, Sŏ Kwang-bŏm, and his nephew Sŏ Chae-p'il (who later became known as Dr. Philip Jaishon), Pyŏn Su, Yun Ch'i-ho, Yi To-jae, and Yu Kil-jun.

27. CS, Vol. VI, Part 4, p. 681; Gordon Haddo, "The Rise and Fall of Progressive Party in Korea," *The Chautauquan*, XVI (1892–1893), 46–49; No. 128,

Foote to Frelinghuysen, December 17, 1884; Tabohashi, *Kindai Nissen kankei*, I, 765; KKD, I, 366–367.

28. Some notable reform measures taken were these: the abolition of the ancient laws that prohibited Korean aristocrats from engaging in commercial enterprises; granting of educational equality to all; the establishment of an English language school; the publication of a modern, tri-monthly newspaper called *Hansŏng sunbo*; the sending of a large number of young Koreans to Japan to study economics and military science; the installation of steamship service between Inch'ŏn and Shanghai by a British firm; the modernization of the silk industry by Western technicians; the founding of an experimental farm called the "American farm" with the land donated by the king, and seeds and stock brought back from the United States; the introduction of modern military training; and the establishment of a modern postal service.

29. *Hansŏng sunbo* was published by Pangmungwan, which was organized by the Progressives with the help provided by Fukuzawa through his students Inoue Kakugorō and Ushiba Takuzō.

30. KKD, I, 275, 276; Kikuchi Kenjō, *Kindai Chōsen shi* ("Recent Korean history") (2 vols.; Keijo: Keimeisha, 1929), I, 649–654.

31. Kim Ok-kyun went to Japan in the fall of 1883, hoping to secure a 3,000,000 yen loan from Japan. He was not successful in this project. He also failed to convince the American minister, John A. Bingham, and an American financier, James R. Morse, in Yokohama, to support the Korean Progressives. The *Jiyūtō* (the "Liberal Party") in Japan, particularly its leaders such as Kobayashi Kusuo and Okamoto Ryūnosuke, attempted to help Kim. Through the members of the *Jiyūtō*, Kim negotiated with the French minister, Joseph A. Sienkiewicz, who "promised" both financial and military aid for Korea. Yamabe Kentarō, a well-informed Japanese writer on Korean-Japanese relations, disclosed to me in our conversations that this was only a make-believe plan dreamed up by the members of the *Jiyūtō*. Ishikawa, *Fukuzawa*, III, 301; Tabohashi, *Kindai Nissen kankei*, I, 908–913; KKD, I, 256, 259; Uda Tomoi (ed.), *Jiyūtōshi* ("History of the Liberal Party") (2 vols.; Tokyo: Gosharō, 1910), II, 334–347; Inoue Kakugorō Sensei Denki Hensankai, *Inoue Kakugorō sensei den* ("Biography of Inoue Kakugorō") (Tokyo, 1943), pp. 50, 51. Hereafter cited as *Inoue Kakugorō den*.

32. The Chinese violated the Li-Fournier agreement of May 11, 1883, and after failing to receive definite reply from Peking, the French declared a blockade of the coasts of Formosa on October 23, 1883, and began belligerent action.

33. Ishikawa, *Fukuzawa*, III, 309; *Inoue Kakugorō den*, pp. 50, 51; HR: CKS, I, 284–294.

34. On October 2, 1884, Minister Takezoe had an audience with King Kojong *à deux*, and presented Emperor Meiji's personal letter and the gift from the Japanese Foreign Minister to the Korean monarch. On November 12, he suggested two alternative plans for Japan in Korea to his government in Tokyo. In his dispatch, "Tai-kan saku kō otsu nian" ("Plans A and B for Korea"), Takezoe, after summarizing the political situation in Seoul, proposed that: (A) since there was no possibility for mutual understanding and cooperation in respect to Korea between Japan and China, and as an open war with China was desirable to curb China's arrogance, it seemed to be best for Japan to *instigate and bring about a civil*

war in Korea; and (B) in order to maintain peace in the Far East and to avoid friction between Japan and China, leave Korea alone, and let nature take its course there. In the latter case, however, Japan's action should be limited to providing some protection for the Progressives and their actions.

On November 18, Takezoe informed his superiors in Tokyo that, according to confidential information, the lives of the Progressives were in grave danger, and concluded that "If the Japanese party (meaning the Progressive Party) fails, and the leaders of that party are dispatched, the hope for Korea's independence would certainly perish completely." HR: CKS, I, 265–287; C. M. Kim (ed.), *Nikkan gaikō shiryō shūsei* ("Collection of sources on Japanese-Korean diplomatic relations") (8 vols.; Tokyo: Kannandō, 1963—), III, 3–6. In HR: CKS, the phrase "Instigate and to bring about a civil war" is missing. However, the unpublished *Chōsen kōshō jiken roku* ("Documents relating to Korean affairs") collected at Gunaishō archives, Bk. III, Doc. 4 included them. GM has no information.

35. Jerome Ch'en, *Yüan Shih-k'ai (1859–1916)* (Stanford: Stanford University Press, 1961), p. 23. See also LWCK: HK, Bk. 20, pp. 23a, 24b.

36. On the eve of November 29, King Kojong summoned Kim Ok-kyun to his chamber and had an audience *à deux*. Kim urged the King to approve his plans against the Chinese and the Min party. He stated that "We must reform our country's system, develop and promote the people's welfare, and establish our country's independence, and open doors to others so that we may import new civilization and increase our national power." King Kojong agreed with Kim, saying, "We have no better opportunity than now to win our independence." Kim, *Kapsin illok*, November 29, 1884.

37. This date was chosen primarily because the Progressives could assemble a large number of government officials at a spot without arousing special suspicion. At the same time, it was thought that the Conservatives would relax their security measures, since almost all the Progressives were scheduled to attend the dinner commemorating the opening of the Postal Administration, given by Hong Yŏng-sik, a leading member of the Progressive Party and first Superintendent of Postal Administration. All foreign representatives, except the Japanese Minister, attended the dinner. Minister Takezoe did not attend the banquet because of his "illness." He was actually preparing to take Japanese soldiers to the palace to support the revolutionaries. *Allen Diary*, December 5, 1884 (in the Horace Allen MSS, collected in New York Public Library); Tabohashi, *Kindai Nissen kankei*, I, 951; "Keijō ihen shimatsu sho" ("Report on the Seoul Incident"), in GM, XVIII, 352–362; No. 127, December 5, 1884, No. 128, December 17, 1884, Foote to Frelinghuysen.

38. Pro-Chinese members of the Min party who were killed were: President of the Foreign Office Min Yŏng-mok; Home Minister Min T'ae-ho; commanders of Palace Guards Han Kyu-jik, Yun T'ae-jun, and Yi Cho-yŏn. An ardent pro-Min and pro-Chinese, Cho Nyŏng-ha, was also killed.

39. Japanese soldiers came to the palace upon King Kojong's request. Takezoe to Foreign Minister Yoshida Kiyonari, December 6, 1884.

40. KKD, I, 366, 367; Kim, *Kapsin illok*; Tabohashi, *Kindai Nissen kankei*, I, 956.

41. It means the "Three Days Mastery of the World by Kim Ok-kyun."

42. Forty-three Progressives perished during the counterrevolutionary retaliation; only nine survived the catastrophe. Among the perished was Hong Yŏng-sik.

Kim Ok-kyun, Pak Yŏng-hyo, Sŏ Kwang-bŏm, Sŏ Chae-p'il, and a few others fled to the Japanese legation first, and then to Inch'ŏn. From Inch'ŏn they sailed for Nagasaki, Japan, despite Minister Takezoe's objection. Some forty Japanese, including Captain Isobayashi Shinzō, were killed by the Chinese and Koreans during and after the coup.

43. As a result of this treaty, Korea was again forced to pay 130,000 yen indemnity to Japan. GM, XVIII, 347, 348.

44. The Li-Itō Convention (Tientsin Treaty) of April 18, 1885, stipulated that: (1) both China and Japan shall withdraw their troops now stationed in Korea; (2) they agree to invite the king of Korea to instruct and drill a sufficient armed force in order to assure Korea's public security; (3) the king of Korea shall engage into his service an officer or officers for military instruction of his troops from a third power; (4) neither China nor Japan shall send any of their own officers to Korea for the purpose of giving military instruction; (5) in case of any disturbance of a grave nature occurring in Korea which necessitates either China or Japan to send troops to Korea, each party shall give previous notice in writing to the other party, showing its intentions of doing so; and (6) when the matter is settled its troops shall be withdrawn promptly from Korea.

45. *Sadae jui* is an ideology or attitude (*jui*) peculiar to Korea's foreign affairs during the nineteenth century. It means literally "ideology of serving, or depending on, a great power." *Mohwa sasang* refers to a thought or belief that worshiped things Chinese.

The Role of the Radical Left Wing in the Japanese Suffrage Movement

JOHN H. BOYLE

Stanford University

For the first twenty-five years of this century, the issue of universal male suffrage occupied the attention and energy of both reformer and revolutionary in Japan. The purpose of this paper is to examine the response of the radical left wing to this issue and to suggest that this group forfeited a position of leadership in this important social and political struggle by its inability to speak with one voice.

The pre-World War I advocates of universal suffrage came, for the most part, from the incipient socialist movements, or were descendants of the popular rights (*jiyū minken*) movement of the early years of the Meiji period. The socialists based their program on the social democratic ideas of the German socialists but also were subject to strong Christian humanistic influences. The most important of the early socialist groups was probably the *Heiminsha* (The Commoners' Society). Its newspaper, the *Heimin Shimbun* ("Commoners' News"), founded in 1903, suffered a precarious existence due to its espousal of "dangerous ideas" such as universal manhood suffrage, a graduated income tax, the abolition of the peerage, and the nationalization of the railways. Its stand opposing the Russo-Japanese War made it extremely suspect by the authorities, and the newspaper was banned, for the first time, in November, 1904, when it published the Communist Manifesto.

The men who were associated with the *Heiminsha*, such as Katayama Sen, Abe Isō, Sakai Toshihiko, and Kōtoku Shūsui, can be considered as the mainstream of the Japanese socialist movement in the first years of this century. Most of these men were commited to peaceful parliamentarianism and regarded a revision of the

81

nation's suffrage laws as one of their chief goals. By virtue of an Imperial Ordinance issued in 1890, suffrage had been given to males over the age of 25 who paid a land or income tax in excess of fifteen yen. The effect of this standard was to enfranchise approximately 450,000 men or about one and a half per cent of the total population. Until after the end of the first World War the only significant revision of the suffrage ordinance was a reduction of the tax qualification to ten yen.

Universal male suffrage was mentioned prominently in the platforms of the political parties formed by the *Heiminsha* group. For example, the *Shakai Minshutō* (Social Democratic Party), formed in 1901, called for universal male suffrage, but this appeal was short-lived; the party's radical program prompted police authorities to order its dissolution just three hours after it was created. The *Nippon Shakaitō* (Japan Socialist Party), created in 1906, managed to survive somewhat longer, in part by a judicious refusal to publish a declaration of its principles at the time of its organization. Within a year, however, it faced not only official disapproval but an even greater threat arising from internal dissension.

The internal threat to the unity of the socialist group came in the form of proposals for a substitution of "direct action" (*chokusetsu kōdō*) in place of parliamentary tactics to achieve political control. The direct action program at this time is usually associated with one man, Kōtoku Shūsui. Kōtoku had been active in the socialist movement since 1897, and like most of the socialists of that time he had stressed the evolutionary nature of socialism and argued for a reduction in the tax qualification in the election law. But by 1907 he had come to lose faith in parliamentary techniques, and in an article entitled "I change my ideas," he outlined his new views on universal suffrage.[1]

Citing the United States as an example, Kōtoku declared that, even in countries which have universal male suffrage, only the wealthy, the brazen, the shrewd politicians are elected to office. Moreover, Kōtoku argued, even assuming that the proletariat did manage to elect someone who might be expected to represent its demands, the person elected would soon become tarnished by his new surroundings and associates and would inevitably betray his trust. Here he cited the British Socialists as an example; as soon as they were elected they "lost their stamp as laborers and became arrogant."[2] Thus, Kōtoku argued, the Japanese must not rely upon these ineffective tactics. "Direct action"—terrorism and the general strike—were the means he proposed as a substitute for universal suffrage, and anarchism was to be the goal.

Kōtoku introduced his newly acquired beliefs to the second annual convention of the *Nippon Shakaitō* which was held in February, 1907, and he very nearly managed to convince the organization of the wisdom of direct action and of the futility of the call for a universal suffrage movement. A draft resolution reflecting a compromise between "direct action" and parliamentary socialism had been drawn up. It included the universal suffrage movement among a list of "optional" activities recommended to its members. Kōtoku was not satisfied with this concession and demanded, in an impassioned, hour-long speech, that the party strike the reference to a universal suffrage movement from its resolution and add a clause affirming its belief in the ineffectiveness of parliamentary action. According to one observer, Kōtoku spoke "with eyes ablaze and a tongue spitting forth fire." He criticized the party's reliance on the Diet and its failure to recognize that the universal suffrage movement was only a "device of the bourgeoisie for toppling the power of the nobility and for exploiting the laboring class."[3] The universal suffrage movement and social reform, as techniques of the bourgeoisie, had no place in the struggle of the working class. "Direct action" was the only way—in spite of the fact that there would be many "victims." Kōtoku continued:

> But were there not 400,000 victims sacrificed on behalf of the capitalists in the recent Russo-Japanese War? Compared to this figure, the number of victims that we will lose in a few weeks, a few months of direct strikes, will be insignificant.[4]

At the very time the convention was in progress an important event was taking place at the Ashio copper mines in Ibaragi Prefecture north of Tokyo.* The mines there had been the scene of frequent labor incidents in the past but the riots which broke out

---

* Sources are not altogether consistent with regard to the chronology of events being discussed here but I believe the following is probably correct:

February 4, 1907   Beginning of riots at the Ashio copper mines.
February 5, 1907   Appearance of Kōtoku's article, "I change my ideas" in the *Heimin Shimbun.*
February 7, 1907   Ashio mine incident reaches most critical stage.
February 17, 1907   Debate over direct action takes place at *Nippon Shakaitō* convention.

in February, 1907, were violent to an unprecedented degree in Japanese history. Over 3,600 miners and sympathizers participated in the riots which arose from dissatisfaction with working conditions and low wages. Extensive damage was done to the mine's properties by workers using dynamite. When local police were unable to cope with the situation the Army was finally called out to suppress the rioters, over 300 of whom were arrested.

The Ashio riots were convincing proof to Kōtoku of the value of direct action and he drove his point home to the convention delegates by contrasting the revolutionary vigor of the miners with the torpor of the Diet:

> We have great respect for Tanaka Shōzō* and I think that we have found it difficult getting men like him into the Diet in the past ten years or so. [But] to what effect has he shouted in the Diet for these past 20 years? Was he able to do so much as lift a finger when it came to [alleviating the situation at] the Ashio copper mines in Furukawa? The laborers at the Ashio mines have done more in three days than he did in 20 years. And, more than that, they have sent a shuddering chill into the hearts of the domineering classes. Violence has always been bad, but we have to recognize that the power of direct action for just these three days was greater than 20 years of parliamentary discussions.[5]

The combination of Kōtoku's persuasive address and the events at Ashio nearly gained the day for the cause of direct action. When the final vote was taken on the convention's resolution, Kōtoku's proposal for direct action received twenty-two votes, with twenty-eight votes cast for the program which included universal manhood suffrage.

The *Nippon Shakaitō* convention of 1907 is an all but forgotten moment in the annals of the proletarian movement in Japan. But it does have some significance—as a landmark—to the historian, for if the genesis of the ideological split over revolutionary methods which plagues the Japanese socialist movement to this day can be traced to one moment in time, that moment would be when the vote was taken on the Kōtoku amendment to the convention's resolution on February 17, 1907.

Kōtoku's extremism assured him of a very small, though very enthusiastic, following. It also ushered in an era of extraordinary

* Tanaka Shōzō (1841–1915), a member of prefectural and national assemblies from 1880, was regarded as a friend of the peasant.

police surveillance and oppression of radicals. Although Kōtoku's program had been rejected by the *Nippon Shakaitō*, the very mention of the proceedings of the conference in the *Heimin Shimbun* so alarmed the authorities that they once again ordered the newspaper's suspension. The party was also ordered dissolved, and it was not until after World War I that the Japanese socialist movement again had a party. These regressive measures tended for a while to strengthen the hand of the direct action advocates, for it was becoming evident that there were no legal avenues of critical protest left open by the government. But police oppression, which had begun to weaken the ranks of the socialists, reached a peak in the *taigyaku jiken* ("treason incident") of 1910. Kōtoku himself was executed for his part in this alleged plot to assassinate the Emperor Meiji. If the radical movement in Japan had walked with the unsure steps of an infant in the first decade, it at least had a lusty voice; after the *taigyaku jiken* even that was gone. When the movement was reborn in the first years after World War I, massive changes were taking place in Japanese society, and these changes gave the suffrage movement a popularity and an impetus it had not previously known.

Shinobu Seisaburo in his multi-volume history[6] of democracy in the Taishō period maintains that the "rice riots" of 1918 marked the turning point in the universal suffrage movement.* The riots had created what amounted to a national sense of exhilaration. People had become aware, almost overnight, that they possessed the capacity to affect the society around them, to bring a government down, to challenge the power of the Army and police, to crush their economic enemies, the rice speculators and usurers. They had, in short, begun to acquire a political consciousness.

Almost immediately the universal suffrage movement began to

* The rice riots (*kome sōdō*) stemmed from governmental failure to control the spiraling cost of rice in the inflated economy of postwar Japan. Violence first erupted when the housewives of a fishing village in Toyama Prefecture ransacked the shops of local rice merchants in August, 1918. The riots, which spread to the metropolitan centers within days, necessitated widespread use of the Army and resulted in the collapse of the Terauchi cabinet in September, 1918. The riots were largely spontaneous occurrences with little or no leadership. For a valuable discussion of their significance, see George O. Totten, "Labor and Agrarian Disputes in Japan Following World War I" in *Economic Development and Cultural Change*, IX (October 1960), pp. 187–239.

display a new character. Not only was its base of popular support now broadened, but new tactics were also utilized. The chief participants in the prewar movement had been a small group of discontented intellectuals, most of whom came from wealthy families. Most of these men were far more at home in a study group than in labor union halls. To them the universal suffrage movement had meant, more than anything else, discussion and appeals—and an endless number of formal petitions presented to the Diet. Symbolic perhaps of the change in technique between prewar and postwar years was the "postal card movement" (hagaki undō) which was under way by late 1918. The avalanche of postal card appeals from commoners to their representatives in the Diet brought a large segment of the population into direct contact with the suffrage movement, and while, as one commentator observed, the postal appeals had little effect on the Hara government, they lit a fire under the nationwide suffrage movement.

What then was the role of the radical left wing during this post-war period when new forces in Japanese society began to be released by the rice riots and also by the Russian Revolution? In particular, to what extent was the radical left interested in gaining control of the movement for universal suffrage? One might think that the leaders of the radical left, conscious of their lack of a broad popular following, would have seized this opportunity to mobilize popular agitation for expanded suffrage and then, after acquiring this indispensable base of popular support, move on to more revolutionary causes. Some leaders of the radical left did of course advocate this plan of action, but one of the most influential spokesmen for the radical left, Yamakawa Hitoshi,* advocated a different strategy.

* Yamakawa Hitoshi (1880–1958) had studied at the Christian Dōshisha (at that time a mission high school, later a university) in Kyoto. There he read about socialism and learned of the Christian concept of God. The latter concept, as he later recalled, had sown the first seeds of doubt in his mind about the nature of the Japanese state, the Imperial institution, in short, about what was called kokutai. He left Dōshisha as a baptized Christian at the age of 17, but soon abandoned his Christian faith in favor of socialism. By the time he was thirty he had been in and out of jails for anti-war protests during the Russo-Japanese War, for his participation in the "Red Flag Incident" in 1907, and in connection with the suppression of the Heimin Shimbun where he had been employed from 1906. Biographic details are taken from "Rōnō-ha to jinmin sensen—Yamakawa Hitoshi o megutte" ("Yamakawa Hitoshi and the Rōnō Faction and the people's front"), by Hanzawa Hiromu, in Tenkō ("Conversion") (Tokyo: Heibonsha, 1962), II, 369 ff.

Yamakawa was the translator of Western works on socialism and communism into Japanese, the editor of half a dozen radical journals, including (in post-World War I years) the Communist Party's theoretical journal *Zen'ei* (Vanguard) and *Shakai Shugi Kenkyū* (Study of Socialism), the unofficial organ of left-wing socialism. The *Nihon Shakai Shugi Dōmei* (Japan Socialist League), formed in 1920, was Yamakawa's creation. He also helped organize the Communist Party in Japan, directed its course for two years, and then brought about its dissolution. He was, in short, at the very center of the radical movement in Japan at this time, and if any one person deserves to be called its spokesman, it is Yamakawa.

In February, 1922, Yamakawa expounded his views on the universal suffrage movement in an article in *Zen'ei*.[7] In good Marxist tradition he maintained that tactics such as the struggle for expanded suffrage could be evaluated only in terms of the present stage of development of capitalism in Japan and the direction in which it was moving. The Japanese bourgeoisie, Yamakawa maintained, was different from the European bourgeoisie in that it had not participated in any revolution. Consequently, government by feudal nobility had not been replaced by a bourgeois democracy in Japan. It had instead been replaced by a "government of bureaucratic and military cliques" (*kanryō gumbatsu no seiji*). No significant bourgeois liberalism, no political democracy had developed in Japan; far from that, it was a shrewd dictatorship that controlled the country. Japan's bourgeoisie had already moved into the reactionary and imperialist stage. "It would be the gravest mistake," he wrote, "to imagine that an age of freedom or democracy is coming to Japan. The bourgeoisie in Japan are without a doubt going to become more and more reactionary, more and more predatory, more and more on the offensive whether we have universal suffrage or not."[8]

Since this was so, Yamakawa argued, there was no possibility of an alliance by the proletariat with the bourgeois forces, no room for proletarian participation in any of the bourgeois programs, because such a coalition would only strengthen the hand of the bourgeoisie: "If we crowd in at the newly opened doors of [some future] Diet we will only lend a new stability to the base upon which the future capitalist rule will rest."[9] He pointed to a recent declaration by representatives of nine Tokyo newspapers who had announced their backing of universal suffrage. Yamakawa quotes them as saying:

The class struggle is not going to be an easy problem for Japan to solve. We do not believe that we can eradicate the problem by universal suffrage but if the proletarian classes are not given some right to expression we have no reluctance in contending that this problem is going to become worse and worse. For this reason, that is, in order to pacify class strife, we urge the realization of universal suffrage. . . .[10]

Here was proof for Yamakawa that the bourgeoisie intended to quiet the voice of the proletariat through the granting of universal suffrage. This was sufficient evidence to constitute the basis for an anti-universal suffrage movement led by the proletariat. "Let the party politicians whistle. We'll not dance to their tune," Yamakawa concluded.[11]

What Yamakawa went on to propose was not that the proletariat should merely stand aloof from the universal suffrage movement but that it should organize a counter-movement which would positively renounce enfranchisement rights. Yamakawa had in fact been advocating this for two years or more, and his February, 1922, article in *Zen'ei* was meant to clarify and justify his views on what had by this time come to be known as the *kiken undō* ("discard [voting] rights movement").

In trying to understand why Yamakawa felt that a *kiken undō* was necessary it would probably be wrong to place too much emphasis on his theoretical analysis of the nature of the Japanese bourgeoisie and the revolutionary situation in general. Not surprisingly, the language and the substance of Yamakawa's theoretical evaluations of Japanese society during this period betray his reliance upon Comintern evaluations. In any case, Yamakawa's February, 1922, evaluation was in complete harmony with the evaluation offered by Zinoviev in January, 1922, when Zinoviev addressed The Congress of the Toilers of the Far East in Moscow.*

The most compelling reason why Yamakawa felt that the proletariat had to engage in a *kiken undō* at that time was that he believed that this movement would heighten the proletarian

---

* The Congress of the Toilers of the Far East, whose sessions were held in Irkutsk and Moscow beginning in the fall of 1921, provided the first opportunity for Comintern leaders to meet with significant leaders of the Japanese proletariat and analyze the revolutionary situation in Japan. See Xenia Eudin and Robert C. North, *Soviet Russia and the East* (Stanford: University Press, 1957), pp. 153–154; 225.

consciousness of the labor unions and other left wing organizations which were just beginning to emerge. A *kiken undō* would be a dramatic means of demonstrating to Japanese radical forces of the left that their goals and tactics had nothing in common with the goals and the tactics of the bourgeois political parties and the forces associated with *minpon shugi* (democracy). The *kiken undō* was, more than anything else, Yamakawa's method of establishing the widest possible gulf, psychological and tactical, between the proletariat and the *minpon shugisha* (democrats).

Yamakawa felt that the *minpon shugisha*, men like Ozaki Yukio* and Yoshino Sakuzō,† were merely anxious to use the energy of the laboring classes to bring about democratic reforms such as universal male suffrage, reforms which would lull the revolutionary forces into a false sense of accomplishment and well-being and set them on the dangerous road to parliamentarianism. Referring to Ozaki's efforts to organize Japanese labor so that he might have a mass audience to which he might transmit his suffrage program, Yamakawa said that, "We [Yamakawa and other radical left wing leaders] saw the danger to the infant Japanese labor union movement and sounded the alarm."[12] Going on, he asked rhetorically:

So, you say that there might once have been a danger—a danger that the labor union movement's vigor might be sapped by parliamentarianism—but isn't the danger gone now? Never! It is all the more present now. The gates of the Diet are blocked firmly to the laboring classes now. But what if the gates are opened. Then, without a doubt a segment of the laboring classes will elect to move ahead on the "smooth road." Moreover, this segment will probably be a surprisingly large one. . . . Labor's road ahead is today more than ever fraught with great peril. We must face up to this peril and examine our beliefs. We must strengthen the camp. We must adopt proletarian tactics.[13]

* Ozaki Yukio (1858–1954), a Diet member for sixty-three years, championed the cause of free speech and resistance to the militarists and the *zaibatsu*.

† Yoshino Sakuzō (1878–1933), a professor of political history at Tokyo Imperial University, was probably the chief publicist for *minpon shugi*. His articles appeared nearly every month for years in the *Chūō Kōron* during and after World War I. He believed that democracy was fully compatible with the concept of the Emperor's sovereignty and was the solution necessary to eradicate the great political evils of the day—political corruption, governmental irresponsibility, and the growth of a powerful plutocracy. Universal suffrage, in turn, was the only way to realize—or at least perfect—democracy.

Yamakawa's resentment over the labor unions' failure to realize that they were being "used" by the *minpon shugisha* was probably inevitable considering the philosophy of the *minpon shugisha*. The foremost spokesman for *minpon shugi* was Yoshino Sakuzō. Yoshino's vigorous espousal of political reforms in the years during and after World War I was matched by—and to a great extent derived from—a fear that political and social inequalities would result in revolutionary upheaval in Japan. In discussing the need for universal suffrage in 1919, Yoshino repeatedly uses the phrase "safety valve" (*anzen-ben*) to illustrate the function of universal suffrage. It would allow the people to express their dissatisfaction and release their energy in a harmless, even beneficial, manner. Lacking such a "safety valve," the masses were a powerful and dangerous force which could wreak great havoc on society. In his 1919 work on the suffrage movement, he wrote:

> It is already evident that the people are dissatisfied with the gradual extension of the suffrage and, moreover, even if they were content today, we have no reason to hope that they will remain content tomorrow. . . . Inequitable social legislation [will be regarded as] arising from limited suffrage and the people will perceive the relevance of all this to be problems of their livelihood and then . . . whatever the cost they will one day act to carry out their demands.[14]

The Japanese historian Shinobu has summed up Yoshino's attitude towards the proletariat by saying:

> Yoshino Sakuzō rejected the idea that the people are sovereign (*jinmin shuken ron*), he rejected the idea that proletarian rights should be extended, and at the bottom of his "social cooperation" (*shakai kyōdō ron*) was a distrust of the masses. . . . He was a disciple of government by the philosophers, of government by the elite. . . . Above all else, he concentrated on the endowment of the masses with the right to political participation—but not with political power.[15]

For Yamakawa, mere "political participation" was not enough. And, in view of the proletariat's woeful lack of "proletarian consciousness," political participation would be not only insufficient but useless and dangerous. For this reason, to heighten "proletarian consciousness," Yamakawa called for a *kiken undō*.

It is difficult to measure how much influence Yamakawa's call for a *kiken undō* and his guidance in general exerted on the labor union movement. There was a pronounced change in the tactics and platforms of the labor unions and federations beginning in late 1919 and becoming more pronounced in 1920 and 1921. But it is impossible to determine whether this increased revolutionary fervor stemmed from Yamakawa's guidance or from two other factors: (1) the angry reaction that set in following defeat of suffrage bills by Hara and the *Seiyūkai* politicians in the 42nd session of the Diet;* (2) an intensification of police suppression of strikes and labor union activities which came in the wake of the postwar economic recession and especially after the stock market crash of March 15, 1920. These factors undoubtedly had the effect of making the labor unions more and more disenchanted with parliamentary and "unionistic" methods and increasingly inclined toward policies of direct action.

Whatever the reasons, such a trend did emerge. Let us take one example, the *Yūaikai* (later the *Sōdōmei*). Until 1918 we might characterize this union as conservatively oriented and solidly under the control of men like Suzuki Bunji and Kagawa Toyohiko. These men, especially Kagawa, were not without their merits as union activists, but their basic philosophy was humanitarian rather than revolutionary. The *Yūaikai* at this time supported the universal suffrage movement. By 1919 the influence of this conservative group was still strong in the Kansai (Kyoto-Osaka) area but its headquarters in Tokyo was being infiltrated by a group of radicals, many of them university students who had only recently supported universal suffrage but who now had come to believe in direct action. Their efforts to change the platform of *Sōdōmei* failed in 1919, and again in 1920, but the strength of the so-called anti-suffrage faction (*fusen-ha*) was clearly growing. In December, 1919, at a *Yūaikai*-sponsored meeting in Tokyo, the aged Suzuki Bunji was shouted down with cries of "Suzuki is not a laborer," when he attempted to address the group on the merits of suffrage.[16] Finally, in 1921, the

---

* This is the view of Nishi Masao who maintains that the period from 1919 to early 1920 was the period of greatest mass participation in the universal suffrage movement, but that labor unions began to abandon the movement and veer towards syndicalism immediately after the rejection of universal suffrage bills by Hara and his subsequent dissolution of the Diet in February, 1922. Nishi Masao, "Saikin ni okeru kaikyū undō" ("Various class movements of recent years") in *Nihon shihon shugi hattatsu-shi kōza* ("Essays on the development of Japanese capitalism") (Tokyo: Iwanami Shoten, 1932–1935), p. 18.

Kansai branch of the *Sōdōmei* capitulated, and universal suffrage was completely dropped from the organization's program. Thus the universal suffrage movement had lost the support of a large segment of organized labor by late 1921.

Paralleling this development was the increasing syndicalization of the labor union movement. Yamakawa had hoped to contain the syndicalist forces, to bring these "troublesome extremists" under the control of what was shortly to become the Communist Party. Therefore, in late 1920 he created the *Nihon Shakai Shugi Dōmei* (The Japan Socialist League) which was to include representatives from the entire spectrum of the proletarian movement. It was an important event because it succeeded, for a while, in bringing together the old line socialists of the prewar days with their more radical postwar counterparts, and because it was the first organizational attempt to bring the socialists and labor union leaders together. But like the *Nippon Shakaitō* before it, its early collapse in 1921 stemmed as much from internal strife brought about by anarcho-syndicalist elements as from police oppression.

In 1922, Yamakawa became increasingly concerned with the danger being posed to the radical movement by the anarcho-syndicalists. These forces, he feared, were rapidly overwhelming the labor movement in Japan. Their violent tactics and anarchistic goals were losing popular support among the proletariat and had already brought about a greatly intensified campaign of police suppression. Thus, whereas in early 1922 Yamakawa had perceived that the greatest danger to the proletarian movement lay in its lack of revolutionary fervor, by August, 1922, he had come to believe that the movement was imperiled by an excess of revolutionary fervor.

As a result, Yamakawa wrote an article for the August, 1922, issue of the *Zen'ei*. The article, "Musan kaikyū undō hōkō tenkan" ("A change of direction in the proletarian movement"),[17] has become a classic in the great body of Marxist polemic literature in Japan and was, at the time of its writing, an exceedingly controversial issue among left-wing ideologues in Japan.*

---

* The origins of the article are controversial to this day. The official history of the prewar communist movement maintains that it was "a propaganda piece" designed to publicize the resolutions of the Communist Party." Ichikawa Shōichi, *Nippon kyōsantō tōsō shōshi* ("A short history of the Japan Communist Party")

The article called for a "return to the masses" (*Taishū no uchi e!*). It advocated, on the basis of a reappraisal of the stage of development of Japanese capitalism, a working class movement based upon mass support. It criticized the isolated and sectarian activities of the leaders of the radical movement. Socialism in Japan, he maintained, was ideologically "the purest in the world" prior to World War I. This was, he said, very praiseworthy, a necessary step in the creation of an elite who possessed an independent "proletarian way of thinking." But, he said, in keeping their eyes fixed on the final goal, the destruction of capitalism, the radical leaders had ignored the means to achieve that goal. Yamakawa concluded: the Japanese socialists had always been concerned with purifying the movement but the more they purified it, the further they isolated themselves from the masses. It was now necessary, he insisted, for the leadership to compromise its ideological purity and identify itself with the masses and their goals, however mundane and short-ranged those goals might be.

While Yamakawa did not specifically advocate support of the universal suffrage movement in his "return to the masses" article—perhaps he could not bring himself so suddenly to such an un-revolutionary step—the implications were clear. The large segment of the radical left which looked to Yamakawa for ideological leadership found justification in his words for support of the universal suffrage movement.

By January, 1923, Yamakawa had come to admit that his *kiken undō* may have been a mistake. The idea of a *kiken undō* had been correct "in principle," he continued to maintain, but there may have been an error "in timing."[18] Whether the proletariat decided

---

(Tokyo: Shōkō Shoin, 1946), p. 61. On the other hand, Yamakawa, on the occasion of a post-World War II public forum discussion on the subject "Fifty Years of Progress in the Socialist Movement in Japan," stated that he wrote it on the spur of the moment the very night before its publication. There had been no directions from the Party, he said. Shinobu Seisaburo, *Taishō demokurashii shi* ("A history of Taishō democracy") (Tokyo: Nihon Hyōronsha, 1955), pp. 666–667. (Hereafter, Shinobu, *TDS*.) Shinobu offers an interesting explanation of the "change of direction." It was a response, he maintains, to Soviet appeals to the proletarian forces in Japan to sponsor a movement which would (1) bring pressure on the Government to call off the Siberian intervention and (2) assist in famine relief in the Soviet Union. These two goals could not be carried out within the framework of a syndicalist-dominated movement. They called for a mass organization. Shinobu, *TDS*, p. 629.

to vote or to refrain from voting was not crucial. Such alternatives were merely tactics and a "choice should not be made on the basis of empty theorizing . . . but by analyzing which of two tactics could better counter the bourgeoisie in the Diet."[19] What was crucial, however, was the attitude of the proletariat in pursuing either a universal suffrage movement or a *kiken undō*. In defining what that attitude must be Yamakawa dwelled on the word "positive" (*sekkyokuteki*). Thus, in a somewhat later analysis of his *kiken undō*, he wrote (in November, 1923): ". . . the proletariat must always be ready, in its future political activities, to shift from positive exercise of voting rights to positive abstention from voting."[20] But he hinted that he would not be issuing another call for a *kiken undō* by making it clear that:

> It is an undisputable fact that positive exercise of voting rights is the ordinary means of opposition [to bourgeois forces] and that positive abstention from voting is an extraordinary means of opposition designed to cope with an extraordinary situation.[21]

The most convincing reason for Yamakawa's decision to abandon his *kiken undō* and "return to the masses" is provided in a deposition Yamakawa wrote for police officials fifteen years later, in 1938, when he was under arrest for engaging in illegal political activities.[22] By late 1922, it had become evident, he wrote, that universal suffrage would soon be realized and it would, therefore, only be a question of time before the masses began to engage in political activities such as the creation of political parties. He discussed this with young people, and found that they were all in agreement about the urgent need for the proletariat to create political parties. The proletarian movement could no longer afford to ignore the enthusiastic demands for participation in the universal suffrage movement and other parliamentary activities. "I feared that we would become isolated," he wrote. "Therefore, in order that we might not lose the masses, we would have to take it upon ourselves to organize political parties."[23]

In summary, it would seem that Yamakawa, up until about the middle of 1922, had endeavored to steer the Japanese proletarian forces clear of involvement in the suffrage movement—and all other parliamentary activities—because he felt that the drift of Japanese society was away from democracy and the proletariat could therefore expect no benefit from "entering the Diet." Far from receiving any benefit, it would lose what little sense of "proletarian consciousness" it possessed and would soon cease to pursue revolutionary goals. From about the middle of 1922 on, however, he began to perceive that revolutionary zealots were isolating the radical movement from an essential proletarian base. Moreover, on the basis of either his own analysis or that of the Comintern he had come to believe that there was hope for development of the radical movement within the framework of the institutions. of bourgeois democracy. As a result, he called for a "return to the masses," for proletarian participation in the suffrage movement.

By this time, however, the passage of universal male suffrage legislation was virtually a foregone conclusion, and when final enactment came in the spring of 1925 the forces of the radical left could take little of the credit. Their vacillation and reluctance to engage in parliamentary tactics had meant that the center of the suffrage movement stayed in the hands of the *minpon shugisha* and, more particularly, the opposition "bourgeois" parties of the Diet.[24]

NOTES

1. The article appeared in the *Heimin Shimbun* in February, 1907. It is discussed in Nobutake Ike, "Kōtoku: Advocate of Direct Action," *Far Eastern Quarterly*, III (May 1944), 222–236.

2. *Ibid.*, p. 233.

3. The description of Kōtoku's rhetorical style belongs to Sakai Toshihiko, quoted by Arahata Kanson in his *Jiden* ("Autobiography") (Tokyo: Ronsōsha, 1960), p. 161. Arahata was also present at the convention and presumably recorded Kōtoku's remarks.

4. *Ibid.*, pp. 161–162.

5. *Ibid.*, p. 162.

6. Shinobu Seisaburo, *Taishō demokurashii shi* ("A history of Taishō democracy") (Tokyo: Nihon Hyōronsha, 1955). Hereafter, Shinobu, *TDS*.

7. Yamakawa Hitoshi, "Futsū senkyo to musan kaikyūteki senjitsu" ("Universal suffrage and proletarian tactics"), *Zen'ei* ("Vanguard"), I (February 1922).

8. *Ibid.*, p. 153.

9. *Ibid.*, p. 156.

10. *Ibid.*

11. *Ibid.*, p. 149.

12. *Ibid.*

13. *Ibid.*, p. 150.

14. Yoshino Sakuzō, *Futsū senkyo ron* ("Discourses on universal suffrage") (Tokyo: Bunshinsha, 1919), p. 48.

15. Shinobu, *TDS*, pp. 496–497.

16. *Ibid.*, p. 878.

17. Yamakawa Hitoshi, "Musan kaikyū undō hōkō tenkan" ("A change of direction in the proletarian movement"), *Zen'ei*, II (August 1922), 16–25. Because the original article was heavily censored, my discussion of the article is based upon a less censored version as it appeared in Yamakawa Hitoshi, *Musan kaikyū no seiji undō* ("The political movements of the proletarian classes") (Tokyo: Kōsei-kaku, 1924), pp. 1–23.

18. Yamakawa Hitoshi, "'Hōkō tenkan' to sono hihan" ("A change of direction" and its criticism), dated January 1923, in Yamakawa Hitoshi, *Musan kaikyū no seiji undō*, p. 60.

19. *Ibid.*, p. 61.

20. Yamakawa Hitoshi, "Nihon ni okeru demokurashii no hattatsu to musan kaikyū no seiji undō" ("The development of Japanese democracy and the political activities of the proletarian classes"), dated November 1923 to April 1924, in Yamakawa Hitoshi, *Musan kaikyū no seiji undō*, p. 244.

21. *Ibid.*, p. 246.

22. Yamakawa Hitoshi, *Shuki* ("Memorandum"), an unpublished manuscript, dated August 1938, written at the Higashi Chōfu police station on official police stationery. It is now in the possession of the Hoover Institution, Stanford University.

23. *Ibid.*, pp. 867–869.

24. A discussion of the role of the political parties in the universal suffrage movement is contained in Peter Duus, "The Universal Manhood Suffrage Issue (1919–1925)," *Papers on Japan*, I (June 1961), published by the East Asian Research Center, Harvard University, pp. 227–260.

Factionalism and the Left Kuomintang

JAMES SHIRLEY
Northern Illinois University

Among factions of the Kuomintang, the *tso-p'ai* ("leftist faction"), more commonly called the Left KMT, stands out as having been discussed far more often than any other faction of the Party. From Stalin and Trotsky on down, the subject has been worked over by communist theorists as well as by many non-communist students of twentieth-century Chinese politics. All the effort devoted to the subject has generally resulted in the observation that the Left KMT, if not the figment of someone's imagination, was so weak as to be insignificant. That so much time and effort should have been devoted to study of this aspect of the KMT, to the neglect of other aspects, is only partly the result of the involvement of the Left KMT in the dramatic events of 1927; it is more the result of the primary concentration of our interests on the history of the Chinese Communist Party. It may be (although I doubt it) that lost causes deserve less attention from historians than successful ones and that the neglect of Kuomintang history is thus normal. In the 1920's, however, the Chinese Communist Party represented the lost cause, the KMT the successful one; and to write the history of the 1920's as if the KMT were no more than an obstacle in the path of the Communists, or a vehicle that the Communists might drive, is to distort the history of the period seriously.

In the 1920's, the KMT rode to power in China with the assistance of the Communists, then attempted to smash its former allies. It may well be true, as Senator Knowland recently remarked, that Knowland and his friends are only using the Birch Society for their own purposes; and that after those purposes are achieved the allies will be cast away like squeezed-out lemons. To pose the question of who

97

is using whom is not entirely accurate—both are attempting to win political control for themselves by using the other. In the 1920's, the Communists clearly hoped to use the Kuomintang to attain their own goals; it is equally certain that the Kuomintang intended from the beginning of the Communist alliance to make use of the Communists for KMT purposes. It is true that the Chinese Communist Party grew rapidly through the alliance, but it is seldom understood that the KMT too profited immensely from Communist support. When Sun Yat-sen formed the alliance in 1922, he was the bitter, defeated leader of a small and dispirited revolutionary party. Before the alliance was broken off, his Party had achieved dominance in Chinese politics.

There is another dimension to this pattern of political alliance that is crucial to an understanding of the Left KMT. No significant political party can be expected to show total unity within; its membership is not likely to be fully committed to exactly the same goals. A political party is usually a collection of groups with competing interests within a common framework of goals. From these competing interests, and from the ambitions of individuals, factions are derived. As the party struggles together against outsiders to achieve its common purposes, there is a parallel struggle for power inside the party. This intra-party struggle is fully as serious and as important as the greater one in the world outside. When the Chinese Communists were admitted, on Sun Yat-sen's order, to the Kuomintang, they entered the Party as a ready-made faction, and came to participate in ready-made factional conflicts. It is true that the Communist faction attempted to make use of the Left KMT to gain its own objectives within the Party; similarly, the Left KMT made use of the Communists, with great success, to achieve its purposes. Properly read, I think, the history of this period shows that the Kuomintang was more successful in making use of the Communists than the Communists were in making use of the Kuomintang, and that the Left KMT was more successful in utilizing the Communist faction than the latter was in utilizing the Left KMT.

In describing the Left KMT as a faction, I am following Chinese usage. To do so, I think, distorts the actuality of the Left KMT a bit. The problem is that the Left KMT was no more a coherent entity than was the Kuomintang. One could think of the Left KMT as something other than a faction, perhaps as a super-faction, or alliance of factions, to emphasize its unstable nature. It is better, however, to continue to think of the Left KMT as a faction, with careful notation of the fact that even factions have factions. The Left KMT was then a collection of groups that wanted to ensure that the Left KMT controlled the Party, but each group of which wanted to control the Left KMT. Once the first objective had been attained, the Left KMT quite naturally fell apart at the seams.

Those who discuss the Left KMT generally think of it primarily as it existed at the end, as the group that controlled the Wuhan regime in 1927, under the leadership of Wang Ching-wei. To insist that the Wuhan group was all there was of the Left KMT is unhistorical; one must look at the situation in considerably greater depth. It may be right, for example, to describe the Left KMT of 1927 as a "pillowcase stuffed with red feathers,"[1] but that is certainly no adequate description of the Left KMT in general. The dramatic conflict of 1927 between the Wuhan regime of Wang Ching-wei and the Nanking regime of Chiang Kai-shek is normally presented as a battle between left and right; it was, rather, an open struggle for Party power between the two chief constituent factions of the Left KMT.

One of the major difficulties in understanding the Left KMT lies in the definition of the term "left": what did it mean in the Chinese context of the 1920's? First of all, we have to recognize that "left" and "right" as political descriptions do not derive from the Chinese political experience. They are terms evolved from European parliamentary experience, and were apparently introduced to the Chinese scene by the Communists. I have never seen them used by Chinese before the Communists began to participate in Chinese politics, and the terms were certainly used more commonly by Communists than by KMT members. Kuomintang leaders seem always to have been uncomfortable with them. Sun Yat-sen, as far as I know, never used them; in 1927, Chiang Kai-shek specifically labelled the usage of such divisive terms as one of the crimes committed by the Communists against the KMT.[2]

Wang Ching-wei's usage of these terms is interesting, since he is generally considered the Left KMT leader par excellence. Wang never made a published reference to the terms until 1926. Then, although demonstrating that he knew the European parliamentary context of the terms, he chose to confuse the issue by citing an ancient Chinese literary reference:[3]

> Han Chou-po told the soldiers: "All in favor of Liu, bare your left shoulders; all in favor of Lü, bare your right shoulders." All the soldiers bared their left shoulders; Lü was destroyed and Liu was restored. We can see that the terms "left" and "right" come from very ancient times.

This passage, I think, suggests some peculiarities about Wang's leftism. Moreover, among the rare examples of Wang's usage of the term "left" is a private letter written at the height of the Wuhan regime. In it, Wang disclaimed any knowledge of what the Left KMT was—precisely at the moment he was being publicly proclaimed its leader.[4] It is true that for the next few years Wang allowed his friends to describe him as a leftist, apparently hoping to attract support away from the Communists. After 1931, however, he abandoned this tactic; as his English-language spokesman, T'ang Leang-li, put it, the choice of the term "left" was unfortunate since it smacked of Communism.[5] After that date, one seldom sees the term used by KMT members except in attacks on Wang, where it appears, derisively, as "the so-called left."

Wang Ching-wei wore the leftist label very lightly indeed, so lightly that we should know, even without the aid of his career, that he was no genuine leftist. His lack of commitment, however, was far from unique—virtually every other Kuomintang leader of the 1920's at one time or another wore the same label with equal unconcern. Through long years of usage in their European context, "left" and "right" acquired meanings which are relative and somewhat vague. In the Kuomintang, where their usage was new, the meanings associated with them were much too precise. A KMT leftist, by definition, was one who supported the Communist alliance; a rightist, one who opposed it from the beginning. In 1922, when that issue was first raised, virtually every KMT leader was a leftist. Wang Ching-wei may have been one of the rare exceptions to this rule; but the most prominent early rightist, Chang Chi, was no exception: in 1922 he was a leading leftist, and stood as Li Ta-chao's guarantor for admission to the Kuomintang.

This easy fluctuation between left and right was possible because the Communists fixed the definition of "leftist" or "rightist" on the single issue of the KMT-Communist alliance. Those who favored the alliance were leftists, those who opposed it were rightists. If that issue had possessed necessary social content, if it had been a genuine test of the revolutionary positions of the various leaders in the Kuomintang, then the terminology would have had significant meaning. Sun Yat-sen chose to ally with the Communists not because he approved of communism, but because he needed desperately the assistance offered by Communists. Other Party members either followed the same logic, or accepted the alliance out of loyalty to Sun, or thought it could contribute to personal or factional advancement in the Party. Their decisions had nothing to do with ideology, and everything to do with tactics.

As a matter of tactics, the decision to support the alliance could be reviewed at any time. When conditions changed, KMT leaders reconsidered regularly the tactical value of the alliance, and, as an increasing number withdrew their support from the alliance, there was a gradual but steady decline in the number classified as leftist. By 1925, this drift had become significant enough to force the coining of the term "new right wing," to distinguish ex-leftists from those who had never held that position. In the spring of 1927, the Communists were reluctantly forced to add Chiang Kai-shek's name to the list of new rightists; that summer, virtually all the rest of the old leftists followed Chiang into that category, and there was nothing left that the Communists could classify as a Left KMT. Old KMT leftists could become new rightists overnight because the transition had nothing to do with their philosophical positions; it had only to do with their decisions on one aspect of revolutionary tactics.

During Sun Yat-sen's lifetime, the drift away from the alliance was insignificant. Sun rewarded those who favored his policy, and the careers of leftists like Liao Chung-k'ai, Wang Ching-wei, and Chiang Kai-shek boomed, while those of Old Comrades like Hu Han-min languished. It should not be surprising that opposition to the Communist alliance developed first among the Old Comrades, men whose power in the Party was already well-established. Hu Han-min was Sun's traditional deputy and expected heir; he could not look with favor on a disturbance of the power arrangements in the Party. Even the Russian advisers (who failed to understand much of what was happening around them) did realize that

Communists who obtained official KMT Party positions would alienate those officials they dispossessed.[6] As long as Sun lived, there was little percentage in opposing him, however, and the dispossessed, the threatened, had to bide their time.

When Sun died early in 1925, Hu Han-min expected to enter into his inheritance. Since Hu was noticeably cool to the alliance, the Communists might be expected to oppose his succession to the leadership. As one might expect, all leftists also opposed Hu; but, unexpectedly, not all rightists supported him. According to the principles of factional conflict, no opposing faction must be allowed to become too powerful, and Hu's domination of the Party was no more palatable to most KMT rightists than to the leftists. The conflict in the KMT that arose after Sun's death was not one of left versus right, because the real issue involved was not that of the Communist alliance, but one more important. It was, who would take power in the Party, and whose factional supporters would receive the spoils of victory. The alliance issue was of crucial significance only for the Communists; and it is only because we have not given Kuomintang history the autonomy it deserves that we constantly misread that history by insisting that issues of importance to the Communists were the ones that mattered most.

In the months after Sun's death, what we must call the real Left KMT was formed with the purpose of bringing down Hu Han-min. It was composed of Liao Chung-k'ai's civilian party supporters; the small but growingly-important military following of Chiang Kai-shek; Wang Ching-wei; and most of the significant warlords of the Canton region. In June, this group pulled off a military coup at Canton that left it in control of the Party, its government, and its military forces.

Histories of the Kuomintang are peculiarly reticent about this coup and the forces behind it. The best official histories pass it over in silence; the worst explain it by blaming it on the Communists. "Borodin controlled everything" is the common dictum that exonerates the leaders of the coup. It is however, false; Borodin did not control everything, and there is no indication that he was even informed of the Canton coup. There is no evidence that the Communists were in any way involved in the coup, and the group that carried it out had no need of their aid—this Left KMT was no paper tiger. It had prestigious leadership, and both political and military backing. Perhaps for that very reason, it was easier for the dispossessed to blame the Communists than the real culprits, and they publicly denounced the Communists. Among themselves, they talked of assassinating Borodin; but they shot Liao Chung-k'ai instead.[7]

By early 1926, the Left KMT had successfully read its opponents out of the Party and solidified its own control, but after Liao Chung-k'ai's death a polarization of forces within the Left developed. Wang Ching-wei emerged in control of the Party apparatus, and Chiang Kai-shek in control of its military forces. Chiang chose to demonstrate the superiority of military over civilian power in twentieth-century China through the Chung-shan Gunboat coup early in 1926, when he forced Wang into temporary exile and inserted his own friends into important Party positions. The Northern Expedition, however, diluted Chiang's power and Wang was able to form an opposition alliance, supported by the Communists, and backed by warlord military power. In the Wuhan regime, the results of Chiang's 1926 coup were undone, and in retaliation Chiang declared war on the Wuhan regime which he characterized as Communist-dominated.

Chiang's charges have generally been accepted by historians, and Wang Ching-wei's denials of them discounted. The common historical judgement argues that the Communists controlled the Wuhan regime through what are called "key lower-echelon positions," a statement that somehow ignores the still-more-key upper echelon positions solidly controlled by pure KMT leaders. Above all, as Chiang Kai-shek and others repeatedly demonstrated, the really key positions in Chinese politics were held by those who possessed military power, and there the Communists were hopelessly outclassed. Chiang easily crushed the Communists, and so did the Wuhan regime three months later. It is worth noting that Chiang's attacks on the Wuhan regime were paralleled a dozen years later by Wang's wartime charges of Communist influence on the Chungking regime.

What this formulation suggests about the history of the Left KMT is that the violent factional conflicts in the years after Sun Yat-sen's death had very little to do with either the activities of the Communists or with ideological conflicts within the Kuomintang. Both Chiang and Wang were leftists not because they favored radical solutions to social problems—neither did—but because both favored, for a time, the tactics of the Communist alliance. On that issue they divided only over the proper moment for breaking the alliance. They were not split on questions of ideology, for both were above all else concerned with the problems of power—of who would control China, and who would control the Kuomintang.

That is not to deny that the Communists played a significant role in Chinese history during the 1920's. It is, rather, to attempt to place proper limits on that role, and to indicate the broader significance of the Kuomintang for the history of this period. To explain the phenomenon of the Left KMT, it is more important that we understand the processes of factional conflict in the KMT than that we follow out Comintern pronouncements, or the smoke-screens thrown up by those involved in power struggles.

NOTES

1. Jerome Ch'en, "The Left Wing Kuomintang—a Definition," *BSOAS*, XXV (1962), 576.

2. Chiang Kai-shek, *Declaration to Kuomintang Members (1927)* (Shanghai: Commercial Press, n.d.), p. 14.

3. "Tso-hsiang chou-k'an hsü" (1926), in Shih Hsi-sheng (ed.), *Wang Ching-wei yen-hsing lu* (Shanghai: Kwang-yih Book Co., 1932), II, 368–369.

4. "Ssu-yüeh liu-jih chi Li Shih-tseng shu" (1927), in *Wang Ching-wei chi* (Shanghai: Kuang-ming Shu-chü, 1929), IV, 6.

5. T'ang Leang-li, *Inner History of the Chinese Revolution* (New York: Dutton, 1930), p. 330.

6. "Stepanov's Report on the March 20th Coup d'Etat," in Martin C. Wilbur and Julie Lien-ying How, *Documents on Communism, Nationalism, and Soviet Advisors in China, 1918–1927* (New York: Columbia, 1956), p. 617.

7. Lei Hsiao-ts'en, *San-shih nien tung-lüan Chung-kuo* (Hong Kong: Ya-chou ch'u-pan she, 1955), pp. 27–28.

A Liberal Nationalist and the Meiji Constitution

BARBARA TETERS
Iowa State University

The liberal potential of Meiji nationalism is nowhere revealed more clearly than in the essays of Kuga Katsunan, spokesman of the national essence movement, newspaper editor and publicist from 1888 to 1906.[1] In those remarkable essays which appeared first in *Tokyo Dempō* and then, beginning on February 11, 1889, in *Nihon Shimbun*, Kuga confronted the problem of ministerial responsibility in Japan. He grappled with its implications, attempted to evade it by developing a curious version of separation of powers, and at last accepted fully both the inevitability and the desirability of ministerial responsibility to a parliamentary majority. His acceptance of political party government came much more slowly.

Convinced that factionalism was inherent in parliamentary and party government just as in *hambatsu* rule, Kuga attempted to develop a theory of constitutional government which would enable Japan to avoid both evils. His effort to adapt the famous principle of Montesquieu to the Japanese national essence failed, and Kuga came in the end to accept both parliamentary and party government as the only feasible alternatives to the *hambatsu* government he abhorred. However, the story of his attempt and failure discloses both the liberal potential of Meiji nationalism and the dilemma of the liberal nationalist in the second half of the Meiji period. The crux of this dilemma was the apparent conflict between representative government and the national essence.

Kuga's short career of eighteen years as a newspaper editor and political essayist coincided with a lively period crowded with some of the most momentous events of modern Japanese history. During this era of crises at home and on the continent, Japan became a world power, and Kuga's curiously liberal character is clearly evident in his views on foreign policy long after the *hambatsu*'s critics in the party movement had become as aggressively national-istic as the oligarchs themselves.[2]

While Japan was moving swiftly into the mainstream of world politics, constitutional issues of equal or greater import were being decided within Japan. From the time of the promulgation of the Meiji Constitution and the establishment of the Diet, one of these critical issues was the fundamental problem of the proper relation-ships between the Emperor, the government, and the people, and between those who exercised executive, legislative, and judicial functions. This problem profoundly concerned Kuga Katsunan because it affected the national essence, the preservation of which was his first concern.

The national essence, *kokusui*, was that peculiar and unique quality which made the Japanese distinct from all other peoples on the face of the earth. Under the leadership of the *hambatsu* with its policy of Europeanization, *kokusui* had been all but lost. "Modern Japan," Kuga lamented, "is losing that essence. . . . This island country called Japan will gradually become just a meaningless name in the atlas. . . . The Japanese nation has lost its footing and is drifting in a whirlpool. We want to save this aimlessly drifting Japan. . . ."[3]

The national essence of Japan comprised all of those things which gave the nation a continuing and distinctive character. Of these the most important by far was the union of Emperor and people represented by the compound *kokumin*. None of the components of *kokumin* had an existence apart from it; none was more important to *kokumin* than the others. "The foundations of the modern nation . . . rest on *kokumin* which means a union of the ruler and his subjects. The nation which is based on the ideal of *kokumin* values the people's rights, and yet does not allow them to conflict with the monarch's powers; it permits the existence of the aristocracy but does not permit it to supersede the commoners. In the ideal *kokumin*, there is no aristocracy, no commoner class, no issue of people's rights, no monarchical power. The ideal *kokumin* is a harmonization, a mixture, a union of all of these."[4]

The perfection of *kokumin* was thus Kuga's goal, not the fulfillment of the individual, the satisfaction of the aims of any particular class, the enhancement of the Imperial power, nor the glorification of the state. Indeed, he felt the importance of this concept of *kokumin* so keenly that he referred to himself and those associated with him as the "Kokumin Rompa" in a remarkable series of essays he published in *Nihon* in July and August, 1890, entitled "Modern Political Thought."[5] Neither the nation nor the individual had an existence apart from the other. Kuga refused to choose between them. "Try to imagine," he exclaimed, "the nation without the individual. . . . An uninhabited house is a dilapidated, abandoned house. A man without a home is a wanderer who cannot protect his life. . . . True liberty is the liberty of the individual within the power of the nation." Thus he rejected the arguments of those few Japanese who took the position that the nation existed for the sake of the individual, and denounced with equal fervor the arguments of those who believed the individual existed for the sake of the nation.[6]

Nevertheless, living as he did in an era in which the nation was exalted and the individual neglected and even abused, he urged greater emphasis on the importance of the individual and greater attention to his rights. Those instances in the past and in the present in which great national power had been achieved while the individual and his rights were ignored were "only temporary flashes, like those which result from lighting the fire with a little oil. Civilized government lies first in by all means expanding the potentialities of the individual, and by that means working for the expansion of the national power."[7] Individualism was thus in Kuga's mind an appropriate means to the end which was *kokumin*. The ultimate objective demanded preservation of a delicate balance between the freedom of the individual and the power of the state; it required a maximum of the former and a minimum of the latter.[8]

The liberty of the individual, however, must be accompanied by equality, and since these principles were often incompatible, one must constantly be balanced against the other. Both were principles which, properly applied, would strengthen *kokumin*. In a brilliant essay, "Jiyū Shugi Ikan," Kuga remarked that "liberty is the brother of equality." Yet, like most brothers, "they are sometimes enemies": "Look at what happens when liberty goes forth alone! As for those who are rich, their wealth becomes almost greater than that of the monarch; those who are poor must sometimes even beg for food. Those who are in high places alone have good fortune;

those without high connections have no influence at all! . . . When liberty goes forth alone, a new class arises at once in society, a new aristocracy, a new wealthy class, and new special privileges emerge in various forms."[9] *Kokumin* thus depended as heavily on the doctrine of equality as on liberalism.

Moreover, absolute liberty was the "empty hope" of dreamers, dogmatists, and revolutionaries.[10] Like equality, individualism, and individual rights, liberalism as an abstract principle held no charms for Katsunan. As a means of realizing *kokumin*, liberalism was useful, indeed essential. However, Kuga was contemptuous of those such as the French who worshiped it in the abstract and so "venerate the wooden idols called the rights of man. . . . Ah, this is the liberalism of theory."[11] Frenchmen, he observed, saw liberalism as an inalienable right, Englishmen, as the product of history, Germans, as the natural companion of ability.[12] To Kuga himself liberalism was a means which, however indispensable, must always be judged by the degree to which it contributed to achievement of the ultimate goal.

Kuga was, of course, like almost everyone else in Meiji Japan, thoroughly committed to the Imperial institution. However, he saw no conflict between liberalism and the monarchical form of government, nor any reason for fearing that liberalism would bring republicanism with it. It could be practiced under any form of government; no form of government guaranteed its practice. In this regard, Kuga once again contrasted, as he did so often, England and France.[13]

What liberalism and therefore *kokumin* did require was constitutional government. Indeed, in Kuga's view, *kokumin* could not be realized without limited government. However, constitutionalism, too, was not an end in itself; it was a method of governing, not the purpose of government.[14]

This being the case, how limitation was accomplished depended on the form of government. In a republic, the president's fixed term of office, for example, was a constructive limitation on the executive power. A monarchy demanded a different solution, in short, "Cabinet responsibility."[15] Answerability, however, to whom? Kuga insisted that the answer to that inevitable question be determined by the national essence. He found in foreign countries no model for constitutional government in Japan. Attracted though he was by the doctrine of separation of powers, Kuga could not fail to reject the republican model of the United States. His scorn for French political life is evident again and again in his essays. He saw about him in Meiji Japan the influence of German political thought and feared and abhorred it as a threat to *kokumin*.

Kuga admired the English parliamentary system greatly, but until 1894 he continued to see it as quite unsuited to Japan. In the English Cabinet government, the Cabinet and the Parliament stood between the monarch and his subjects, whereas in Japan "'the Imperial House must be brought close to the people and the barriers between them diminished as much as possible.'"[16] Cabinet government on the English model depended on common understandings and self-restraints rooted in the English tradition and character, a part, indeed, of the English national essence. It provided few if any safeguards in a country where English traditions did not exist and where constitutionalism did not arise in protest against monarchy but in a sense in defense of the Imperial institution. "Constitutionalism as in England is impossible," he wrote. "England is England. To copy the old system of an old country and hope for results is extremely foolish. Still more, simply to copy without taking the results! Still more, not to make a true copy or to copy only superficially!"[17] Kuga and his colleagues, the *kokumin rompa*, hoped instead "to establish constitutional government in Japan in a Japanese form."[18]

It is hardly surprising that in his quest for a Japanese form in which limitations might be placed on the executive power, Kuga turned first to the doctrine of separation of powers. As he himself recalled, Kido Kōin and others in the early Meiji period had been attracted by Montesquieu's famous principle.[19] Kido's disciple, and one of Kuga's patrons, General Miura Gorō, had joined with his fellow "Discontented Generals," Tani Kanjō, Torio Koyata, and Soga Yujun,[20] to develop it further in their 1881 memorial to the Throne.[21] Tani Kanjō, also *Nihon*'s patron, based his 1887 memorial[22] on the same principle in attempting to secure amendments to the draft constitution presented to the Privy Council in 1888.[23]

Writing in the winter of 1888–1889, Kuga argued that immediate separation of executive, legislative, and judicial powers was essential if constitutional government were to be realized and the goal of *kokumin* achieved: "Independence of powers is an essential element of a liberal form of government, and is an indispensable condition if we are to guarantee individual rights and prevent the arbitrary use of political power."[24] The Ishin attempt to accomplish separation of powers had failed and, as a consequence, all the reforms of Ishin had resulted in a "beautiful house built on mounds of sand."[25]

In Meiji Japan the one concept which could not of course be questioned was Imperial sovereignty. Kuga conceded that sovereignty was by its very nature unlimited, and yet insisted that *kokumin* demanded limited rather than unlimited government. Accepting the official doctrine that the Constitution was the gift of the Emperor, he used it to extricate himself from this apparent dilemma, arguing that the Emperor was limited by the Constitution itself because he was limited by the will of his ancestors present in that document: "Although the monarchical power of foreign countries is limited in regard to the subjects, the Imperial power of Japan is unlimited in regard to the subjects and limited in regard to the teachings of the ancestors. Therefore, the great power of the Japanese Emperor is on one hand the so-called sovereignty of Western jurisprudence, that is, unequalled and supreme, while on the other hand, it is the monarchical power of a constitutional country, that is, limited and moderate power."[26]

In a constitutional monarchy, unlike a country suffering under a despotic rule, the sovereign's will reflected that of the public. This, Kuga said, was achieved "by means of the Diet which is the organ of public opinion. . . ."[27] The primary function of the Diet was thus to reflect public opinion to the Emperor and to keep watch over the performance of administrative officials. It should be very careful not to attempt itself to exercise the executive powers for which the Cabinet, not the Diet, was responsible to the Emperor. For example, *Nihon* criticized sharply the First Diet's attempt to use its budget powers to secure changes in administration. Kuga and his colleagues condemned such action on the ground that it "diminishes the responsibility of the Cabinet."[28]

The Cabinet or executive body was directly responsible to the Emperor for its exercise of administrative and executive powers. If it was to fulfill that responsibility, it must listen always to public opinion as expressed through the medium of the Diet: "If this is not the case, the Cabinet will behave presumptuously, using the supreme power of the Emperor to deal with the people arbitrarily, playing with their fortunes, taking advantage of their confidence, and usurping the supreme power of the Emperor. And on this account, the unity of *kokumin* will break down. Still more, those who are in name responsible will in fact misgovern." [29]

Members of the third branch of the government, the judiciary, must also be answerable to the Emperor alone for the proper conduct of their offices. During the Ōtsu Incident of 1891, Kuga, like Prince Konoe,[30] was among those who protested vigorously the government's interference in the judicial process.[31]

No one branch of the government could be entrusted with the full powers of government nor allowed to regard itself as being *the* government. Each branch had a vital but partial role to play. "The executive branch," wrote Kuga, "inclines always toward taking matters into its own hands; the legislative branch always inclines toward joint discussion. The weakness of the former is that it sees only the nation and ignores the individual; the weakness of the latter is that it sees only the individual and ignores the nation." [32] The vision of both was needed for the fulfillment of *kokumin*; somehow, they must be fused. That, in Kuga's judgement, was the most important function of the Emperor: "If the Emperor does not perform this function, enmity and distrust will naturally arise between the three powers and there can be no unity." [33]

Kuga's Emperor, therefore, clearly had to have more than "the right to be consulted, the right to encourage, the right to warn." The national essence and the times required that he play a larger role. In a system of separation of powers, conflicts would inevitably, and indeed should, arise between the three branches of the government. In such circumstances, the Emperor must serve as moderator, synthesizer, and harmonizer. And, no less important, it was the Emperor who must see that the necessary balance was preserved between the needs of the state and the rights of the subjects. The Emperor's power was the "highest" and therefore he alone could provide the essential unity. As Kuga himself described the Imperial role, "The governing power of the Emperor transcends the legislative, executive and judicial powers; on the one hand, it harmonizes the relationships between these three powers; on the other, it mediates between these three powers, that is, the powers of the state, and the rights of subjects." [34]

Kuga's early insistence on the need for separation rather than fusion of powers resulted in part from his deep-seated aversion to, and fear of, the political parties of his day. Parties, or more accurately, factions, were the inevitable products of man's nature, and strife between them was as natural as that between individuals, from which, indeed, it sprang. But this was, in Kuga's view, not an attribute of human nature, but a weakness, and so to be controlled, not encouraged. This was all the more so since party strife imperiled the unity of *kokumin* and thus *kokumin* itself.[35]

Since the so-called parties of the day were in fact factions based on factional interests, not true parties committed to the fulfillment of *kokumin*, they were thus in essence just like the *hambatsu*. All were factions whose activities threatened *kokumin* itself. Consequently, there was nothing to be gained from the establishment of the principle of ministerial responsibility to a parliamentary majority. Kuga put his case vividly: "For us to go through the years just changing those who govern would be like using wolves and wild dogs to fend off wolves and wild dogs. That is what will happen if the responsibility doctrine is enforced."[36]

In fact, if the executive had the support of a majority in the Diet, the unchecked government by faction which would result, "herd government," "swarm government," Kuga called it,[37] would be even worse than *hambatsu* rule. Since strong discipline prevailed in the parties and they were "almost organized as troops," there was little hope that they would survey critically proposals submitted to them by an executive body which represented the same interests as they. Instead, they would give "almost unlimited obedience" to the party leadership. "If such parties should come to power," Kuga warned, "they would not only not oppose the government when it was wrong, but would rather feel the obligation to protect it. . . ."[38]

Kuga also argued, although less often and at less length, that acceptance of the legal doctrine of ministerial responsibility to a parliamentary majority could only lead to deterioration of moral accountability since people would come to understand responsibility only as meaning they could do as they liked so long as their actions resulted in no consequences damaging to themselves.[39]

Kuga thus rejected parliamentary and party government which was, he said, no better than "government by *soroban* [abacus]."[40] He made instead the case for separation of powers and concluded,

"In a situation like today's in which men are dominated by self-interest we do not want an executive body united with the Diet, but rather want to have them a little opposed."[41]

Nonetheless, in February, 1894, Kuga published in *Nihon* an essay entitled "Ministerial Responsibility," in which he lamented that the principle of ministerial responsibility to the Emperor directly had resulted in totally irresponsible government. The separation of powers doctrine assumed the full acceptance by all the members of the government of their varying responsibilities to the Throne. That full acceptance was manifestly lacking in so far as the ministers were concerned, and it now seemed to Kuga that the ministers' ultimate responsibility to the Emperor and to *kokumin* might better be secured through the medium of the Diet, particularly through the ministers' acquiescence in the will of the people expressed in the election of a new Diet following dissolution of the previous one.[42]

While this new approach required drastic modifications in the separation of powers doctrine as Kuga had developed it earlier, it did not compel him to renounce altogether or in essence his original position. Nor did it reflect any sudden insight into the inadequacies of the separation of powers doctrine under Japanese conditions.

Kuga's reaction to a series of events beginning in 1891 with the Ōtsu Incident had revealed an increasing awareness of the *hambatsu*'s intention to disregard separation of powers[43] and a growing alarm over the rapidly developing power and influence of the *hambatsu*'s military faction.[44] Moreover, as the months went on, he became more and more closely associated with Prince Konoe Atsumaro, leader in the House of Peers of a group to whom *Nihon* gave the flattering title, "the people's party of the House of Peers." Konoe, who eventually assumed the financial responsibility for *Nihon*, had returned to Japan in 1890 from Germany where he had written his doctoral dissertation on the doctrine of ministerial responsibility. His biographers have remarked that although he was educated in Germany Prince Konoe was attracted instead by the political thought and institutions of England.[45]

The events which occurred during and immediately after the Fifth Diet completed this phase of Kuga's political education and led him finally to attempt to reconcile his original theory of separation of powers with the doctrine of ministerial responsibility to a parliamentary majority, a principle which he had not long before rejected as being totally unsuited to Japan.

The story of the short-lived Fifth Diet, convened on November 28, 1893, twice suspended, and dissolved on December 30, 1893, really began in late 1892. At this time the nation had become aware of the price Mutsu Munemitsu, now Foreign Minister, was preparing to pay for treaty revision: in exchange for legal and tariff autonomy, the new Foreign Minister was willing to concede mixed residence. Opposition sprang up in many quarters, from the left-wing of the party movement to such groups as the "Discontented Generals" and Konoe's circle in the House of Peers, from the organs of the parties to *Nihon* and *Nihon Jin*. This resentment crystallized in the establishment in the spring of 1893 of the Dai Nihon Kyōkai, or Great Japan Society, which formed the nucleus of a Strong Foreign Policy Faction in both houses of the Diet. This strangely conglomerate assembly included Ōi Kentarō and others of the left-wing party movement and still others such as Kuga's patrons, Konoe and Tani. Together and supported by *Nihon*, they vigorously opposed mixed residence and pressed for strict enforcement of the existing treaties. They argued that if the government applied consistently and rigorously those provisions of the unequal treaties which restricted the activities of foreigners, the treaty powers would be willing to grant legal and tariff autonomy without insisting that their nationals be permitted to reside freely throughout Japan.[46]

When the Fifth Diet convened in November, 1893, Abei Iwane, a leader of the Dai Nihon Kyōkai, had just risen in the House of Representatives to urge strict enforcement, when the government suspended the Diet. At the end of the suspension period, Foreign Minister Mutsu himself appeared in the House to argue against a strict enforcement policy. This personal appearance failed to persuade the Strong Foreign Policy Faction. The *hambatsu* again suspended the Fifth Diet, and on December 30, 1893, thirty-three days after it convened, dissolved it. In dissolving the Fifth Diet, Itō compounded the damage by failing to follow the precedent established by Matsukata who had published his reasons for advising the Emperor to dissolve the Second Diet.[47]

The *hambatsu* quite accurately regarded the Dai Nihon Kyōkai as the source of much of its troubles. The government suspended its meetings, censored and suspended its organs, and on the day following dissolution of the Fifth Diet ordered the Dai Nihon Kyōkai disbanded on the charge that it disturbed the public order. When part of the membership formed the Dai Nihon Kurabu, or Japan Club, the *hambatsu* disbanded it also.[48] The oligarchy took steps to prevent election of the Dai Nihon Kyōkai's leaders to the following Diet. *Nihon* itself, silenced for long periods, felt directly and painfully the force of the *hambatsu*'s anger.[49]

A little more than a month after the late December, 1893, dissolution of the Fifth Diet and suppression of the Dai Nihon Kyōkai, Kuga published in *Nihon* his essay called "Ministerial Responsibility." Here he clearly and unequivocally argued that the ministers' responsibility to the Emperor and *kokumin* could only be achieved through their responsibility to the Diet.

The effect of the actions of the *hambatsu* in recent years had been to destroy constitutional government, just as a "revolution" from below would do. He saw no fundamental difference between the two situations. "If we call those among the people who agitate the breakdown of constitutional government traitors and rebels, how," he asked, "can we call those in the government who act to break down constitutional government loyal subjects and faithful retainers? If A protects order and prevents harm, B must also be a defender of order and preventer of harm."[50] The difficulty Kuga suggested, lay in confusion regarding the nature of ministerial responsibility, a confusion which resulted from the fact that some discussed the doctrine from the standpoint of law and others from the viewpoint of morality.

The legal argument was that the ministers were responsible only to the Emperor. Kuga admitted that ministerial responsibility, that is, the responsibility of the ministers to the Emperor and the people through the Diet, could not be defended on the basis of law. The Constitution itself offered no means whatsoever of enforcing such responsibility, no basis, indeed, for justifying it. According to the Constitution, the ministers were appointed by the Emperor and responsible to him, and he was sacred and inviolable. The appointment and dismissal of ministers belonged to the supreme power of the Emperor and was not subject to interference by the Diet or the people.

However, in actual fact, as Kuga demonstrated in some detail, this meant that the ministers operated without any restraint, claiming always to be exercising the Imperial will. Kuga's disillusionment with his theory of the separate and direct responsibility of each of the three branches to the Emperor is nowhere more apparent than in the passage in which he said: "When those who are ministers themselves wish to leave office, they obtain an Imperial order; when they wish to remain in office, they do so in the name of the Emperor. They remain, or they depart, on the basis of the legal doctrine. They say, 'How can we be governed by public opinion and general consultation? We serve the Emperor.' So they come and go freely under the pretext of the law. . . ."[51]

The legal doctrine thus served as a cover for irresponsibility. However, while he found it very difficult, if not impossible, to justify ministerial responsibility on legal grounds, Kuga was attracted by the moral argument. The ministers' responsibility to the Emperor could best be fulfilled by means of their responsibility to the people, manifested both in their acquiescence to the popular will and in their attempts to guide it. Their acceptance of both obligations, in fact, was nothing more than their duty as loyal subjects.[52] The two obligations were inseparable: "We do not say that the ministers should act automatically according to public opinion. If they believe public opinion to be wrong, they must on occasion oppose it by the proper methods, and of course it is proper for them to attempt to guide public opinion. If they are unable to guide it, then it is also proper for them to leave office."[53]

This practice, he argued, was inherent in the establishment of constitutional government and the opening of the Diet: "Those who are opposed to this . . . can not refute the moral argument. Their excuse is simply the dignity of the government and the self-confidence of the Cabinet. . . . If we say that by going along with public opinion and acting on the basis of general consultation we injure dignity and self-confidence, then it would have been better in the first place not to have established the Constitution or opened the Diet."[54]

At this point, February, 1894, Kuga was sufficiently sophisticated to recognize that the Emperor's use of his sovereign power to dismiss a minister on his own initiative would create an "extraordinary political crisis" which surely none would want as a regular occurrence.[55] The ministers must instead fulfill their responsibility to *kokumin* by asking to be relieved of office in certain circumstances:

"When they are incapacitated in mind or body, have made mistakes in the administration of the government, or are opposed by the Diet, ministers must, obeying the moral law, ask to be relieved of their offices. When they themselves ask to be relieved, that is the time to relieve them." [56]

Their resignations should be the result of their relationship with the people, not the monarch, since "the ministers are not personal servants of the Emperor's Court but are elder statesmen of the nation and should leave office whatever the Emperor's feelings toward them. Moreover, leaving office in such circumstances would be the best reply to His Majesty's benevolence." [57]

However, the ministers should not hold and leave office simply on the basis of a count of votes in the House of Representatives. To do so would be to govern by *soroban*, as Kuga has remarked on an earlier occasion. According to him, "If they [the ministers] govern simply according to public opinion and general consultation, and leave office on the vote of the Diet, not only will the dignity of the government of course be injured, but there is also the danger of stimulating changes in the form of government. However, those who advocate responsibility do not make that request at all. They do not go beyond asking that public opinion be consulted, their demand being based on the spirit of the establishment of the Constitution and the opening of the Diet." [58]

Therefore, in circumstances in which the ministers were convinced that the course they followed was correct even though they were opposed by the Diet, they must "fulfill their responsibility to the people" by requesting dissolution of the Diet and election of a new House of Representatives. The purpose of dissolution must be to fulfill their responsibility to the Emperor and to the people by ascertaining the true condition of public opinion. Dissolution for any other reason would be unconstitutional:

> The dissolution of the Diet, whatever the circumstances and whatever the reasons, is always nothing other than a means of examining public opinion and making certain what it really is. Since this method is a very extraordinary one, and one which is very expensive to the people, it should not be used unless the government is sure it is right. If the government uses it improperly, it is a hundred times worse than when the statesmen of the arbitrary period built huge useless public works to parade their extravagance!

Still more when they dissolve, however reluctantly, simply in order
to protect mutual relations within the government![59]

The only justification for dissolution was to determine the state
of public opinion. What did political morality require if in the new
Diet the ministers confronted the same hostile majority as previously?
Clearly, immediate resignation of the ministers: "Even though the
Constitution contains no provision limiting the number of dissolutions, to dissolve, even time and time again, until the government obtains a Diet which is in agreement with it, is nothing but
irresponsibility."[60]

In the four and a half months which followed dissolution of
the Fifth Diet and the convening of the Sixth on May 15, 1894, the
burden of opposition to the *hambatsu* was carried largely by the
House of Peers and shared by *Nihon*, with notable effect if one may
judge by the resentment of the *hambatsu*.

Thirty-eight of the aroused Peers, led by Kuga's friends and
patrons, Konoe Atsumaro and Tani Kanjō, presented a letter of
advice to the Cabinet ministers charging that the government had
evaded its constitutional responsibility of defending itself before
the Diet by twice suspending and then dissolving the Diet.

Itō replied that the responsibility for dissolution belonged entirely
to the lower house which had intruded on the function of the
Cabinet by proposing strict enforcement, and said that by doing
so at this particular time, the Diet had endangered treaty revision
which was one of the nation's most urgent needs.

This answer inflamed rather than soothed the resentment of the
thirty-eight Peers who therefore deputized Konoe and Tani to send
the Cabinet a statement of the reasons they found the Prime
Minister's reply so very unsatisfactory. Kuga's view of the proper
relationship between Diet and Cabinet is clearly reflected in this
document in which the Peers denied Itō's contention that there
must always be cooperation between the branches of the government. Exercise of the independent powers of the Cabinet and Diet
would naturally and inevitably sometimes produce friction between
them, and it was inevitable that in a country such as Japan "in
transition from arbitrary to constitutional government . . . friction
between the executive and the Diet will sometimes be great."[61]
This was almost a paraphrase of Kuga's March, 1893, assertion
that "in a situation like today's, in which men are dominated by

self interest, we do not want a government united with the Diet, but rather want to have them a little opposed."[62] As Foreign Minister Mutsu pointed out in a letter to Itō, the Peers' position was exactly the same as that of the *Nihon* faction.[63]

The Sixth Diet, convened on May 15, 1894, was the shortest yet. Its dissolution on June 2, 1894, was the second dissolution in five months. It came within twenty-four hours of unanimous passage by the House of Representatives of a resolution presented by the Strong Foreign Policy Faction which insisted on the Diet's right to approve foreign policy decisions which required the passage of new laws, changes in existing law, or new taxation.[64] Sometime afterwards, reflecting on 1894, Kuga wrote, "1894, which should be remembered as a particularly bad year in the history of constitutional government, was accompanied by unreasonable dissolutions."[65]

1894 was also the year which marked a fundamental and tragic change in the nature of Japanese nationalism, as Professor Maruyama and others have demonstrated. Kuga was one of the few Japanese who did not now turn their attention, their energies and their resources toward the continent and aggressive nationalism. For Kuga, for example, the Sino-Japanese War was rather an excuse to demand a more effective role for the Diet.[66] However, the Seventh Diet was in session for only five days and by the time the Eighth Diet met, the war was nearly over. The war with China had provided the *hambatsu* with a rationalization for minimizing still further the importance of the Diet.

The end of the war brought a renewal of domestic hostilities but with a new and most significant change. The members of the oligarchy who headed postwar governments now sought to reduce party opposition and Diet obstruction by allying their Cabinets with one or the other of the parties, the Jiyūtō in the case of the second Itō Cabinet, the Shimpotō in the case of the second Matsukata Cabinet. Moreover, postwar governments engaged in military expansion on a large scale. Kuga found the implications of both developments frightening.

Nonetheless, in 1898, Kuga at last recognized the inevitable, inescapable link between constitutional or parliamentary government and party government: "If we oppose party cabinets, we must also be against a representative assembly and against constitutional government itself. This is just in the nature of things."[67] Thus Kuga acknowledged, as he had been unwilling to do when writing "Ministerial Responsibility" in the spring of 1894, the inseparability of parliamentary and party government. That he delayed so long in taking this last step was due to his view of the parties of his day as in fact factions, as incapable of perfecting *kokumin* as was the *hambatsu* itself.

When he came at last to advocate party government, he found no party to which to give his support. Japanese nationalism unaccompanied by Kuga, had undergone a profound change since the spring of 1894. The postwar parties to his dismay acquiesced in and supported militarism, were oblivious to the ever more serious threats to the independence and integrity of China, and welcomed Japan's deeper and deeper involvement in conflict with Russia. In domestic affairs, they allowed themselves to be "'bewitched'" by the oligarchs into alliances with the *hambatsu* which led to greater and greater abuses of the rights of individuals.[68] Although Kuga was hopeful that first one and then another "faction" might develop into a "true party," he was again and again disheartened and disillusioned.[69]

By the time he came to long for party government, the parties themselves had abandoned liberal nationalism and liberalism had all but vanished from the Meiji scene. Kuga was one of the few and isolated survivors, abandoned indeed by most of his former comrades in the national essence movement.

Ironically, his leadership, and *Nihon*'s, of the national essence movement had stimulated the growth of an aggressive and jingoistic nationalism which was in many and fundamental ways abhorrent to Kuga himself. Moreover, in defining the national essence, he had developed a relatively sophisticated and coherent theoretical foundation for opposition to both *hambatsu* and party government. In doing so, Kuga eloquently reinforced the deep and traditional distrust of government by faction which vitiated the growth of representative government in Japan before World War II. His eventual conversion to advocacy of parliamentary and party government manifested the strength of the liberal potential in Meiji nationalism. Nonetheless, while in his case the liberal impulse proved in the end to be the stronger force, the late nineteenth century vigor of the ancient inhibition against factionalism was clearly revealed in the earnestness and persistence of Kuga's efforts to develop an alternative theory of representative government.

NOTES

1. Kuga Minoru (Katsunan) was born in Tsugaru *han* in 1857 and received his early education in *han* schools distinguished for Western studies as well as for traditional learning. After attending Sendai Normal School and the Ministry of Justice Law School in Tokyo, he entered the Dajōkan Documents Bureau (later the Gazette Bureau) and later served also in the Torishirabe Kyoku under Inoue Ki. In April 1888, he left the government service to take over the newspaper *Tokyo Dempō*, and ten months later he became editor of the new *Nihon Shimbun*, which in its early years was financed largely by General Tani Kanjō and his associates. Konoe Atsumaro later contributed heavily to *Nihon's* support and finally took over its ownership in December 1901. In June 1906, *Nihon's* editorship was transferred to Itō Kinsuke because of Kuga's illness, and Kuga died September 2, 1907, at the age of fifty-one. Twenty-one members of Kuga's *Nihon* staff jointly resigned in dissatisfaction with the new management, and joined *Nihon's* sister publication, the magazine *Nihon Jin*, which then became *Nihon oyobi Nihon Jin*. For further biographical information, see *Shinsen Jimmei Jiten*, ed. Shimononakaya Saburō (Tokyo, 1937–1941), II, 400; Kawabe Shinzō, *Katsunan to Sohō* (Tokyo, 1943).

2. Maruyama Masao, "Meiji Kokka no Shisō," *Nihon Shakai no Shiteki Kyūmei*, ed. Rekishigaku Kenkyū Kai (Tokyo, 1949), pp. 181–236. Maruyama Masao, "Kuga Katsunan-Hito to Shisō," *Chūō Kōron*, February, 1947, pp. 37–44. Yasui Tatsuya, "Kuga Katsunan ni okeru Nashonarizumu," *Shakai Kagaku Kiyo*, No. 8, March 31, 1959, pp. 1–76.

3. Kuga, "Nihon Sōkan no Shushi," *Nihon*, February 11, 1889, in *Katsunan Bunroku*, ed. Suzuki Torao (Kyoto, 1933), pp. 365–366. This collection of Kuga's essays will be cited hereafter as *Bunroku*.

4. "Kokuminteki no Kannen," *Nihon*, February 12, 1889, *Bunroku*, p. 374.

5. "Kokumin Rompa" in "Kinji Seironkō," *Nihon*, July–August 1890, *Bunroku*, pp. 137–149.

6. "Jiyū Shugi Ikan," *Nihon*, January 1890, *Bunroku*, p. 63.

7. "Shimmin no Kenri" in "Kinji Kempōkō," *Tokyo Dempō*, December 28, 1888–February 8, 1889; *Nihon*, February 28–March 30, 1889, *Bunroku*, pp. 46–52.

8. "Jiyū Shugi Ikan," *Bunroku*, pp. 63–64.

9. *Ibid.*, pp. 66–67. See also "Kokka Teki Shakai Shugi," *Nihon*, March 22–29, 1897, *Bunroku*, p. 457.

10. "Jiyū Shugi Ikan," *Bunroku*, pp. 63–64.

11. *Ibid.*, p. 66.

12. *Ibid.*, pp. 59–60.

13. *Ibid.*, p. 70.

14. "Keizai Hōritsu Shimpo Shugi" in "Gensei," *Nihon*, March 6–22, 1893, *Bunroku*, p. 188. See also "Kokumin Rompa," *Bunroku*, pp. 143–149.

15. "Jiyū Shugi Ikan," *Bunroku*, p. 71.

16. Maruyama, "Kuga Katsunan," pp. 39–40.

17. "Eikoku Seiji to Shimpo Shugi" in "Gensei," *Bunroku*, pp. 208–209.

18. "Kokumin Rompa," *Bunroku*, p. 145.

19. "Taiseishugi oyobi Shinashugi no Chūnyū" in "Kinji Kempō Kō," *Bunroku*, pp. 16–20.

20. Kojima Kazuo, *Ichirō Seijika no Kaisō* (Tokyo, 1951), p. 23. Kojima, himself a member of *Nihon*'s staff, here labeled Generals Tani Kanjō and Miura Gorō the "Discontented Generals," referring to their disaffection beginning after the Satsuma Rebellion when the *hambatsu* reorganized the armed forces on the German model.

21. Shimanouchi Toshie, *Tani Kanjō Ikō* (Tokyo, 1912), II, 87–88.

22. *Ibid.*, pp. 89–121.

23. Shimizu Shin, *Teikoku Kempō Seitei Kaigi* (Tokyo, 1940), pp. 295–312.

24. "Seikenryoku no Tōitsu oyobi Kaishoku" in "Kinji Kempō Kō," *Bunroku*, pp. 15–16.

25. "Taiseishugi," *Bunroku*, p. 20.

26. "Tennō no Taiken oyobi Kōshitsu" in "Kinji Kempō Kō," *Bunroku*, pp. 44–46.

27. "Gikai Ron," Part I, *Nihon*, December 7, 1890, *Bunroku*, pp. 433–434.

28. "Kanshōteki Setsugen no Hi wo Ronzu," *Nihon*, February 3, 1891. See also "Gikai Ron," Part III, *Bunroku*, p. 437.

29. "Kokusei no Yogi," Part I, *Nihon*, November 30–December 3, 1889, *Bunroku*, pp. 408–409.

30. Konoe Kazan Kai, *Konoe Kazan Kō* (Tokyo, 1924), pp. 49–51.

31. Hirao Michio, *Shishaku Tani Kanjō Den* (Tokyo, 1935), pp. 642–646.

32. "Kokka no Kenryoku" in "Kinji Kempō Kō," *Bunroku*, pp. 54–55.

33. "Tennō no Taiken," *Bunroku*, p. 46.

34. *Ibid.*, p. 45.

35. "Seitō no Hei-Kokueki to Tōri," Part I, *Nihon*, June 28, 1889, *Bunroku*, p. 397. See also "Shoron" in "Kinji Seironkō," *Bunroku*, p. 78.

36. "Sekininron to Hōritsu oyobi Keizai" in "Gensei," *Bunroku*, p. 205.

37. "Gyōsei Kikan to Seiji Tōha" in "Gensei," *Bunroku*, p. 198.

38. "Eikoku Seiji to Shimpo Shugi" in "Gensei," *Bunroku*, pp. 208–209.

39. "Sekininron," *Bunroku*, pp. 203–205.

40. *Ibid.*, p. 205.

41. "Eikoku," *Bunroku*, p. 208.

42. "Daijin Sekinin Ron," *Nihon*, February 2–4, 1894, *Bunroku*, pp. 445–455.

43. See p. 111.

44. "Bushin Kansei Ron," *Nihon*, July 30, 1892, *Bunroku*, pp. 439–445.

45. *Konoe Kazan Kō*, p. 39.

46. Otsu Junichiro, *Dai Nihon Kensei Shi* (Tokyo, 1927), IV, 34 ff.

47. *Teikoku Gikai Shi*, ed. Kudō Takeshige (Tokyo, 1901), pp. 302–303.

48. *Ibid.*, pp. 324–325.

49. Maruyama, "Kuga Katsunan," pp. 40–41; Kojima, *Ichirō Seijika no Kaisō*, p. 27.

50. "Daijin Sekinin Ron," Part I, *Bunroku*, p. 445.

51. *Ibid.*, II, pp. 449–451.
52. *Ibid.*, p. 450.
53. *Ibid.*
54. *Ibid.*, III, p. 453.
55. *Ibid.*, p. 452.
56. *Ibid.*, pp. 452–453.
57. *Ibid.*
58. *Ibid.*, p. 453.
59. *Ibid.*, p. 454.
60. *Ibid.*
61. *Teikoku Gikai Shi*, pp. 308–315.
62. See p. 113.
63. Letter from Mutsu to Itō, January 29, 1894, *Itō Ke Bunshō*, Vol. 53, p. 256.
64. *Teikoku Gikai Shi*, p. 341.
65. Yasui, "Kuga Katsunan ni okeru Nashonarizuma," p. 38.
66. *Ibid.*, pp. 30–31.
67. *Ibid.*, pp. 61–62.
68. *Ibid.*, pp. 46–48.
69. *Ibid.*, pp. 66–70.

The Origin and Nature of the Genro

JACKSON BAILEY

Earlham College

INTRODUCTION

In nearly all discussions in Japanese or in English of the development of political institutions in Meiji Japan, mention is made of the Genro as the crucial policy- and decision-making body in the political process. However, little information has been gathered and systematically presented as to the origin, nature, and role of this powerful group of men. The Genro was not a legally constituted body; neither its membership nor its functions were formally defined. As a result definitive statements about it are difficult to make; historical evidence is scanty and at times leaves the student to speculate on matters of process and definition. However, in view of the increased interest in Meiji political history, especially interest in the political leadership of the period, it is important to review the available evidence in an attempt to establish as clearly as possible the origin and nature of the Genro as a political institution. When did it become a recognizable and definable body? Who belonged to it? What were the conditions which produced it? What were its primary functions and how did these fit into the total process of political life in Japan in the Meiji period? These last two questions are open-ended and would require investigation far beyond the confines of a brief article. However, some attempt will be made to raise questions in this area of analysis and interpretation and to point out possible avenues for further exploration.

This article will attempt to establish the date from which the term Genro becomes an accepted and clearly defined designation for the small group of men at the center of political power in Meiji Japan. It will attempt to establish who these men were and what their functions were as members of the Genro. It will further attempt to analyze the political process out of which the Genro as an institution evolved, relating this process to the larger fabric of political history. This is, to my knowledge, the first attempt in English to focus on this problem and, therefore, will need correction, addition, and supplementation. If this study can effectively draw attention to the necessity for further investigation of the nature and function of the Meiji leaders and their roles, individually and as a group, in the process of political development in modern Japan, it will have served a worthy function.

The sources for any study of the Genro are at the same time too voluminous and extremely scanty. Much primary source material in the form of documents, diaries, and letters (in particular such collections as the Ito and Yamagata-Ke Monjo) is available for each of the members of the group. In addition, political biographies, analyses of the events of Meiji history, and studies of political institutions (e.g. Oka, *Kindai Nihon seiji-shi*, Tsuji, *Nihon kanryo-sei no kenkyū*)[1] all deal in one way or another with the role and actions of the Genro. However, none of this material, with one or two notable exceptions which will be discussed later, focuses substantial attention on what factors produced the institution and when it became a definable reality. For the purposes of this study, therefore, most of this material is of little help. Fortunately there is one source of information which is directly relevant to this investigation, and on which I have relied heavily; this is part of a book by Yamada Shikazō, *Seiji kenkyū* ("The Study of Politics").[2] The first half of this book contains an essay entitled "The Process of the Establishment of the Cabinet System in Japan as Viewed in the Press" ("Shimbun-shi yori mitaru Nihon ni okeru naikaku seiritsu no keishiki"). Yamada was a promising young political scientist at Tokyo University in late Taisho. He carried out this research as part of a program of graduate study there. His work is carefully documented and represents a major contribution to the study of Meiji leadership. The other major source of information for this study has been the newspaper files held in the Meiji Shimbun Zasshi Bunko at Tokyo University. Through the references provided by Yamada, I have been able to check carefully, not only his statements but those of others who have written more casually about the Genro. In addition to these two sources I have consulted the standard bibliography in Japanese in the field of modern Japanese political history for interpretive and analytical statements about the Genro. In most of these there is a surprising lack of attention given to the institution. In the twenty-volume *Nihon rekishi daijiten* there is not even an entry. Only in two books, Professor Oka's *Kindai Nihon seiji-shi* ("A Political History of Modern Japan") and the *Taiheiyō sensō genin ron* ("A Discussion of the Causes of the Pacific War"), compiled by the Nihon Gaiko Gakkai,[3] is there significant discussion of the Genro. Both of these treat its origin, nature, and role only briefly.

Before dealing in some detail with the results of my investigation let me state briefly the conclusions I have reached. First, I have established with some certainty that the term Genro was first used in 1892 by the press independently in a well-defined context to refer to a particular group of men as an institution. It would be unwise to attempt to set the date too exactly since the use of such a term in common parlance could only be established over a period of time. It appears in the *Chōya shimbun* for August 9, 1892. I have not been able to find the term used independently before this date, so it seems reasonable to suggest the year 1892 as the period within which the term appeared as a distinct designation for the group. Second, the Genro emerged in the years 1885–1892 as a result of the interplay of complex political forces. Its role is directly related to the establishment of the cabinet system in 1885, and its prototype performed the function of mediator and adjustor of the roles of the formal organs of government in a variety of contexts until its clear acceptance and identification as an institution. This much can be stated with some certainty. In addition, I have attempted to construct a framework within which the origin and emergence of the Genro could be analyzed in their relation to the political process as a whole.

THE GENRO DEFINED

Until recently a common mistake in discussing the Genro has been to assume that the group was related to the legally constituted body known as the Genro-in. There is no relationship between the two that I have been able to find, and I am aware of no serious scholarly research which suggests such a link.

The Genro-in was established by an Imperial command on April 14, 1875, as part of a reorganization of the Dajōkan; it was charged with legislative functions. Its first president was Prince Arisugawa; Gotō Shōjirō was appointed vice-president. In September, 1876, it received an imperial command to draft a memorandum on the establishment of a national constitution, and a Constitutional Investigation Bureau was set up by it. Its importance declined rapidly after 1881, and it was finally abolished October 20, 1890.

The term Genro (elder or senior statesman) is an old one originating, as so many such appellations and phrases do, in the Chinese classics; specifically, it appears in the *Shih Ching* (Shi Kei). Most dictionary discussions of it relate it to the term Genkun (veteran statesman) and say that both terms are used to refer to men who have served the state with distinction. Even in the dictionary the terms are both usually linked with the Meiji leaders by some reference to "Meiji no Genkun; Genro Seiji-ka." There is much in both the dictionary and encyclopedia discussions to suggest that Genkun is the prior and more general term, the use of Genro evolving during the Meiji Period and acquiring more specific institutional meaning. Moreover, the historical evidence which I have found supports this interpretation. Therefore, I shall deal briefly with the term Genkun before discussing the emergence of the Genro as a separate and identifiable term.

The term Genkun derives from a poem by the Chinese emperor Liao Chien (sixth century) in which he uses it to refer to a distinguished servant of the state. More specifically, in Japan it comes to be used for those direct advisers of the emperor who were expected to answer Imperial queries regarding matters of state. The *Seijigaku jiten* ("Dictionary of Political Science")[4] says that the term was applied generally to those who served with distinction during and after the Restoration. By the mid-1880's it was widely used in the press in the phrase "Isshin no Genkun" to refer to the members of the oligarchy. It is certain members of this group who, in the 1890's, come to be designated as the Genro. Let us see how this transition took place.

Through several pieces of evidence, we can trace the process of change from the use of Genkun to refer to the oligarchs as a whole, to the use of Genro to refer to a clearly defined, though never legally constituted, group in the inner circle of Meiji politicians. The first piece of evidence appears in the Imperial Rescript of April 28, 1888, which announced the establishment of the Privy Council. The

Rescript begins, "I hereby select veteran statesmen (*Genkun*) and other skilled and able persons . . ." Commentators are agreed that this use of the term Genkun becomes a specific point of reference from this time on. Furthermore, it is used to refer to eight men (Ito, Yamagata, Inoue, Ōyama, Kuroda, Matsukata, Yamada, and Saigo). This view is supported by the imperial letters sent in turn to Ito, Kuroda, and Yamagata after they had resigned from office as premier. Ito and Kuroda each received such a letter on November 1, 1889. Ito's letter read, "I look upon you, Count Ito Hirobumi, Imperial Adviser, noble of the rank of Jū Ni-i Kun Itto, as one to whom I can continue to look for advice as a minister of state. I further hereby make clear that it is my pleasure to consider you a Genkun." Yamagata received the same letter May 7, 1891, at the time of the announcement of the first Matsukata Cabinet.

The formal designation of these three men as "Genkun" seems, in hindsight, to have been an important step in the transition to the use of the term Genro. Insofar as these letters gave formal definition to the term Genkun, they made it less satisfactory as a general term for the oligarchy as a whole, or for the inner group who held political power. At the same time, in the period from 1889–1892, with the promulgation of the Constitution and the establishment of parliamentary government, the public identification of this small group of oligarchs as the true holders of power called forth the use of a new term and helped to give it clear definition. The emergence of the institution and the establishment of the term reflected the process of struggle and adjustment among the various factors in the political equation, a process that had been clearly identifiable from the time of the establishment of the cabinet system in 1885. We shall return to some discussion of this process later. It is important now to establish when the term was first used, to whom it referred, and what functions the Genro as an institution performed.

I have checked carefully the key issues of two of the leading newspapers of the period 1885–1892 (the *Tokyo nichinichi shimbun* and the *Chōya shimbun*). The first use of the term appears to have been in the issue of August 9, 1892, of the *Chōya shimbun* where the following entry appears:

> The Genro have been meeting regularly since August 2 in order to settle the question [of the new cabinet] while the people have been waiting and wondering . . . If this cabinet is a lineup of the Genkun

> then . . . As they established the new Cabinet [the second Ito Cabinet] the various Genro must have been thinking deeply about the problems [of instability] which have plagued previous cabinets. These have resulted from internal division not external attack . . .

Here in two separate places the term is used independently to designate an institutional grouping with a clearly implied function, that of creating the new cabinet. It is also noteworthy that the term Genkun is used in this context with a meaning that is clearly distinct and lacks any institutional nuance.

There are a number of other earlier references to the Genro, but these are not well substantiated, and in some cases seem to be premature uses of the term. Yamada Shikazō in his book refers at a number of points to the growth in the power of the Genro. In discussing the formation of the first Yamagata Cabinet in 1889 he says, "One finds no mention of the Genro Kaigi in the newspapers, but there are numerous references to secret meetings of various ministers."[5] In reference to the formation of the first Matsukata Cabinet in May, 1891, he says, "From this article [from the *Tokyo nichinichi shimbun* for May 8] one can see clearly that this is the time of the emergence of the power of the Genro." Actually the article itself deals more with Ito's individual role as a mediator in the formation of the cabinet than with the oligarchs as a group, so that Yamada appears to be drawing a more substantial inference from this than is justified.

For a period of several years before the term Genro became established, several other colloquial references were current in addition to the use of Genkun. One of these was Rokuhaku— referring to the six counts who were the so-called "Genkun." There are frequent references in the press to meetings of the "Rokuhaku Kai."[6] Often Sat-Cho was added to Genkun and their meetings were referred to as the Sat-Cho Genkun Kai. Another common term for these meetings was the Kuromaku Kai. (Kuromaku means the black curtain and refers to those who met in secret. It also suggests a manipulator behind the scenes.) The individuals were sometimes referred to as the Kuromaku Genkun.[7]

It is clear that the formation of the second Ito Cabinet represents an important landmark in the development of Meiji political institutions and especially in the emergence and public identification of the Genro as an institution. The Cabinet itself was known as the last Genkun Cabinet. The term Genro came into use from this time on, so that by 1896, when the second Matsukata Cabinet was formed, a newspaper headline read "Shōhaku, Genro to Beibetsu" ("Matsu-kata Breaks with the Genro").[8] Newspaper discussions of political affairs by this time carry frequent references to the Genro so that the term has come to have a well-accepted institutional meaning.

The clearest, most direct summary analysis of the emergence of the Genro is given by Yamada in the last section of his essay which is entitled "The Constitution and Convention." He says:

> My thought is that those various rules of custom which are especially associated with cabinet formation cannot be considered either speci-fically constitutional or specifically unconstitutional. There I should next like to set forth examples of these rules which I shall call the "conventions" related to the process of cabinet formation in Japan. . . .
>
> Section I Those who recommend candidates
> for the post Premier-designate
>
> (1) Genro By about 1892 it appears that the new candidate for premier was being selected and recommended to the throne . . . through consultations carried on extra-legally by a group of older politicians in meetings known variously as the Kuromaku-Kai, the Sat-Cho Genkun-Kai, and the Roku-haku Kai. In time these meetings came customarily to be called the Genro Shūkai and finally today they generally are called the Genro Kaigi. Those who were included in this group and designated as Genro appear to have been the following ten : Ito Hirobumi, Yamagata Aritomo, Inoue Kaoru, Kuroda Kiyotaka, Yamada Akiyoshi, Ōyama Iwao, Saigo Tsugumichi, Matsukata Masayoshi, Katsura Tarō, and Saionji Kimmochi. There were, of course, in addition one or two others who may have received the imperial summons for questioning but it is not clear whether these "Genkun" actually received the summons or not. In addition [it should be noted that] except for Saionji, these ten were all from the Satsuma or Choshu Han. There are such elder politicians as Ōkuma Shigenobu and Itagaki Taisuke who are omitted from those referred to as "Genro." In short, I believe that this situation resulted from the special circumstances and events of history after the Restoration, and from the power and personalities of those men who are included as Genro.

Yamada says in commenting on the establishment of the second Yamagata Cabinet of November, 1899 :[9]

> The thing we must note in this is that the power and influence of the Genro in the process of cabinet formation is more and more being

systematized. This is perhaps because the comparative ease with which political power—power which they had passed to the parties [at the time of the Ōkuma-Itagaki Cabinet in June, 1898] in a moment of wavering self-confidence—had returned to them gave them a sense of the position which they as Genro had attained.

A piece in the *Tokyo nichinichi* for November 5, 1898, further substantiates such a view. It said:

Since the establishment of the Meiji Constitution it has almost without exception become the settled practice for the veteran politicians known as Genro or Genkun to be summoned for questioning by the Emperor whenever a cabinet crisis occurs. When this happens it is more common for these men to consult together and report jointly than for them to present their view individually. Occasionally their conference takes place as an imperial audience [Gozen Kaigi] as, for instance, in June of this year when Marquis Ito resigned. Therefore the Genro actually carry responsibility as [political] advisers of the highest rank although they do not have any status in the administrative system, nor is such an organization provided for in the Constitution. This status has been conferred only through natural evolvement and convention.

In distinguishing between who is a Genro and who is not there is no absolute criterion [by which to judge]. If you use the criterion of those who clearly received the Imperial designation as "Genkun who would henceforth be regarded as Daijin" then there are only two, Ito and Yamagata. [Actually Kuroda also received such an imperial letter.] If one considers those who received imperial letters of appreciation for their service when they resigned, Ōkuma and Itagaki as well as Count Hijikata must be included. However, the group actually has always been restricted to the Sat-Cho group of four Marquises (Ito, Yamagata, Ōyama, and Saigo), and three Counts (Kuroda, Matsukata, and Inoue). Essentially the name Genro is used exclusively for those elder politicians who had served as Sangi [in the old Dajōkan]. [Actually Ōkuma and Itagaki had been Sangi, so the author of the article is confused on this point.]

Of course these men did not designate themselves as Genro. The Emperor selected the seven as recipients of imperial questions, and accordingly the public, too, attached this name to them. So it appears that in point of fact, we have a unique organ for response to imperial questions about the most important matters of state, which has been added to the highest political institutions of the Empire without any constitutional provision having been made for it.[10]

Yamada later quotes an Asahi press correspondent, Hayashida

Kametaro, who wrote an article entitled "Direct Conversations with Prince Ito on the Position of the Genro." Hayashida says that Ito told him:

> There was no provision [for the Genro's position] in the Constitution itself. However, it developed because the Meiji Emperor gave to the [members of the] Genro commands to the effect that in the matter of cabinet formation the Genro and others (nado—) after consulting among themselves should obtain imperial sanction [for their candidate].[11]

With these contemporary analyses and Yamada's comments in mind it is appropriate to turn to present-day analyses and interpretations of the Genro system. Professor Oka comments on the Genro as follows:

> One thing related to the establishment of the cabinet system of which we must take note is the Genro system. After the cabinet system had been set up the Emperor sought the advice of a few men who were known as the "Isshin no Genkun," in order to decide who should be designated to organize the next cabinet when a political change was in order. In this way it became the custom for the premier-designate to be the man whom these men recommended after consultation among themselves. As a result the men who answered the formal Imperial inquiry came by popular custom to be called the Genro. Ito Hirobumi, Yamagata Aritomo, Inoue Kaoru (all of Choshu) Matsukata Masayoshi, Saigo Tsugumichi, and Ōyama Iwao (from Satsuma) were the ones so recognized. The Genro thus constituted occupied a de facto position; their position had no legal basis in the political system. Nevertheless these men actually performed a very important function as "cabinet makers." However, the Genro, as I have indicated, were all men from either Satsuma or Choshu, and so the power of the Hanbatsu through this position of their members as Genro continued very strong in political affairs.[12]

It should be noted that Professor Oka omits Yamada Akiyoshi from his list, whereas Yamada Shikazō had included him. This can be explained, perhaps, by the relatively minor role which Yamada played in political affairs. He was a military man who made an important contribution to the Restoration cause, but he does not seem to have been an important member of the so-called Genkun group. Further research is needed on the roles of Yamada, Saigo, and Ōyama.

The one other statement of significance which I have found in secondary sources appears in the book, *Taiheiyō sensō genin ron*. An early chapter in the book includes a discussion of the role of the Genro as part of an analysis of the position of the Emperor and his chief advisers. This is a careful and enlightening analysis. I quote from it at some length:

Next we turn to a discussion of the Genro. When was the unique position of the Genro established? It goes without saying that from the beginning the Meiji government was in actuality a Sat-Cho Hanbatsu government. Then, by the revisions of December, 1885, the structure of the Dajōkan with the Sa- and U-daijin, which posts had been held by various members of the Kuge and other nobility, was abolished. From then on we had a Sat-Cho government in both name and fact. The first Ito Cabinet, and the Kuroda Cabinet which followed it, were staffed from the beginning by the Sat-Cho Genkun (Ito, Yamagata, Inoue, Kuroda, Matsukata, and Saigo). However, in the next cabinet [Yamagata's first which was organized in December, 1889] while Ito, Inoue and Kuroda stayed outside, Ito was frequently consulted by the Emperor regarding a variety of matters. When in 1891 Yamagata announced to the Emperor his intention to resign, the Emperor first sent the Imperial Household Minister, Hijikata, to Ito to ask his consent to the move. Ito replied, "It is inappropriate and rather awkward for one who is outside the government to receive an imperial question on such an important matter of state as the resignation of cabinet ministers . . ." Nevertheless he did reply and recommended that either Saigo or Matsukata would be [proper] candidates. In due time the first Matsukata Cabinet was formed. Ito, Yamagata, Inoue, and Kuroda stayed out of this cabinet but worked behind the scenes (in the so-called Kuromaku-Kai) as its guardians or sponsors, and Ito and the others responded frequently to imperial questions.

In July, 1892, when Matsukata resigned, Ito, Yamagata, Kuroda, and the others received the Imperial query regarding a successor, and as a result of their joint consultation the second Ito Cabinet emerged. Thus it was because the so-called Sat-Cho clique held political power that the conventions of having the top Sat-Cho men recommend the next premier, reply to imperial queries, and become the sponsors of the cabinet came into being, in spite of the fact that there was no legal basis for such action.

The Genro group originally consisted of Ito, Yamagata, and Inoue of Choshu, and Kuroda, Matsukata, Saigo, and Ōyama of Satsuma, but with Kuroda's death in 1900 and Saigo's death in 1902, by the time of the first Katsura Cabinet we entered a time called the five Genro

Period (Go-Genro Jidai) (i.e., Ito, Yamagata, Inoue, Matsukata, and Ōyama). Since Katsura was a protégé of the five Genro they answered imperial questions on secret matters of state and took an active role as sponsors of the Katsura cabinet itself. During the Russo-Japanese War Ito, as President of the Privy Council, and Yamagata, as Chief of the General Staff, participated in the Supreme War Council. At the same time there were many conferences which included the five Genro and the important ministers of state. Thus from the time of the first Katsura Cabinet the Genro system became clearly established. Since a comparatively junior follower of the Genro had become Premier the weight of the Genro's influence increased, and they came to participate not only in the selection of the next premier but also in decisions on important matters of foreign affairs and internal politics. It looked as if they had become the top leaders in the political affairs of the nation. This situation continued even after 1900 when the top Genro, Ito, died, and the system remained strong on into the Taisho Period. In 1915 Inoue died and the next year [1916] Ōyama also, but Yamagata remained in good health and preserved the dignity and power of the institution. In 1922 when he died, as might have been expected, the institution began to fade. (In 1924 after Matsukata died, Saionji Kimmochi alone was left.) [13]

The above analyses and comments are, I believe, sufficient to indicate the nature and importance of the role the Genro played, as well as the composition of the group. Further discussion of the effects of the Genro system on constitutional government would be appropriate were we to consider in detail political developments in the Taisho and early Showa periods. Professors Minobe and Yoshino both take the position that the Genro performed an essential function, given the immature state of Japanese political institutions during Meiji, Taisho, and early Showa. However, for the purposes of this article it is perhaps sufficient to make note of this as an important question needing further attention. It would be particularly helpful in studying the matter to examine the period after the deaths of Yamagata (1922) and Matsukata (1924) when Saionji was left as the only Genro. There appeared in the mid-1920's an idea, perhaps supported by Saionji himself, known as the Genro Muyo Ron (the thesis that the Genro [system] was no longer essential).

THE GENRO AND THE POLITICAL PROCESS

Having traced the emergence of the Genro, attempted to establish when the term became a definable concept, and indicated the formal role of the institution in Meiji politics, I should like to suggest very tentatively a framework within which the evolution of the Genro can be analyzed as part of the total political process in Meiji Japan.

A review of the political events of the seven-year period from 1885–1892 reveals certain striking organizational and theoretical innovations. The organizational innovations included the establishment of the cabinet system itself in 1885, the creation of the Privy Council in 1888, and the promulgation of the Constitution in 1889. Among the theoretical innovations were the idea of a Genkun Cabinet (1885), the concept of *Dōi Shugi* in cabinet formation (1888), and finally, bridging organization and theory and tying them together, the institution, and the idea of, the Genro. In the end the Genro as an institution came to play the role of mediator and adjuster within the government. In turn the oligarchs had created the cabinet system and the Privy Council in the expectation that they would be able through these to adjust their differences and maintain their power. These two structural devices failed to perform this function satisfactorily, and, after the promulgation of the Constitution, having turned once more, in desperation, to a Genkun cabinet, they settled finally upon the informal device of the Genro as the best means to accomplish their end.

With the death of Iwakura Tomomi in 1881 effective political control passed to the second generation of Meiji leaders—Ito, Yamagata, Inoue, and Matsukata. During the next decade this group, while formally grappling with the problems of creating a new political system, were informally experimenting with devices which could function as means of adjustment, compromise, and maintenance of political control by the group. The establishment of the cabinet system and the Privy Council were two evidences of this experimentation, but the public recognition of the existence of the Genro from 1892 on provides evidence of the ultimate device for control upon which the leaders settled.

The establishment of the cabinet system on December 22, 1885, was an event of major importance in Japanese political history. It represented a significant developmental stage in the transition from the use of *ad hoc* or traditional institutions and official titles such as Dajō Daijin, to the modern political system which came into being with the promulgation of the Meiji Constitution February 11, 1889. This announcement of 1885 also reflected the interaction of forces which were emerging in internal politics, and was one formalization of the same response which also produced the Genro.

The challenge of the *Jiyu Minken Undo* (usually referred to as the Popular Rights Movement) in the early 1880's had shaken the Meiji leadership and forced the promise of constitutional government. This was followed by the establishment of the Constitutional Investigation Committee, and in 1885, by the setting up of the cabinet system. A brief examination of this latter event and some interpretations of it gives insight into the informal adjustments which were taking place within the group of leaders.

Professor Oka Yoshitake in his book says:

> The setting up of the cabinet system was, as the foregoing explanation would indicate, a structural reform of great importance. However, it did not bring any change in the already firmly established political control exercised by the "Hanbatsu."[14]

Yamada quotes from the *Jiyu-to shi* ("History of the Liberal Party"), to the effect that "the implementation of the cabinet reform . . . represented the transfer of actual power at last into the hands of Ito, Inoue, and Yamagata as the successors to Okubo and Iwakura."[15] As Professor Tsuji points out in his discussion of the establishment of the cabinet system, there were critics who saw it only as the tool of the Hanbatsu, but others such as Fukuzawa welcomed its creation as a step toward a full-fledged constitutional system.[16] The *Jiji Shimpo*, which reflected Fukuzawa's position, spoke of the cabinet as performing the function of "Kanmin Chōwa" (bringing harmony to relations between the government and the people). Even the sharp critics in the Jiyuto and Kaishinto welcomed its creation as a step toward constitutional government while suggesting that in practice Hanbatsu control would be secured and strengthened. The *Chōya Shimbun*, which represented the Jiyu-to position, in an article entitled "Administrative Reform" (Byōdō no Kaikaku), saw in the changes a step forward in the preparation for establishing the Diet while at the same time emphasizing that the nature of Hanbatsu control would remain unchanged.

Whichever interpretation one accepts, it seems clear that the cabinet system represented a recognition of the realities of Japanese politics while the former pattern had not. The new system provided what the leaders hoped .would be a way to preserve their own positions in fact while in form they moved toward constitutional government. It enabled them to carry on policy deliberations within a satisfactory formal framework. The first cabinets were known as Gen-kun cabinets and represented the oligarchs' first response to the new system. (The emergence of the Genro in the 1890's was the final stage in this adjustment process as far as the Meiji Period was concerned.) The primary need in order to make the system function properly was a means of consultation and adjustment of differences among the members of the oligarchy. The cabinet was supposed to provide a framework for this and did so for a time. However, by 1888 this device was no longer working satisfactorily, and two new elements of theory and practice appear. One was the establishment of the Privy Council, announced in an Imperial Rescript on April 28, 1888; the other was the appearance of a theory of cabinet formation known as Dōi-Shugi (the theory that the cabinet should be made up of men who were in agreement on matters of policy).

The creation of the Privy Council provided the formal structure for this new development. Instead of having all the group that had come to be known as the "Genkun" enter it, the cabinet was organized and run by a nucleus of the oligarchs, while the remaining ones took posts in the Privy Council. This appears to have been done in an attempt to provide for smoother day-to-day governmental operation while preserving the total position of the oligarchy. There is evidence to support this in Ito's biography,[17] as well as in secondary interpretations of the role of the Privy Council. In a letter to Inoue on April 20, 1888, Ito said:

> This [the Privy Council] is my own invention . . . [and he continued] When we consider the principles of our Constitution, we see that sovereignty resides with the Imperial institution. Ultimate decision-making authority has been conferred on the Emperor through a specific clause in the Constitution. In any situation in which the cabinet and the Diet reach an impasse, there are two alternatives open to the Emperor. One is to receive the resignation of the cabinet; the other is

to dissolve the Diet. In such a case there is a need for an advisory organ which can give adequate advice to the Emperor after considering the total national picture and the feelings of the public. We must create the Privy Council to perform this function for there is no other adequate institution. This is what I have decided.

The Kuroda Cabinet took office on April 30, 1888, just two days after the establishment of the Privy Council. Ito became the first president of the Privy Council and thus, far from withdrawing from a political role after his resignation as premier, he was in a position to participate actively in politics from this new post. The absence of Ito and Inoue Kaoru from important positions in the Kuroda Cabinet is evidence of this new approach in which the cabinet is composed of a nucleus of oligarchs who can agree on day-to-day policy, the remainder operating behind the scenes and in the Privy Council. This mode of operation continued through the first Yamagata Cabinet and the first Matsukata Cabinet, but by then the pressures on the oligarchy from the opposition in the Diet and in the country as a whole caused this arrangement to break down. The Privy Council did not play an important role again until the 1920's and 1930's. (Appointment to it became a sinecure. Remember Ito's resentment over being forced to become president of the Privy Council in 1903?) Evidence that this was the case is provided by the following excerpt from the *Tokyo nichinichi shimbun* of November 5, 1898. This editorial criticizes the Privy Council and the Genro system saying:

... This being the case [the Privy Council now has little function]. If we are to remove its deficiencies should we not reform it, changing its membership to include all of the so-called Genro and Genkun. ... We deplore the fact that even though the Privy Councilors exist as members of the highest advisory organ, they do not assume the role of advisers in dealing with such important matters as cabinet changes, and instead, that role is assumed by the Genro Kaigi, an institution which looks like the Privy Council but has no constitutional status. After the next cabinet takes office, we hope that it will reconstruct the Privy Council, incorporating in its membership the real veteran states-men and other men of ability, so that in the future when a cabinet crisis occurs, the issues in which imperial decision is necessary can be handled by the highest advisory organ.

The second Ito Cabinet was a return to the original Genkun principle of active participation in the cabinet by all the oligarchs (though Matsukata was not a member) in an attempt to meet the internal political crisis precipitated by the repressive policies of the first Matsukata Cabinet.

This last Genkun Cabinet provided a solution to the immediate crisis, but for the long run a new device was needed. The emergence of the Genro was an *ad hoc*, but effective, means of providing for the adjustment of differences and the mobilization of support for the formal organs of government. Despite repeated challenges from the parties and the Diet it remained the locus of political power throughout the Meiji Period and continued to hold the balance of power in political decision-making well into the Showa Period.

The nature and significance of the Genro and its function as I have outlined it above can perhaps best be seen in the following analysis by Professor Inada in the *Taiheiyō sensō genin ron*: [18]

> Although the existence of the Genro system originally was the reflection of the political power of the Sat-Cho clique, we should not lose sight of the fact that national political unity was preserved by this means.

The author then goes on to say that the Meiji Constitution was modeled on the Prussian, not the English, system and therefore left important areas of state which could not be controlled by either the Cabinet or the Diet. The Meiji Constitution assumed that the Emperor would give active leadership in these areas particularly, providing the needed unifying element in relations between the civil and military arms of government. In fact, however, the Meiji Emperor himself did not provide dynamic leadership, and so the Genro, as the men closest to him, began to assume this role on his behalf. Professor Inada then continues:

> The reason that the inherent problem of dualism in the Meiji system did not appear at this time (i.e., in the Meiji Period) lies clearly in the fact that by means of the Genro, who were from the Sat-Cho clique, unified national political leadership was provided through their advice to the Emperor and to the Cabinet and the military.

He then points out, supporting his stand with specific examples, the fact that at the time of both the first Sino-Japanese War and the Russo-Japanese War, important decisions were made, and unity was preserved, through the active participation of the Genro. As Professor Inada has so well stated, the Genro were the mediating and unifying element without which the Meiji system could not have worked. The unsatisfactory experience which the Meiji leaders had in their attempts to use first the Cabinet and then the Privy Council is further evidence of the vital role which the institution came to play in this period.

This explanation of the origin and function of the Genro has attempted to indicate how it can be related to other events of the period. It suggests that much more work must be done on the roles of individuals as well as in institutional analysis. I hope it can serve as a spur to further study of political leadership in Meiji Japan.

NOTES

1. Oka Yoshitake, *Kindai Nihon seiji-shi*, Vol. I (Tokyo: Sōbunsha, 1962); Tsuji Kiyoaki, *Nihon kanryo-sei no kenkyū* (Tokyo: Kōbun-sha, 1963).

2. Yamada Shikazō, *Seiji kenkyū* (Tokyo: Iwanami, 1926).

3. Oka, *Kindai Nihon seiji-shi*, I, pp. 254–255, 304; Nihon Gaikō Gakkai (comp.), *Taiheiyō sensō genin ron* (Tokyo: Shimbun Gekkan-sha, 1953).

4. *Seijigaku jiten* (Tokyo: Heibonsha, 1957), p. 358.

5. Yamada, *Seiji kenkyū*, p. 35.

6. *Ibid.*, p. 86.

7. *Tokyo nichinichi shimbun*, August 2, 1892.

8. *Ibid.*, September 20, 1896.

9. Yamada, *Seiji kenkyū*, p. 49.

10. Quoted in *ibid.*, pp. 49–50.

11. Quoted in *ibid.*, pp. 87–88.

12. Oka, *Kindai Nihon seiji-shi*, I, 254–255. Oka adds that in the Taisho Period Katsura Taro and Saionji Kimmochi were added to the Genro. Katsura was a Choshu man and so only Saionji, a Kuge, of all those who became Genro, was not from the Sat-Cho group.

13. *Taiheiyō sensō genin ron*, pp. 32–33.

14. Oka, *Kindai Nihon seiji-shi*, p. 253.

15. Yamada, *Seiji kenkyū*, p. 32.

16. Tsuji, *Nihon kanryo-sei no kenkyū*, pp. 84–86.

17. Shumpo-kō Tsuishō Kai, *Ito Hirobumi den*, Vol. II (Tokyo: Tōseisha, 1943), pp. 585–586.

18. *Taiheiyō sensō genin ron*, p. 34.

The Japan Medical Association and the Liberal Democratic Party: A Case Study of Interest Group Politics in Japan

WILLIAM E. STESLICKE

University of Illinois

One of the striking features of contemporary Japanese politics is the great number and variety of organized groups and associations actively engaged in efforts to influence public policy-making.[1] Largely a postwar development, the so-called *atsuryoku dantai* ("pressure group" or "interest group") first attracted widespread public attention in 1957 and 1958 during the drafting of the annual budget bill. The activities of a number of groups were highly publicized, and many political commentators concluded that the *atsuryoku dantai* were "running wild."[2] Included in this category was the Japan Medical Association (*Nihon Ishikai*).

The JMA has continued to attract the interest of journalists and scholars and the Association is often pointed to as a "typical" *atsuryoku dantai*, i.e., an organization engaged in political activities designed to promote the "selfish interests" of its members. It is often asserted that the JMA is more influential than most organizations engaged in similar activities, and that the secret of the Association's "success" is its ready access to the high command of the Liberal-Democratic Party (*Jiyū Minshutō*). Some observers argue that, in matters related to the nation's system of medical care and health insurance, the JMA is able to manipulate the LDP more or less at will. The assumption is that effective access guarantees favorable action on policy claims and demands.

Basing his observations mainly on American political experience, David B. Truman has written of political interest groups and the problem of "access" as follows:

> Power of any kind cannot be achieved by a political interest group, or its leaders, without access to one or more key points of decision in the government. Access, therefore, becomes the facilitating intermediate objective of political interest groups. The development and improvement of such access is a common denominator of the tactics of all of them, frequently leading to efforts to exclude competing groups from equivalent access or to set up new decision points, access to which can be monopolized by a particular group. Toward whatever institution of government we observe interest groups operating, the common feature of all their efforts is the attempt to achieve effective access to points of decision.[3]

Like their counterparts in the West, JMA leaders seek to develop their "access" to key points in the governmental process. Unlike many other groups in Japan, however, the JMA has found it difficult to work through bureaucratic channels. As a result, JMA leaders have tended to concentrate their energies in developing and maintaining access to top leaders in the LDP, and through them, to the Cabinet. It is important to note that such "access," in and of itself, is not the basic objective. As phrased by Truman, it is the "facilitating intermediate objective." By and large, the JMA has been successful in maintaining access to the LDP. When important decisions are made, JMA leaders normally occupy a seat at the bargaining table. Contrary to the assumption commonly held in Japan, however, such access does not always lead to favorable action.

The objective of this paper is to describe some of the basic factors which contribute to the JMA's relative ease of access to the LDP and, through a case study, to describe some of the tactics which have been employed to further develop and maintain this access. The case study will also illustrate the general proposition that effective access to key points in the decision making process facilitates—but does not guarantee—achievement of policy objectives.

I

Truman has suggested that the relative ease with which a particular political interest group is able to gain access to key points in the governmental process is affected by at least three major variables: (1) the social status of the group or of its spokesman; (2) the effectiveness of its organization; and (3) the qualifications and skills of its leaders.[4] The JMA's success in establishing and maintaining access to the leadership of the Liberal-Democratic Party during the past several years may be partially explained in terms of these three variables.

Since the establishment shortly after the Meiji Restoration of a system of medical care based on Western medical science, the Japanese doctor has occupied a position near the top of the nation's social prestige hierarchy. Although tending to agree that there has been a slight decline in the past several years, most observers feel that, in comparison with that of other occupational groups in contemporary Japan, the social prestige of doctors remains high. This impression is supported by the limited empirical evidence which is available, e.g., in the well-known national survey of 1955, doctors were ranked second among all occupational groups.[5] Of course, social prestige is not always an asset in the political arena since esteem can also provoke resentment and hostility. There is evidence to indicate that Japanese doctors, as a group, have been the object of considerable resentment and even hostility in the past few years.[6] Doctors have felt this rather intensely and have reacted defensively to what they generally perceive as a loss of social prestige. As the organized spokesman of the medical profession, the JMA has been the beneficiary of the high social prestige of its membership and at the same time the focal point toward which feelings of resentment and hostility have been directed. Therefore, the JMA is able on the one hand, to command respect and on the other, to provoke resistance, when it seeks to represent the interests of the medical profession.

In assessing the relationship of social status to ease of access to key points in the governmental process, however, social prestige is not the only factor to be considered. In fact, what might be termed the group's "strategic" position in society is of greater significance. With respect to Japanese doctors, two points should be noted. First, there is a growing concern with matters related to individual health and welfare in contemporary Japan. As the group having the training, skills, and exclusive *legal* right to render modern, scientific medical care, doctors perform a social function of great importance.

Second, at a time when the improvement of public health and welfare is an important political issue as well as an important part of overall governmental policy, the cooperation and aid of the medical profession is vital. This is particularly true with respect to the functioning and improvement of the system of compulsory health insurance. It is this "strategic" position of the medical profession in Japanese society which is a major factor in facilitating the JMA's access to policy-makers.

An assessment of the effectiveness of the JMA's organizational structure would require far more space than is available here. Only a few of the more significant points will be noted.

Since its reorganization in 1947, the JMA's claim to represent the medical profession has not been seriously challenged. Employed doctors have been reluctant to join labor unions, thus eliminating one potential source of competition, and other would-be rivals have not been able to attract more than a limited regional or ideological following. In 1960, of the 103,131 duly licensed medical practitioners in Japan, 72,981 or roughly 70.7 per cent were members of the JMA. Also, of 50,298 private practitioners (48.8 per cent of all doctors), roughly 99.4 per cent were members.[7] Therefore, the extremely high organizational rate and the absence of other rival organizations supports the JMA's claims to represent the medical profession both in the psychological sense and in the sense of participation in either governmental or non-governmental councils, committees, and other agencies where doctors as a group are represented. One example is the Social Security System Council (*Shakai Hoshō Seido Shingikai*) attached to the Office of the Prime Minister (*Sōri-fu*) where the medical profession is represented by an officer of the JMA. In short, wherever the medical profession is "represented" in an official sense, the JMA selects the representative.

The JMA is, of course, the "peak association" in a more or less federated type of structure consisting of medical associations at the prefectural level and at the county, city, or special ward (*gun-shi-ku*) level. Membership is voluntary at all three levels and the entire structure is cast in what might be termed the "democratic mold." Each level has its own set of elected officers and representative bodies. At the national level, this consists of a House of Delegates (*dai-giinkai*) composed of representatives elected by prefectural medical association assemblies. The House of Delegates elects national officers including a president, two vice-presidents, and a fifteen-member board of directors (*jōnin-riji*). The JMA Constitution also provides for an annual General Assembly (*sōkai*) which is open to all members.[8] Although responsible to the House of Delegates for its management of Association affairs, the executive group (president, vice-presidents, and board of directors) enjoys all the usual advantages of an active minority so that, in practice, direction of the JMA is highly centralized. In effect, the executive—and in particular the president—speaks for the JMA and thereby, the medical profession. The implications of this are obvious and need not be commented upon here.

A further feature of the JMA organizational structure which should be noted is the so-called Japan Doctors' League (*Nihon Ishi Remmei*). In a strict legal sense, the Japan Doctors' League is a completely independent organization. It is not mentioned in the JMA Constitution and, although unincorporated, it has its own charter and registers according to the provisions of the Regulation of Political Funds Law (*Seijishikin Kitei-hō*). The Charter of the Japan Doctors' League (*Nihon Ishi Remmei Kiyaku*) provides for an elaborate organization at the national, regional, prefectural, and local levels based on the principle of two-way communication of information from top to bottom and one-way transmission of instructions and direction from top to bottom. At the national level, the officers of the JMA and the Japan Doctors' League are one and the same and this tends to be the case at other levels. Thus in a functional sense, the Japan Doctors' League is the political action committee of the JMA. The arrangement provides for greater flexibility than is allowed by the organizational structure of the parent group as well as for a measure of functional specialization while, at the same time, fusing leadership and direction.

It should be noted, finally, that the democratic character of the formal organizational structure of the JMA has an important bearing on the problem of "access" in two ways. First, it conforms with the expectations of perhaps the majority of the Japanese community that political groups should be "democratic" in some respects—thereby making it "respectable" for political leaders and/or bureaucrats to deal with JMA leaders. Secondly, the fact that JMA leaders are elected by representatives of the national membership, and that their policies and activities are subject to the formal stamp of approval of those same representatives, strengthens their claim to speak for the medical profession as a whole.

To what extent then is the JMA effectively organized? The points noted above provide at least a partial answer to the question. However, as noted by Truman, "The relation between group organization and access is not . . . a matter of just being organized but equally of being organized appropriately for the problem at hand."[9] A complete answer to the question would thus require a case by case consideration of particular problems. In a general sense, however, it can be said that JMA leaders are in a position to support their claims and demands with the kind of organizational strength that a political party cannot afford to ignore.

What of the qualifications and political skills of those who are in a position to speak for the medical profession and to utilize the organizational strength of the JMA? This is, of course, the most difficult variable to assess. In general, leaders of organized interest groups and associations in Japan tend to be of two types. First, many groups select elderly persons of some distinction in a field other than politics to serve as more or less titular leaders. Second, other groups prefer ex-bureaucrats or politicians with important connections to serve as actual leaders. From the standpoint of maximizing access to decision-makers in the bureaucracy and the political parties, the second type seems the wiser choice and the trend appears to be in this direction. Nevertheless, the more traditional titular leadership continues to attract many groups for a variety of reasons.[10]

Until the election of President Takemi Tarō in 1957, JMA leaders tended to be distinguished doctors with no particular political qualifications. On two occasions, however, dissatisfaction with their failure to exert leadership led to the forced resignation of JMA presidents. On the second occasion, the opposition was led by Dr. Takemi. Although he was not an ex-bureaucrat or party politician, Dr. Takemi is related to former Prime Minister Yoshida Shigeru by marriage and is personally acquainted with most influential Conservative Party leaders. In fact, it is said that almost every prominent figure in Japanese political life has been a patient of Dr. Takemi at one time or another. His clinic, located on the Ginza, is both prestigious and prosperous.

Dr. Takemi is a very aggressive and dedicated leader who has inspired a kind of charismatic loyalty among his followers. Since 1957 he has become a celebrity, and the mass media have created an image of him as "Kenka Takemi" ("contentious Takemi"), i.e., a clever, fighting, but somewhat irresponsible champion of the interests of private practitioners—and the enemy of the Welfare bureaucracy. While the picture has been overdrawn by both journalists and scholars, there can be little doubt of Dr. Takemi's qualifications and skills as a group leader.[11] One measure of this is the fact that, in spite of a consistently "bad press" and bitter opposition both within the medical profession and from the outside, he has been re-elected as president of the JMA three times. In short, Dr. Takemi is not a political amateur, and the tactics employed by the JMA in the political arena are a reflection of his insight and skills—as well as of his limitations.

On balance, it may be said that the JMA scores high on the three variables described above. The combination of social status, effective organization, and Dr. Takemi provides the basis for the JMA's relative ease of access to key points in the policy-making process and, in particular, to the leadership of the Liberal-Democratic Party.

II

On January 5, 1961, the Liberal-Democratic Party's Special Committee for Medical Care Policy (*Iryō Taisaku Tokubetsu Iinkai*), by a unanimous decision, approved of a proposal which had been submitted by the committee's chairman Yamanaka Sadanori.[12] This proposal, known as the "Yamanaka Plan," was an attempt to settle a dispute on various issues related to the nation's system of health insurance between the Welfare Ministry and a number of allied groups on the one side and the Japan Medical Association on the other. Although not entirely satisfied with the "Yamanaka Plan," JMA leaders regarded it as an acceptable compromise and demanded that it be adopted and acted upon by the Liberal-Democratic Party and the Ikeda Government. They had good reason to believe that such would be the case.

Beginning in August, 1960, the JMA had waged a vigorous campaign to secure favorable government action on four specific demands. These "four demands" included: (1) elimination of certain restrictions on health insurance medical treatment; (2) a thirty per cent raise in health insurance medical fees; (3) integration of the two separate health insurance medical fee schedules then in use and the ending of regional differences in medical fees; and (4) simplification of the complicated health insurance paperwork.[13] The issues raised by the "four demands" were not new, and had been the subject of bitter dispute between the JMA and the Welfare Ministry for several years. For a number of reasons, however, JMA officials felt that the time had come to mobilize the resources of the Association for an all-out fight on those issues.

The reshuffling of top leadership posts in the Liberal-Democratic Party following the stormy events of May and June and the subsequent formation of the first Ikeda Cabinet provided the immediate stimulus for their decision to act. Prime Minister Ikeda came into office with promises of a "new beginning," "deeds not words," and a "new policy." Also, he announced that he would call for a general election before the end of the year—and before the preparation of the budget for the next fiscal year. This was the opportunity for which JMA leaders had long waited. In the words of President Takemi, an election campaign was a time when politicians "could be forced to learn something of the problems of medical care."[14] During the latter half of 1960, he and the other JMA leaders would act as teachers.

JMA leaders began to make preparations for the electoral campaign in early August. At a meeting of the Association's board of directors on August 11, President Takemi outlined a general plan which had already been discussed informally. Pointing out that the forthcoming general elections would be different from general elections in the past in that they would mark the beginning of a "new generation," he suggested that the strategy of the JMA and the Japan Doctors' League be changed accordingly. In addition to endorsing individual candidates and contributing to their campaign funds and to that of the political parties, the JMA would take every opportunity to publicize its position on health insurance and attempt to gain a greater measure of public sympathy and support. For two or three months prior to the elections, teams of JMA officials would be dispatched to various parts of the country to give public lectures, to meet with city, town, and village officials, and to talk with representatives of local organizations—especially women's organizations. Moreover, JMA officials at all levels would be encouraged to engage in similar activities in their respective localities. During this time, every opportunity would be taken to argue the JMA's position in the mass media. If this program of public enlightenment could be effectively organized and carried out, President Takemi declared, the positive effects would last far beyond the election itself: "Whether or not the existence of the Japan Medical Association will be appreciated or made light of in the new generation depends a great deal on the activities of the Association in the coming elections." [15]

On the same day, a meeting of Japan Doctors' League representatives was held for the purpose of electing new officers, discussing strategy, and hearing from a guest speaker—Mr. Hori Shigeru. A member of the Sato faction of the LDP, Hori had held a number of important Party and Cabinet posts in the past and was then the chairman of the Party's Executive Board (*Sōmukai-cho*) and a member of the Party's "big three" (*san'yaku*). The fact that a figure of Hori's political stature was present at a JMA function of this sort not only indicates the Party's concern with the JMA as a group, but also indicates the Association's ready access to the higher echelons of the Party.

Hori's address was brief and politically to the point. He noted the success of the Party's Special Committee for Medical Care Policy, which had been organized in 1959, in securing the establishment of the Medical Care Finance Corporation (a move for which the JMA had long agitated) and thanked President Takemi for his cooperation in this venture. He went on to appeal for continued cooperation and mutual understanding in the future and announced that the Party had decided to assign responsibility for policy related to medical care to the Special Committee under the chairmanship of Yamanaka Sadanori. [16]

Later in the day, Hori and a number of other Party leaders were guests at a dinner party held at the JMA headquarters in Kanda. A glance at the guest list suggests that the dinner party was more than an idle frolic. Included were Welfare Minister Nakayama Masa, Welfare Vice-Minister Tanaka, Lower House Social-labor Committee chairman Ōishi Buichi, LDP Policy Board member Hatta Sadayoshi, International Trade and Industry Vice-Minister

Kimura Morie, Foreign Vice-Minister Katsumata, and the chairman of the Party's Special Committee for Medical Care Policy Yamanaka Sadanori. While the frequent JMA social functions of this sort differ in atmosphere from the "smoke-filled rooms" of American politics and the Geisha parties so common in Japanese business and political circles, their objective is very much the same, i.e., the influencing of public policy-making.

A few days after the presentation of the "four demands" to the Welfare Ministry, President Takemi delivered a radio address entitled, "What We Expect of the Ikeda Cabinet in the Field of Social Security." Setting the tone for the JMA's campaign, Takemi's speech was, for the most part, an appeal for public understanding of the position of the medical profession vis-à-vis health insurance. He discussed a number of specific problems and referred often to the "interest of the people." With respect to the JMA's claims, however, his tone was uncompromising. He warned that the JMA would not be satisfied with half-way measures for reform: "One thing which I should like to emphasize is that, even though the Ikeda Cabinet may show a great deal of willingness to increase the budget, this is not enough to insure improvement of Japan's social security system. The Ikeda Cabinet should understand that in order to do this, it must give fullest consideration to the formulation of a drastically new social welfare policy, and not simply patch together policies from the past."[17] Indicating that he had lost patience with the "insurance bureaucracy" and, in particular, the Insurance Bureau of the Welfare Ministry and the Federation of Health Insurance Societies (Kenkō Hoken Kumiai Rengō-kai)—the "new insurance zaibatsu"—Takemi added: "During this time, what measures has the Diet taken with respect to the negligence of the insurance administration?"[18] Without providing a direct answer, he warned that, with a general election near at hand, both he and "the people" would carefully observe the activities of Dietmen and the results of Diet deliberations. He urged that Dietmen who leave social security problems in the hands of insurance bureaucrats be removed from office. Finally, Takemi concluded: "I demand that the Ikeda Cabinet take strong action to correct the present situation in which the welfare bureaucracy and especially insurance bureaucrats resort to petty tricks, engage in political intrigues, and ignore the welfare of the people."[19]

These were the circumstances in which the JMA's campaign got underway, and President Takemi and other Association leaders had reason to be optimistic over the future. In the original statement of the "four demands," October 1, 1960, had been specified as more or less a due date for governmental action. However, October 1 passed with no conclusive action having been taken by either the government or the JMA. Takemi first explained this turn of events at a meeting of the board of directors on October 12. Noting that Prime Minister Ikeda seemed to have a "very good understanding" of the problems involved in executing the government's "Health Insurance for the Whole Nation" (*Kokumin Kai-Hoken*) policy as well as the nature of the medical fees controversy, Takemi went on to point out that the Prime Minister was well aware of the fact that the various issues would have to be seriously considered in connection with the formulation of the so-called "doubling the national income" plan. Also, he indicated that in his opinion, Prime Minister Ikeda had been "kind," "honest," and "sincere" in considering the JMA's demands. For this reason, the JMA's claims for immediate action had not been pressed. By way of further explanation, Takemi pointed out that the policy-making machinery of the LDP had been gradually "penetrated," and it would therefore be unnecessary to engage in *hade* (showy, loud) activities. Finally, he noted that the Emergency House of Delegates meeting (*Rinji-Daigiinkai*) scheduled for October 15 would provide an excellent opportunity to unify the opinion of the medical profession and to thereby confront the LDP with a demonstration of the strong determination of Japanese doctors to achieve their goals.[20]

The House of Delegates meeting was held as scheduled and the representatives enthusiastically passed formal resolutions in support of President Takemi and the national leadership and in support of the "four demands." These resolutions were then incorporated into a petition, copies of which were personally delivered to various government and party leaders by small groups of JMA officials and representatives. In each case, the petition was handed to the party leader or Cabinet member by a JMA delegate from the former's electoral district. That evening the delegates attended a cocktail party at the JMA Building and mingled socially with LDP Executive Board Chairman Hori, former Welfare Minister Watanabe and a number of other Dietmen from both political parties. Photographs published in the Association's journal (*Nihon Ishikai Zasshi*) showed a beaming Takemi flanked by Chairman Hori and other Dietmen and suggested to readers that everything in the "medical family" was in good order.[21]

By the time of the House of Delegates meeting, the JMA's electoral campaign was well underway. Officials at all levels were encouraged to hold public meetings to present the Association's point of view in terms which would be meaningful to the layman and which would suggest that the JMA was working in the public interest. Also, teams of national officials were dispatched to a number of areas in order to present "An Evening of Films and Lectures" and to distribute a specially prepared pamphlet, "Your Medical Care" (*Anatagata no Iryō*). There is no record of how many such meetings were held or how much was spent. However, from the reports given at board of directors meetings, sessions conducted by two national officers in Kōchi were more or less typical. While one member of the "team" met with JMA members and others closely related to the medical profession, the other spoke to a group of about one hundred and fifty laymen (mostly women). The pamphlet was distributed and discussed and the problem of restrictions on health insurance medical treatment was emphasized. According to this officer's report, the audience appeared to be impressed and there were many who declared: "This is the first time that I have heard of the actual state of health insurance. I won't be able to cooperate with something like that in the future."[22] Such meetings continued to be held until the election of November 6, and JMA officials appear to have been satisfied with the results. This was the "public enlightenment" phase of JMA electoral strategy.

While there was considerable talk at JMA meetings to the effect that only those candidates who had demonstrated some sympathy for the Association's position would be officially endorsed, there is no evidence to indicate that this practice was actually followed. A list of endorsed candidates was published in the Association's journal only ten days before the elections. As indicated in Table I, a total of 326 candidates were given the JMA stamp of approval. This included 259 candidates affiliated with the Liberal-Democratic Party, 44 candidates affiliated with the Japan Socialist Party, 19 candidates affiliated with the Democratic Socialist Party, and 4 Independents. Of the total number, 269 or 82.5 per cent were actually elected. This included 218 Liberal-Democrats (84.2 per cent); 41 Socialists (93.2 per cent); 9 Democratic Socialists (47.4 per cent); and one Independent. The JMA endorsed the candidacy of all seventeen doctors in the race, of whom fourteen were elected— six in the Liberal-Democratic Party and nine in the Socialist Party.

TABLE I

NUMBER OF CANDIDATES OFFICIALLY ENDORSED BY THE JAPAN DOCTORS' LEAGUE:
GENERAL ELECTIONS OF NOVEMBER 20, 1960

	LDP	JSP	DSP	Independent	Total
Endorsed	259	44	19	4	326
Elected	218	41	9	1	269
Failed	41	3	10	3	57
Rate	84.2%	93.2%	47.4%	25.0%	82.5%

Source: *Nihon Ishikai Zasshi* (December 1, 1960), p. 775.

One often encounters the saying in Japan that "Every doctor carries one hundred votes in his medical bag." There is little evidence to support this nor is there any evidence to suggest that the JMA endorsement in any manner contributed to the success or failure of particular candidates. In effect, the JMA endorsement was little more than an attempt to court the good will of individual candidates and, for the most part, candidates who seemed assured of victory. Much more important than the JMA endorsement, however, were the contributions made to individual candidates and to the political parties. Here the JMA was quite generous.

According to the report filed by the Japan Doctors' League, a total of 42,010,000 yen was contributed to organizations and individuals during the period of August 31 to November 30, 1960. Of this, 32,700,000 yen or 77.7 per cent was donated to the Liberal-Democratic Party and to factions and individuals associated with the Party.[23] An analysis of the JMA's contributions would require much more space than is available here. It should be noted, however, that the Japan Doctors' League was a very important source of financial support for candidates affiliated with the Liberal-Democratic Party, and JMA leaders felt confident that they could expect something in return.

In fact, JMA leaders appear to have been quite pleased with their efforts during the campaign, and, in a post-election report to the board of directors, President Takemi expressed his optimism for the future. Following the opening of the special session of the Diet on December 5, a cocktail party was held at the Akasaka Prince Hotel to which all the victorious candidates endorsed by the JMA were invited. According to the JMA count, two hundred appeared. Again, photographs published in the Association's journal showed a beaming Takemi surrounded by Dietmen of the three political parties.[24]

By the end of the year, however, the optimistic attitude changed to one of "wait and see." On December 20, Takemi reported that he had talked with the medical Dietmen of both parties and that they had expressed their support and assured him of their willingness to work for the JMA's cause. A disappointment was the fact that Dr. Hatta, one of the more influential doctors in the Diet, was appointed Vice-Minister of the Agriculture-Forestry Ministry and not of the Welfare Ministry as Dr. Takemi had hoped. He indicated that he had not attempted to pressure the LDP in any way on appointments to Party and Cabinet posts since this would be interfering in internal Party affairs.[25]

Prime Minister Ikeda came into power in July, 1960, in the wake of the United States-Japan Security Treaty fiasco, and with the cooperation of five of the Liberal-Democratic Party factions. His basic political objective was to consolidate his position within the Party and at the same time to develop a new public image both at home and abroad. In the general elections of November 20, the Liberal-Democratic Party—under Ikeda's leadership—was given an absolute majority of seats in the Lower House of the Diet, and Ikeda was once again nominated to form a government. Thus the period from July to November was largely a preparatory stage for the Ikeda forces and a transitional phase in Japanese political life. Little was accomplished in the way of policy outputs. With the electoral victory and the formation of the Second Ikeda Cabinet, Japanese politics entered a new phase, and the first item of business was the drafting of the budget bill for fiscal 1961.

As indicated earlier, JMA leaders had decided to drop their claims for immediate action on the "four demands" and to concentrate their energies on the election campaign in the hope of penetrating the Liberal-Democratic Party's policy-making apparatus. Throughout this period, President Takemi insisted that the "four demands" were inseparable. However, as the drafting of the budget progressed, the JMA's demand for a raise in the health insurance medical fee assumed paramount importance. All parties were in agreement that the nation's doctors were entitled to a raise. The issue became, how much and in what way. The "Yamanaka Plan" provided one answer.

According to this proposal, the value of each point in the Medical Fee Schedule would be raised fifteen per cent—from ten yen per point to 11.5 yen per point—with all regional differences in fees to be eliminated. Moreover, the raise in medical fees was not to be accompanied by a raise in the insuree's contribution. While this was a long way from the thirty per cent raise that the JMA leaders had been demanding, they were nevertheless willing to compromise. The objective thus became that of encouraging the Party's Policy Planning Board (*Seimu-kai*) and then the Cabinet to adopt the "Yamanaka Plan."

In this, however, the JMA and its sympathizers in the Party ran into the vigorous opposition of the Health Insurance Bureau of the Welfare Ministry. On January 6, the Bureau's Planning Section chief held a press conference and bitterly criticized the Party's Special Committee and political party politics in general. Pointing out that in accordance with the provisions of the various health insurance laws, any change in medical fees was subject to the prior approval of the Central Social Insurance Medical Care Council (*Chūō Shakai Hoken Kyōgikai*) attached to the Welfare Ministry, he insisted that the Special Committee had completely ignored the legally established procedures. Also, while granting that doctors were entitled to a raise, he argued that it should be a raise of only ten per cent and—most important—that it be a "rational" raise. In brief, the Insurance Bureau's position was that hospitals be given a raise of twelve to fifteen per cent and clinics a raise of five per cent, and that this would average out to a ten per cent overall raise. In effect, the value of each point would remain the same but the number of points awarded for certain services would be increased. Later in the day, Bureau officials attended a meeting of the Party's Social Affairs Division of the Party's Policy Board in order to argue this position.[26]

JMA leaders were enraged. In the first place, they had been boycotting the Central Social Insurance Medical Care Council and refused to lift their boycott until the structure and functions of the Council were totally revised. Secondly, since the over-whelming majority of JMA members were private practitioners and owners of clinics, a discriminatory raise in favor of hospitals and organized medicine was regarded as completely unacceptable. The problem now came down to a conflict on fundamental issues. JMA leaders branded the Welfare Ministry plan an attempt to enforce state control of medicine and insisted that if the Welfare Ministry's proposal was adopted by the Party and by the Cabinet, they would call upon their membership to refuse to cooperate with the system of health insurance—in brief, a general resignation on the part of doctors. This was the JMA's "ultimate weapon" and they were now prepared to use it. On January 11, the *Nihon Keizai Shimbun* noted that the medical care issue had entered a "critical stage."

It is interesting to note that the new Welfare Minister Furui Yoshimi had not given his authorization to the actions being taken by officials of the Ministry's Insurance Bureau. The latter were acting on their own initiative! After conferences with Prime Minister Ikeda and other Party officials in which he was urged to bring his Ministry under control and get on with the business of preparing a set of realistic budget demands, Welfare Minister Furui called for a Ministry conference on January 15 and managed to secure agreement on a definite proposal. This was then immediately sent to the Finance Ministry as the Welfare Ministry's final word. This plan called for a ten per cent raise in medical fees as of July 1 with details to be worked out after the budget bill had secured final Diet approval. Moreover, the exact allocation of the raise would be deliberated upon in the Central Social Insurance Medical Care Council, and the JMA would be urged to cooperate in the deliberations. Thus Furui's move was prompted by the desire to get over this crisis and to force the issues out of the political arena and into administrative channels. This was precisely what the JMA did not want.

Early the next morning, an eighteen-member delegation of JMA officials from Prime Minister Ikeda's home prefecture of Hiroshima —who had rushed to Tokyo the evening before—called on the Prime Minister and urged him to intervene in the dispute on behalf of the JMA. As reported by members of the delegation, the Prime Minister spoke with them "frankly" and expressed his sincere hope that the JMA and other groups concerned would work out their differences. He pointed out that the handling of the medical fee problem had been entrusted to Welfare Minister Furui, whom he had known for a long time, and that he trusted Furui completely. The latter, he emphasized, was a very capable person and he urged that President Takemi meet with him often in the future to calmly discuss the various issues. Finally, Ikeda pointed out that Furui had been appointed Welfare Minister on the basis of a strong recommendation from Party Secretary-General Masutani. Therefore, any decisions made by Furui would be supported by the Party—or, at least, he (Ikeda) would take that attitude.[27]

Prime Minister Ikeda's firm support of his Welfare Minister was a blow for the JMA and, with the preparation of the budget bill entering its final stage, there appeared to be only two possibilities for changing the drift of events. A number of LDP "Medical Dietmen" called on Welfare Minister Furui and urged him to change his position—but with no success. A final possibility remained. The Policy Board of the LDP had not yet made its recommendations to the Cabinet with respect to the health insurance medical fees issue. On January 18, while the members of the Cabinet were meeting to make a final decision on the budget bill, the Party's Policy Board and Executive Board held a joint meeting in order to discuss outstanding issues. During this meeting, Policy Board Chairman Fukuda Takeo and Executive Board Chairman Hori argued in favor of the JMA's position but, despite their strong insistence, no decision was made. Instead, the matter was referred to the Policy Board's Social Division for further deliberation. However, the latter did not meet. Late in the evening, the Policy Board forwarded its final report to the Cabinet meeting which was still in session. This report made no mention of the medical fees issue. Therefore, in the absence of any objections to the contrary from the Policy Board, the Cabinet approved the proposal which had been submitted by Welfare Minister Furui.[28] The budget would provide for a ten per cent raise in health insurance medical fees, but the exact method for executing the raise was to be determined at a later date by Minister Furui after consultation with the Central Social Insurance Medical Care Council.

III

If a full and even sympathetic hearing of its case by persons in a position to make authoritative decisions may be regarded as a measure of "effective access," the JMA was successful in achieving that objective. From August, 1960, to January, 1961, JMA leaders employed a number of tactics designed to maintain and further develop their access to LDP leaders and hence to the government. These tactics included a campaign to enlist general public support, personal contacts with LDP leaders including the Prime Minister, endorsement of candidates and financial contributions to campaign funds prior to the general elections, lobbying on the part of the so-called "Medical Dietmen," development of internal group unity and cohesion, and, of course, threats of reprisals. At one point, JMA leaders felt that they had been successful in penetrating the LDP's policy-making mechanism, and the decision of the Party organ which had been assigned responsibility for dealing with the Association's demands, while not entirely satisfactory, was acceptable. However, the "Yamanaka Plan" was not adopted by the LDP Policy Board, and the Cabinet decision of January 18, 1960, completely ignored it. In brief, JMA leaders occupied a seat at the bargaining table but their arguments had not prevailed.

President Takemi and other JMA leaders looked upon the Cabinet decision as a complete defeat for their cause. Not only had they failed to obtain favorable action on their "four demands" or the "Yamanaka Plan" but they had also suffered a "loss of face." In a bitter post-mortem to the Cabinet decision, President Takemi declared that Welfare Ministry officials had, in fact, insulted the JMA.[29] If other *atsuryoku dantai* were "running wild," the JMA had, at least momentarily, been effectively corraled. Curiously enough, however, Japanese political commentators concluded that the JMA had once again been successful in obtaining concessions from the LDP and the government.

NOTES

1. This is a revised version of a paper originally read at the October 1964 meeting of the Midwest Conference on Asian Affairs. The paper is based on research conducted in Japan during 1960–1963 under a Ford Foundation Foreign Area Training Fellowship.

2. For a discussion of scholarly and popular attitudes toward political interest groups in Japan, see Tsuji Kiyoaki, "Atsuryoku dantai" ["Pressure Groups"], in Arizawa Hiromi, *et al.* (eds.), *Keizai shūtaisei kōza—shakai II* ("The Industrial Man in the Industrial Age—Society II"), Vol. IV (Tokyo: Chūō Kōron Sha, 1960), 232–248.

3. David B. Truman, *The Governmental Process* (New York: Alfred A. Knopf, 1955), p. 264.

4. *Ibid.*, pp. 265–270.

5. Research Committee, Japan Sociological Society, *Social Mobility in Japan: An Interim Report on the 1955 Survey of Social Stratification and Social Mobility in Japan* (Prepared for the Third World Congress of Sociology, ISA, May 1956, mimeo), pp. 2–3.

6. See, for example, Ōwatari Junji, *Isha no erabikata* ("How to Choose a Doctor") (Tokyo: Hoken Dōnin Sha, 1962).

7. Based on Kōseishō Daijin Kambō Tōkei Chōsa-bu, *Iryō shisetsu chōsa: ishi; shikaishi; yakuzaishi chōsa* ("Medical Care Facilities Investigation: Doctors; Dentists; and Pharmacists") (Tokyo: Kōsei Tōkei Kyōkai, 1962), p. 151; and *Nihon Ishikai Zasshi* ("Japan Medical Association Journal") (April 1, 1961), p. 759.

8. *Nihon Ishikai Teikan* ("Japan Medical Association Constitution"), November 1, 1947.

9. Truman, *The Governmental Process*, p. 269.

10. Cf. Ishida Takeshi, *Gendai soshiki ron* ("Modern Organization Theory") (Tokyo: Iwanami Shoten, 1961), pp. 84–102.

11. For a recent appraisal, see: Nitto Shūichi, "Itansha: Takemi Tarō Ron" ("Heretic: A Discussion of Takemi Tarō"), *Chūō Kōron* (July 1964), pp. 246–258.

12. *Nihon Ishikai Zasshi* (November 1, 1962), p. 830.

13. *Nihon Ishikai Zasshi* (August 15, 1960), p. 1.

14. Interview with Dr. Takemi Tarō, December 27, 1962.

15. *Nihon Ishikai Zasshi* (August 15, 1960), p. 292.

16. *Ibid.*, p. 295.

17. *Ibid.*, pp. 267–269.

18. *Ibid.*

19. *Ibid.*

20. *Nihon Ishikai Zasshi* (October 15, 1960), pp. 598–604.

21. *Ibid.*, pp. 529–530.

22. *Ibid.*, pp. 597–598.

23. Risō Senkyō Fukyūkai Hakkō, *Shūgiin Sōsenkyō no Senkyō hiyō sōkesson, Showa 35nen Ilgatsu 20ka shikkō* ("General Statement of Election Expenditures of the General Election for the House of Representatives, Carried out November 20, 1960") (Tokyo: Risō Senkyō Fukyūkai, 1961), pp. 169–170.

24. *Nihon Ishikai Zasshi* (December 1, 1960), p. 775.

25. *Nihon Ishikai Zasshi* (January 1, 1961), pp. 74–77.

26. *Nihon Ishikai Zasshi* (January 15, 1961), pp. 359, 370–371.

27. *Nihon Ishikai Zasshi* (February 1, 1961), pp. 417–418.

28. *Ibid.*, p. 421.

29. *Nihon Ishikai Zasshi* (February 15, 1961), p. 473.

Business Political
Participation in Japan:
Continuity and Change

JAMES R. SOUKUP

University of Texas

Prior to World War II—especially during the 1920's—Japanese business circles strongly influenced government decisions. This business power, however, was concentrated in the hands of executives from the Mitsui, Mitsubishi, Sumitomo, and Yasuda combines. Furthermore, these so-called Zaibatsu leaders generally confined their activities to economic problems; they rarely issued statements on such political matters as party organization, electoral machinery, etc.

Rather than involve themselves directly in government or party affairs, prewar businessmen preferred to rely on the assistance of politicians or bureaucrats with whom they had family and/or financial ties. Political donations were regarded primarily as necessary company expenditures and only secondarily as expressions of personal political preferences. A considerable number of Diet members had business connections, but few such national legislators were from large, established firms, and many began their careers as politicians or bureaucrats.

This prewar pattern of business political participation is now being altered. Specifically, slow but significant changes are occurring in the organizations through which businessmen articulate their interests, the content of their demands, and the amount and forms of their political involvement. The purpose of this article is to reveal the extent and nature of these changes and their impact upon the reigning Liberal-Democratic Party.

The Organization of Business Interests

The range and number of business firms involved in politics has increased substantially. In 1960 no fewer than 143 companies contributed one million or more yen to political organizations. More important, the political influence of the aforementioned "old Zaibatsu" combines has diminished. Among the ten companies making the highest political donations in 1960 only one was closely affiliated[1] with Mitsui, Mitsubishi, or Sumitomo interests.[2]

Occupation reforms only temporarily halted the Japanese tendency toward economic concentration, but they did create an opportunity for new business leaders to emerge. Among today's main-current businessmen,[3] for example, the four who are known most for their political activities—Ataru Kobayashi, Shigeo Mizuno, Shigeo Nagano, and Takeshi Sakurada—attained prominence with little, if any, Zaibatsu assistance. Moreover, they consistently stress the need for business leaders to act independently of any one group.[4]

Of late, there has been considerable speculation that the "old Zaibatsu" will again have a commanding position within the business community. Through mergers and other forms of combination Mitsui, Mitsubishi, and Sumitomo interests have been reconsolidated. By April, 1965, for example, Mitsui & Co. was to have absorbed Kinoshita & Co., thereby becoming the largest trading concern in Japan.[5] It is not likely, however, that the old style relationships and controls will be restored. The Zaibatsu combines of prewar Japan were owned by families, organized around holding companies, and tightly controlled through financial arrangements. They were also bound together by a network of arranged marriages and personal knight-vassal relationships. In contrast, today's Zaibatsu combines are no longer family-owned and controlled, and participating companies are much more independent in finances and management.[6] Ties among company executives within a combine are motivated less by personal considerations than by managerial necessity (e.g. joint participation in the formation of petrochemical kombinats).[7]

When broad issues are involved, particularly those with direct political repercussions, businessmen have been turning with increasing regularity to their national federations. A case in point is the inauguration and operation of Keizai Saiken Kondankai

(KSK), an organization designed to pool business political donations and to reduce questionable personal ties between individual firms and politicians. In 1954, following newspaper reports that ship-owners gave Diet members, LDP executives, and Transportation Ministry officials large sums of money to expedite the passage of favorable shipping legislation, Keidanren (The Federation of Economic Organizations) and Keizai Dōyūkai (Economic Friends Association, more commonly referred to as Japan Managers' Association), jointly sponsored the formation of the KSK. From 1955 until its final dissolution in 1961, funds for the KSK were collected by Keidanren officials who *assessed* member firms and industrial associations on the basis of their capital assets and yearly profits.[8] Equally indicative of this new trend is the fact that, after the 1954 scandal, shipowners shifted from their previous strategy of working independently through friendly Diet members and Ministry officials toward greater reliance on Keidanren efforts.[9]

The most prominent business federations are Keidanren, Keizai Dōyūkai, Nikkeiren (The Japan Federation of Employers' Associa-tions), and Nisshō (The Japan Chamber of Commerce and Industry). Among these four federations, the two with the greatest political significance are Keidanren and Dōyūkai. Nikkeiren confines its activities to labor policy, while Nisshō contains such a wide variety of firms and regional groups that it encounters great difficulties whenever it strives to formulate concrete demands. As a rule, Nisshō is also more effective in representing regional than nation-wide interests.[10]

Keidanren members are older and more attached to big business than their Dōyūkai counterparts. They are also less inclined to express their personal views and to examine new avenues of activity. The latter difference stems in part from the fact that businessmen join Dōyūkai as individuals, while in Keidanren they represent their companies or trade associations.

From the standpoint of policy, Keidanren is often equated with the National Association of Manufacturers and Dōyūkai with the Committee for Economic Development in the United States. Specifically, Dōyūkai is more inclined than Keidanren to accept business self-regulation, cooperation with government authorities, earlier and more comprehensive trade liberalization, trade union-ism, and social welfare programs.[11]

Although real, the differences between Keidanren and Dōyūkai are probably not as great as those that separate the NAM and CED in the United States. When interviewed by the author, both Kogoro Uemura, vice-chairman of Keidanren, and Seiichi Yamashita, secretary-general of Dōyūkai, argued that journalists exaggerate their organizations' differences.[12] The facts that the median age of Dōyūkai members rose from forty-eight in 1949 to fifty-eight in 1962, and that some Dōyūkai officers[13] have also attained responsible positions within Keidanren lend support to such contentions.

At present, Keidanren is the primary promoter of concrete business legislation. Dōyūkai is largely a generator of new ideas rather than a synthesizing interest group. For instance, a comparison of Keidanren and Dōyūkai resolutions from 1951 to 1961 shows that Dōyūkai proposals are more vaguely worded and less frequently refer to specific legislation.[14] In the future, however, Dōyūkai's influence is likely to increase substantially. Already many of Dōyūkai's ideas are stimulating thought within political circles. Moreover, past Dōyūkai leaders are also gradually entering the highest echelons of the business community.[15]

Neither Keidanren nor Dōyūkai can hope to exercise the same degree of control over today's businessmen as the "old Zaibatsu" did in prewar Japan. As indicated earlier, Japanese entrepreneurs have greater financial and managerial independence today, and their inter-personal relations are no longer as semi-feudal in character. Officials of national federations will also have to overcome the traditional tendency of Japanese businessmen to regard such associations as social friendship agencies rather than as service organizations.[16] Nevertheless, there are ample grounds for expecting the role of Keidanren, Dōyūkai, and similar federations to expand. In Japan's rapidly growing economy, businessmen are likely to become more aware of their service potentials. Pressures generated by trade liberalization are also forcing business executives to turn to such organizations for guidance and coordination. Businessmen have been expressing a variety of views on how to cope with trade liberalization, but the main debate has taken place within the business federations, and the general consensus is that broad-gauged cooperation among business circles is mandatory.

In anticipation of an expansion of their functions, both Keidanren and Dōyūkai have recently consolidated their decision-making apparatus and strengthened their professional staffs. Nikkeiren in the labor field has also stepped up its public relations' services to member firms.[17]

THE NATURE OF BUSINESS DEMANDS

Japanese businessmen still tend to confine their remarks to economic issues and to refrain from discussing political developments unless they have clear-cut economic implications. From 1951 to 1959 Dōyūkai resolutions referred to such matters as foreign policy, party organization, and electoral machinery on an average of only twice a year, while Keidanren did so but once a year.[18] When asked about the activities of his organization's Foreign Policy Committee in 1962, Kiichiro Sato, second vice-president of Keidanren, replied that the committee, now inactive, had been formed at the request of Mr. Aiichiro Fujiyama when the latter served as foreign minister under Kishi. Fujiyama had concentrated on inserting "business cooperation" clauses in the revised U.S.-Japan Security Treaty.[19]

The most persistent political request of business circles is for unity within conservative party ranks. After a disorderly Diet session in 1954, Keidanren, Dōyūkai, Nikkeiren, and Nisshō issued a joint declaration urging conservatives to "unite against the menace of left-wing extremism." Faced with this business pressure and alarmed by the reunification of the Socialist Party, conservative politicos joined hands and formed the Liberal-Democratic Party in November, 1955. Similarly, one of the major reasons for businessmen organizing the KSK was their desire to reduce the flow of funds to intra-party factions.

In accordance with their desire to preserve conservative unity, main-current business leaders advocate an orderly transfer of power from one conservative prime minister to the next. On occasion, they have even intervened when they felt that a prime minister had lost the public confidence. After the 1960 Security Treaty demonstrations, for example, the big four business federations jointly apologized to President Eisenhower and intimated that Mr. Kishi should resign from the premiership, which he promptly did.

One should not, of course, jump to the conclusion—as many Japanese Marxists do—that a hard core of businessmen *dictates* who will be Japan's prime minister. Business circles can, and have, made it difficult, if not impossible, for a prime minister to remain in office. But they have encountered difficulties in the process of determining a successor and, particularly, the timing and method of his succession. Most main-current business executives endorsed the Yoshida-Kishi-Ikeda-Sato line of succession; some, however, retained close personal-financial ties with rival faction heads. Business groups advised against an Ikeda-Sato showdown in the LDP presidential election of May, 1964, but the strong-willed bureaucrat-politicians decided otherwise.

Business organizations are beginning to take a more active interest in party modernization and programs to increase individual political participation. Dōyūkai, in particular, has initiated such moves. It has endorsed proposals to change the present middle-sized, multi-member election districts to smaller, single-member units; it has urged the LDP to eliminate internal factions and to expand its contacts with the masses; and Dōyūkai has encouraged businessmen to make political donations on an individual, rather than a company, basis.[20]

On balance, it can be concluded that high ranking businessmen are still inclined to think that their efforts should be concentrated heavily on economic matters, but they are starting to realize that they must concern themselves with political problems formerly left to the discretion of friendly politicians and bureaucrats.

INDIVIDUAL POLITICAL PARTICIPATION

The business and political elite are still linked by networks of personal relationships. The frequency of marriage alliances, however, has declined. More often these interlocking ties result from career-centered connections. Former Prime Minister Ikeda formed firm alliances with financial circles when he served as Finance Minister; Eisaku Sato, the present Premier, established friendly relations with transportation firms during his term as Transportation Minister; and Sato's chief rival, Ichiro Kono, did the same with fishery and agricultural interests while he was Minister of Agriculture and Forestry.[21]

The central question, of course, is not whether the business elite have political "connections," but whether or not businessmen are now more inclined to "enter" government and party affairs as individuals.

According to Professors Scalapino and Masumi, among Liberal-Democratic Diet members in 1947 approximately 52 per cent had business affiliations, while 64 per cent and 52 per cent had such connections in 1949 and 1953, respectively.[22] A check of LDP members of the 1960 House of Representatives likewise indicates that 52 per cent had, or were holding, positions in business firms and associations.[23] Among the twenty Lower House standing committee chairmen in 1961, half had current business ties;[24] and within the Liberal-Democratic Party itself about half of the thirty Executive Committee members had been or were then associated with business.[25]

The above figures plus the fact that no less than 90 per cent of the LDP's funds are derived from business sources certainly illustrate that businessmen have excellent "access" to both the Liberal-Democratic Party and the Diet. As measures of individual participation, however, these facts should be used with caution. One must differentiate between Diet members who enter politics "from" business (businessman-politicians) and those who relate to business "after" they have spent time as bureaucrats (bureaucrat-businessmen) or as politicians (politician-businessmen). Of the 155 business-connected LDP Dietmen in 1960, only 55 could be classified as businessmen-politicians; no fewer than 42 were bureaucrat-businessmen, and 32 were politician-businessmen.[26] Moreover, few of the businessmen-politicians hailed from large, established firms.

Very few business executives leave their enterprises to serve as temporary government administrators. In Japan, bureaucrats frequently resign their posts to enter the business world, but the reverse route of business to bureaucracy is contrary to custom. Nevertheless, bureaucrat-businessmen are playing an increasingly significant role in business circles;[27] and as their influence increases, they may encourage fellow businessmen to take a more active part in politics.

The latest and most significant effort to promote individual political participation has been the organization of the People's Association (Kokumin Kyōkai). Like its predecessor, the KSK, Kokumin Kyōkai is designed to pool business donations to the LDP; but it also seeks to reduce the flow of funds to intra-party factions, to replace company with individual contributions, and to stimulate personal political action.[28]

Since its inauguration in July, 1961, until December, 1963, Kokumin Kyōkai contributed 1,600,000,000 yen to the Liberal-Democratic Party.[29] Also, in January, 1964, it claimed a total of 41,317 individual members.[30]

As yet no figures have been released on how many of Kokumin Kyōkai's members are businessmen. There can be little doubt that the business community is the backbone of the organization. Almost all of its funds were supplied by business, and in 1962, at least fourteen of its thirty-five board members were from the business world—among them such prominent leaders as Ataru Kobayashi, Takeshi Sakurada, Kogoro Uemura, and Tomiji Yamazaki.

In May, 1962, the five companies with the highest number of individual Kokumin Kyōkai members were Kubota Iron and Steel, Nomura Securities, Fuji Iron Manufacturing, Fuji Bank, and Mitsubishi Trading Company. Bank employees were among the first to enroll. As often as not, however, their membership resulted from the persuasive powers of their bank presidents and supervisors.

There is evidence, therefore, of a slight increase in political participation by businessmen. Yet several problems persist. At least 75 per cent of the Kokumin Kyōkai's funds come from corporate, not individual, members. (The largest corporate donation in December, 1962, was 300,000 yen.)[31] It is safe to assume that 90 per cent of these corporate contributions came from companies and industrial associations. Membership drives within business enterprises have proceeded from the top down and have not progressed very far down. Few company section chiefs (*kachō*) can be found among the membership of Kokumin Kyōkai, and several of the department heads (*buchō*) and members of boards of directors (*torishimari*) joined because of loyalty to the company and hopes for promotion.

Most Keidanren officers agree with Kokumin Kyōkai's aim of reducing donations to intra-party factions; a few of them even believe that individual contributions should replace those from companies. But they are skeptical of the Association's drive to push direct individual participation. A vice-chief of the Liberal-Democratic Party Secretariat remarked that Keidanren's position is "we will contribute money but we cannot engage in other individual activities."[32] One problem is the natural inclination of business executives to concentrate on their economic tasks—a tendency which is more marked in Japan than in the United States. Another barrier to individual participation is that many Japanese businessmen have a low regard for politicians.[33]

Despite these difficulties, an increasing number of business leaders —especially those associated with Dōyūkai—are beginning to urge more active political participation by top and middle management. Kokumin Kyōkai could be reduced to just another collection agency, but it may very well be a forerunner of newer, more individual-action-oriented organizations.

The Impact of Business Groups

As indicated earlier, the business elite certainly have excellent "access" to political decision makers. By virtue of their financial resources and networks of personal ties with the government and party elite,[34] they are assured of ample opportunities to explain their views.

On economic questions, political leaders are careful to court business support before making any important moves. Although they are considerably less disposed to *act* on business proposals for party reform, the political elite are beginning to *think over* such suggestions.

Business attacks upon factionalism within the Liberal-Democratic Party have not put an end to such behavior. Factionalism is, after all, a deeply ingrained characteristic of Japanese political and social life. Even many of the businessmen who criticize the divisions within LDP ranks still feel the need for a personal political champion or to "play it safe" by donating to several factions. Nevertheless, there has been a slight drop in the financial receipts of factions, and several faction leaders have found it expedient to give up separate and elaborate headquarter facilities. One newspaper even commented that "division commanders" within the LDP were experiencing difficulties in holding their groups together before the Party presidency election of May, 1964—so much so that the newspaper predicted that LDP members were likely to vote as regiments rather than divisions.[35]

Party executives are also beginning to take a second look at business-backed organizations like Kokumin Kyōkai. They are now advocating, for example, that party officers be sent in to direct Kokumin Kyōkai and that the Party and Kokumin Kyōkai publications be merged. However, officials of the organization insist that no such steps be taken as long as the Party regards the Association as merely a fund-raising agency and refuses to recognize that its *primary* function is to promote individual participation.[36] Especially noteworthy is the fact that young party secretaries are interested in joining younger business executives in efforts to facilitate wider and deeper contact with the masses. As a matter of fact, Kokumin Kyōkai is in many ways a *joint* effort of young party executives and businessmen to effect this.

Business influence upon party and government decisions— particularly those of an economic nature—is obviously substantial. But the Marxist image of business domination is an exaggeration. Such thinking ignores the fact that bureaucrats (e.g. Finance Ministry) and especially bureaucrat-politicians can and sometimes do resist business pressures. After completing a case study of business efforts to secure bank reforms, Frank Langdon concluded; "In the case of central bank reform, business, especially banking, was fully consulted and able to take part in the formulation of policy. It was not able to prevail. On monetary policy, at least, even with finance, industry, and the central bank in agreement, business and its allies could not overcome the position of the Ministry" (Finance Ministry).[37]

Marxists also forget that the business world has problems of "cohesion" and "depth." Referring to the problem of business cohesion, Taizo Ishizaka, president of Keidanren, noted that "gaps are developing among various segments of industry."[38] Numerous examples of this fact can be cited. The Ministry of International Trade and Industry (MITI) has failed in several attempts to pass a Specific Industries Promotion bill. This failure is due in part to disagreements among business leaders: one group fears bureaucratic controls, while another argues that business-government collaboration is needed, and that, at the very least, businessmen should make an effort to "adjust autonomously."[39] Banking, industrial, and trade circles each expressed diverse views regarding the raising of the bank discount rate in 1964. Bankers felt that the move was long overdue; industrialists admitted that it was inevitable, but complained the new rate was too high for growth industries; and trading company executives referred to the change as "treacherous."[40]

Most Japanese businessmen favor economic relations with Communist China on a "business as usual" basis, but they have divergent views on specific steps for promoting such trade. Small and medium enterprise owners, merchants in the Kansai area, and trading firms are the most willing to make political concessions—perhaps even recognition of the communist regime. In contrast, executives of large scale firms, Tokyo businessmen, financiers, and most industrialists are more cautious. In deference to the United States they insist that care must be taken not to imply recognition, and accordingly, no government funds should be used to finance any system of deferred payments. A few Keidanren and Nisshō officials have also been in the forefront of activities to promote Japanese-Nationalist Chinese friendship.[41]

In the long run, the greatest difficulty confronting business circles may be the attitudes of middle management—especially section chiefs and their assistants. Interviews with forty department and section leaders in one of Japan's major steel companies indicated that middle-level executives have ambivalent attitudes toward politics.[42] On questions designed to measure their political interest and sense of political efficacy, the respondents scored high. Nevertheless, they seldom, if ever, attended political speeches or meetings. Very few had heard about Kokumin Kyōkai and those that had were not interested in joining. When asked their reactions to the possibility of their companies organizing political education seminars, several of the respondents expressed interest; but they thought in terms of programs for workers rather than ones for themselves. And many remarked that they did not wish to revive prewar types of political education which involved indoctrination.

A common explanation for this gap between expressed political interest and actual participation of middle-management can be made in terms of role concepts. Management personnel at middle levels feel that they should concentrate on economic chores and leave political tasks to their company presidents. A second point is that white-collar workers in Japan have a tendency to sympathize with socialist, as much as with conservative, politicians. Respondents in our survey usually favored Liberal-Democratic candidates, but several revealed that their ideals were closer to those of the Democratic-Socialist Party. Vice-chiefs of sections, in particular, seem to be caught between the socialist proclivities of workers under them and the assumed conservative attitudes of higher company officers.

As the importance of mass contact and activity gradually increases in Japanese politics, business executives will have to probe more "deeply" and to mobilize middle-management if they are to maintain even their present level of influence. They can presently count on the fact that managerial personnel tend to become more conservative with age and promotion, but they may need more active commitments in the future.

CONCLUSIONS

Japanese businessmen still cling to their enterprises and tend to regard trade associations as social gatherings rather than as service organizations. Slowly, however, national business federations like Keidanren and Dōyūkai are taking a more positive role in coordinating business views on economic policy. In fact, these federations appear to be replacing the old style Zaibatsu combines as the major organs through which businessmen express their demands to the party and government elite. The more conservative and cautious Keidanren is the leading federation today. But the more progressive and activist views of Dōyūkai may well prevail in the future.

The traditional practice of tending to business and leaving politics to friendly politicians and bureaucrats lingers. Also, businessmen are still prone to donate political funds on a company, not an individual preference, basis. But with Dōyūkai in the forefront some business executives are beginning to make suggestions about party modernization and electoral reform; and with Kokumin Kyōkai as the focal point they are making *individual* contributions to the Liberal-Democratic Party.

Through a network of financial and personal ties the business elite have ready "access" to the party and ministry elite. They can be assured, therefore, that their views on economic issues, at least, will receive careful consideration. Some party leaders—particularly younger secretaries—are even interested in business suggestions for the reform of their own organizations. Yet, the Marxist assumption that business controls government and party leaders must be qualified, if not discarded. On a number of occasions, business moves, even in the economic realm, have been thwarted by resistance from bureaucrats and bureaucrat-politicians. Moreover, the business world itself is bothered by less internal cohesion than it possessed during the prewar era; and middle-management personnel are not interested in political activities.

The future ability of the business community to maintain and to increase its political influence may well depend on the success or failure of organizations like Kokumin Kyōkai; for in an open, expanding society like Japan's, political power is increasingly dependent upon one's ability to mobilize rank and file members and to make alliances with other groups—especially with elements within the middle class.

NOTES

1. A firm was considered to be "closely affiliated" if one or more of the following conditions were met:

   a. Over twenty per cent of financial resources of company provided by Mitsui, Mitsubishi, or Sumitomo financial institutions (including stock and insurance companies as well as banks).

   b. Ten per cent or more of company stock held by Mitsui, Mitsubishi, or Sumitomo financial institutions and/or other firms in the group.

   c. The company's president attends the regular presidents' meetings of Mitsui, Mitsubishi, or Sumitomo group.

Statistics on financial and stockholding arrangements were found largely in Keizai Chōsa Kyōkai, *Keiretsu no kenkyū* (Tokyo, 1960).

2. Data on company donations was reported by Fusae Ichikawa in *Shūgiin giin sō senkyo no senkyo hiyō sō kessan* (Tokyo, 1961), pp. 175–183. For a more comprehensive analysis of political donation patterns see J. R. Soukup, "Comparative Studies in Political Finance: Japan," *Journal of Politics*, 25 (November 1963), pp. 737–756.

3. When describing the main-current members of the business community a distinction should be made between those whose interests and contacts are narrowly confined to matters related to their particular firms and industries, and those whose interests and contacts are broader and, consequently, of greater political import. Also, among the latter group, daily *activists* and general *advisers*, who have great prestige and are consulted by the activists, should be differentiated. With these distinctions in mind, the leading businessmen can be tentatively listed and classified as follows:

   A. *Broad Interests and Contacts: Advisers*
      Tadashi Adachi, Taizō Ishizaka, Kiichirō Satō, Michisuke Sugi, and Kōgorō Uemura.

   B. *Broad Interests and Contacts: Activists*
      Noboru Gotō, Shōzō Hotta, Hiroki Imazato, Yoshizano Iwasa, Ataru Kobayashi, Tokusaburō Kosaka, Shigeo Mizuno, Shigeo Nagano, Motohira

Nakayama, Takeshi Sakurada, Nobutaka Shikauchi, Haruo Suzuki, and Hiroshi Usami.

C. *Enterprise and Industry Leaders*

Kichihei Hara, Yasuzaburō Hara, Kichitarō Hagiwara, Sazō Idemitsu, Shojirō Ishibashi, Shōjirō Kojima, Taizō Kurata, Kōnosuke Matsushita, Eiichi Ogawa, and Tarō Yamashita.

The above listing and classification of business leaders is based on the author's interviews with newspapermen and businessmen during the spring of 1962; Kunio Fukumoto, "Zaisei shuryūha no yukue," *Tōyō Keizai* (1963), No. 4, pp. 54–60, and "Sengo zaisei no shisō to kōdō," *Chūō Kōron* (January 1964), pp. 170–192, and Hideo Ōkuma, "Zaikai sekiwake monogatari," *Chūō Kōron* (January 1962), pp. 202–217.

4. Fukumoto, "Sengo zaisei no shisō to kōdō," pp. 182, 185.

5. *Japan Report*, Vol. 10, No. 16 (August 31, 1964), p. 10.

6. See Kozo Yamamura, "Zaibatsu, Prewar and Zaibatsu, Postwar," *Journal of Asian Studies*, XXIII, No. 4 (August 1964), pp. 539–554.

7. Iwao Hoshii, "Trends in Japanese Industrial Organization," *Orient/West*, Vol. 8, No. 6 (November–December, 1963), pp. 32, 33. Referring to decision making within the petrochemical kombinats Hoshii writes, ". . . the kombinats, although identified with particular groups, sometimes had to put economic rationality ahead of group preferences."

8. Soukup, "Comparative Studies in Political Finance: Japan," p. 749.

9. This switch to Keidanren channels was confirmed by the author in interviews with the executive director of the Shipowners' Association, Fujio Yoneta, and the vice-chief of the Transportation Ministry Shipping Bureau (July 12 and July 24, 1962, respectively).

Dōyūkai, acting on the assumption that rehabilitation of the shipping industry is essential to continuous economic growth, was the first to propose a renewal of efforts to pass favorable legislation. Shortly thereafter, Keidanren took a direct interest in coordinating diverse views and proposing specific legislation.

10. This view was expressed to the author by top Keidanren officials in the spring of 1962.

11. Fukumoto, "Sengo zaisei no shisō to kōdō," pp. 172–173, 188–189. The original Dōyūkai leaders—Kobayashi, Mizuno, Nagano, and Sakurada—are firmly anti-communist and not very receptive to proposals for mixing socialism and capitalism. Younger elements, led by such men as Haruo Suzuki and Seiji Tsutsumi (Fukumoto refers to them as "second generation" leaders, emphasizing the fact that they are the sons of former prominent business executives), are more receptive to a full-scale welfare state and even moderate socialism per se.

12. Interviews by author, June 12, 1962, and June 19, 1962, respectively.

13. Shigeo Nagano and Takeshi Sakurada were the first to move into Keidanren. Now, prominent officers of Dōyūkai who simultaneously have responsible positions in Keidanren are Yoshizane Iwasa, Kazutaka Kikawada, and Tatsuzō Mizukami.

14. This comparison was made by the author from materials found in *Keidanren no jūnenshi*; *Keidanren jigyō hōkoku*, Nos. 17, 18, 19, 20, covering the period 1957–1960; and *Keizai Dōyūkai jūgonenshi*.

15. All of the business leaders listed under category B in note 3 are Dōyūkai

members. Fukumoto, in particular, stresses the rise of Dōyūkai members to prominence within business circles.

16. Japan Productivity Center, *Organization and Activities of Business Groups* (September 20, 1961), Chapter 6, mimeographed.

17. Japan Federation of Employers' Associations, *JFEA News*, No. 15 (September 1963), pp. 5–8.

18. Keidanren resolutions averaged twenty per year, while Dōyūkai issued statements on an average of seven times per year.

19. Interview by author, March 7, 1962.

20. "Resolution for the Protection of Parliamentarianism," November 10, 1958, *Keizai Dōyūkai jūgonenshi*, p. 379, and "Political Funds to be Collected Through Party Organizations, Thorough Revision of the Election System Needed," *Keizai Dōyū*, No. 153 (February 1, 1961).

21. Kaneji Miura, Asahi Shimbun Political Section, interview with author, March 26, 1962, and "How the Eight Liberal-Democratic Party Divisions Raise Their Funds," *Keizai Ōrai* (February 1963) as translated by the United States embassy in Tokyo in *Selected Summary of Japanese Magazines* (SSJM) (March 11, 1963), p. 3.

22. Robert Scalapino, *Parties and Politics in Contemporary Japan* (Berkeley: University of California Press, 1962), p. 63.

23. Compiled by author on basis of data in *Shūgiin Yoran* (1961) and *Kokkai benran* (1962).

24. "Biographical Sketches of Lower House Standing Committee Chairmen Designates,"*Sankei Shimbun*, as translated by the U.S. embassy in Tokyo, *Daily Summary of Japanese Press* (DSJP), May 3, 1961.

25. In the less significant Policy Research Council (*Seichōkai*) eleven of the twenty-five committee members and six of the fourteen bureau chiefs had business ties. The third Ikeda Cabinet (1963) contained nine bureaucrats, five politicians, two journalists, and two businessmen, while the fourth Ikeda Cabinet (1964) was composed of eight bureaucrats, four politicians, four businessmen, and two journalists. See *Japan Report*, 9, No. 14 (July 31, 1963), and 10, No. 13 (July 20, 1964).

26. Among the sixteen Liberal-Democratic Party Executive Committee members with business backgrounds only six could be considered businessman-politicians.

27. Seicho Matsumoto, "Discourse on the MITI Bureaucracy," *Bungei Shunjū* (October 1963), pp. 223–224.

28. Soukup, "Comparative Studies in Political Finance: Japan," p. 754.

29. "LDP Leaders and the People's Association at Odds over the Fund Raising Issue," *Tōkyō Shimbun* (evening), February 3, 1964, *DSJP*, February 11, 1964, p. 6.

30. *Ibid.*

31. *Nihon Keizai*, May 13, 1962.

32. Interview with author, May 17, 1962.

33. This assessment of businessmen's attitudes was made by Tatsuzō Mizukami, President of the Mitsui Trading Company and a leading figure in Dōyūkai (interview with author, April 5, 1962).

34. Businessmen do serve on numerous Ministry advisory committees and government officials, in turn, are often invited to attend business federation meetings.

35. "Internal Factions of the Political Parties Still Survive," *Yomiuri Shimbun*, February 17, 1964, *DSJP*, February 27, 1964, pp. 3–8.

36. "LDP Leaders and the People's Association at Odds over the Fund Raising Issue," *Tōkyō Shimbun*, February 3, 1964.

37. Frank Langdon, "Big Business Lobbying in Japan: The Case of Central Bank Reform," *American Political Science Review*, LV, No. 3 (September 1961), p. 538.

38. *Japan Times*, August 5, 1962.

39. "Specific Industries Promotion Bill to be Shelved for the Third Time," *Yomiuri Shimbun*, *DSJP*, June 27–29, 1964, pp. 6, 7, and "Specific Industries Promotion Bill to be Presented to the Diet Again," *Nikkan Kōgyō*, *DSJP*, January 10, 1964, p. 1. Dōyūkai officers have been inclined to favor the latter view while Keidanren executives expressed the former opinion.

40. "Reactions of Economic Circles and Socialist Parties to Raising of the Bank Rate," *Nihon Keizai*, March 18, 1964 as reported in *DSJP*, April 12, 1964, p. 8. A notable exception to trading circle reactions was that of Tatsuzō Mizukami. He stated that major trading companies should act from a national standpoint instead of turning their eyes toward expanding the volume of goods they handle.

41. "Keidanren Leaders on Economic and Trade Problems," *Mainichi Shimbun*, *DSJP*, April 15, 1964, p. 3. See also *Mainichi Shimbun*, April 8, 1964, and *Nihon Keizai*, April 9 and May 31,1964.

42. This survey of middle management attitudes and activities was conducted by the author and a team of Japanese undergraduate and graduate students from March–May, 1962.

True Structural Change and the Time Dimension in the North Indian Kinship System

HAROLD A. GOULD

University of Pittsburgh

Studies of urbanization and industrialization have widely assumed that the adoption of city living causes the automatic dissolution of extended families and their replacement by nuclear, neolocal units. Economic, demographic and ideological conditions allegedly make this transition inevitable. Thus Mukerjee and Singh, in their social survey of Lucknow, assert:

> The urban family at present is in transition towards the natural family [*sic*] comprising the couple and their unmarried children. But the transition is in no way complete, and many families still exhibit the features of a joint family—with several generations and a large number of relations living together.[1]

The trouble with such a viewpoint is that it has been derived from an uncritical application of generalizations appropriate to the West's experience with industrialization. This is a dangerous procedure on a number of grounds, but particularly so in a country like India where unilineal kinship systems and caste, both rare or nonexistent in even the preindustrial West, occupy such important places. Bloch has pointed out that medieval feudalism arose in Europe in part as a response to the weakness of kinship institutions at a time when wider principles of interdependence and mutual obligation were required.[2] What is most important, however, is that in no society are all of the changes that occur in the composition of kin groups through time *structural* changes. Therefore, since the transition from a nonindustrial to an industrial society represents a major series of changes in the structure of technology and significant social groups, it becomes essential that genuine structural change be differentiated from other structural activities, whether in regard to kinship or any other feature of society, if a truly accurate assessment of change is to be made. Furthermore, it will always be important to learn how much structural alteration in a given dimension of society is actually *necessary* to fulfill basic functional requirements of mechanized, bureaucratized productive activities. This latter may, in fact, become a most crucial variable in determining the eventual form which non-Western societies will take after they have achieved their maximum absorption of industrialization.

The need for distinguishing between true structural changes in kinship systems and merely normal rearrangements of personnel through time has been cogently stated by Fortes. He declares:

> ... what are the institutional mechanisms and customary activities of social reproduction in a particular society and how do they operate? ... In all human societies, the workshop, so to speak, of social reproduction, is the domestic group. ... The domestic group goes through a cycle of development analogous to the growth cycle of a living organism. The group as a unit retains the same form, but its members, and the activities which unite them, go through a regular sequence of changes during the cycle which culminates in the dissolution of the original unit and its replacement by one or more units of the same kind.[3]

Such an approach is decidedly essential if we are to understand the true nature of kinship organization in Indian urban areas today. In our effort to demonstrate this, we must first begin by stating the general features of the traditional kinship system found in northern India, the region where my field work was done. We must do so because, as is well known, any social structure varies in relation to what it has been in the past, as well as in relation to what it is becoming, due to the effects of forces of change. In fact, as we shall see, the evidence is especially compelling that such an approach is necessary when talking about India.

An entire tradition of Hindu law, ultimately traced back to Manu, lies behind and legitimizes the principles of relationship, descent and inheritance prevalent in this part of northern India; this is known as Mitakshara Succession.[4] In brief, the following principles are included: (a) the "normal condition"[5] of the Hindu family is jointness, that is, it is a "coparcenary unit" which owes maintenance to all its members "in severality"; (b) property is inherited through male agnates; (c) females may not inherit the chief wealth of the joint family; (d) females become members of their husbands' joint families upon marriage and cease being members of their natal families; (e) residence is patrilocal/virilocal; and (f) any adult male agnate may call for partition of the coparcenary any time he deems it in his interests to do so.[6]

The rule permitting any male agnate to call for partition appears to have been a means of assuring that younger brothers could not be deprived of a share in the property of the joint family after the father's death. For without such a rule, the leadership of the family, devolving upon the eldest brother as next in line of succession, might be used as a weapon against younger generational equivalents. With the coming of European rule, modern technology, bureaucracy, modern jurisprudence, the pecuniary economy, rapidly growing populations, and rising property values, a definite pattern or cycle of fission got established in domestic groups and persists up to the present time, especially in the rural areas, where most Indians live and where land is the chief form of heritable wealth. Basically it is this: Domestic groups divide in every generation, because after the father dies the sons eventually invoke their right to partition the coparcenary. There are a number of interrelated reasons for this. As the father ages, the sons are maturing, marrying, and having children of their own. This works counter to the unilineal interests of the kin group because it means that each son progressively develops conjugal loyalties to his own wife and children which often lead to conflicts with his lineal loyalties. With the removal of the father's strong patriarchal authority, these conflicting sets of loyalties become overwhelming because no basis exists for the reassertion of this authority with equal force at the intragenerational level. The right to partition nullifies the possibility of an all-powerful eldest brother who could use effective coercion to hold the unit together.

Viewed in the overall, we can say that contemporary social conditions, male agnatic succession, the right to partition, and the denial of major inheritance rights to women have combined to produce a characteristic developmental cycle consisting of a series of phases. During some of these phases, the personnel of the domestic group accord with the standard description of the nuclear family, while in others they accord with that of the compound or extended family. This means that a mere counting of the number of simple and compound households displayed by groupings of North Indians would be wholly useless as a basis for ascertaining "modern" influences.

The phases through which the North Indian domestic group passes, therefore, are ultimately a reflection of certain fundamental events. Once again it must be emphasized that these events manifest themselves most ideally in the villages, where property and social relationships remain largely what they have been throughout Indian history. Thus, we are essentially saying that the village pattern of today constitutes an ongoing structural model for kinship relations, which is the frame of reference for modifications in kinship organization that may be observed in cities. This, of course, arises from the fact that the population of cities is growing rapidly and that this growth is being sustained primarily by migrants from the villages. These milestone events in the typical developmental cycle are: (a) the breaking of the heterosexual sibling tie by the out-marrying of sisters after puberty and their replacement by in-marrying wives; (b) a transitional phase during which efforts are made to keep the domestic group together despite the loss of the patriarch; (c) the breaking of fraternal ties through partition of the coparcenary following the death of the father. The full developmental cycle arising from these events follows:

PHASE I: The replacement of female siblings in the domestic group by wives.

> *Subphase A:* (Nascent Period) From the moment of the first *gauna*, when the first sister leaves for, or the first wife comes to, her husband's household, until half of the *gaunas* have occurred. During this nascent period, households contain a mingling of brothers, sisters, and brothers' wives, together with parents who are normally in transition from Young Adulthood (21–35)[7] to Later Adulthood (36–50). The incoming wives are beginning to bear children, and the socialization of the next generation is commencing.
>
> *Subphase B:* (Mature Period) From the point where more than half of all potential *gaunas* have occurred, until the complete

replacement of sisters with brothers' wives. Here the domestic group is reaching its maximum size and generational depth. All brothers are acquiring conjugal units, and members of the parental generation are moving from Later Adulthood to Old Age (above 50) and death.

PHASE II: A period when the coparcenary unit is a fraternal extended family after the death of the patriarch (normally the father of ego but occasionally a father's brother, or other collateral agnate). This phase is bypassed whenever there is only one surviving son, of course. When present, it can comprise a large, complex domestic group consisting of the brothers' conjugal units and sometimes, in addition, a widowed mother and/or other widowed female kins-women.

PHASE III: Brothers partition the joint family and establish separate domiciles, thus breaking the fraternal sibling tie as a basis for corporate activities. Frequently, this occurs due to quarrels among brothers in which pulls of loyalty between conjugal and lineal ties become irreconcilable.

Subphase A: From the establishment of separate domestic groups by recently divided brothers until the marriage of the first child. Marriages occur early among traditional Indians and do not lead to immediate cohabitation. Gaunas await the onset of puberty. Thus, married children continue living in their natal household, but their marriages signify the movement of the domestic group toward repetition of the first phase in the developmental cycle—viz., breaking of the heterosexual sibling tie. Subphase A is normally "nuclear" in structure and must be seen as a normal period in the life cycle of the Indian domestic group and in no sense indicative of structural change.

Subphase B: From the marriage of each brother's first child until the occurrence of the first gauna. With this latter event, the developmental cycle has come around full circle, and the original domestic group has been replaced by however many new ones arose in the aftermath of the patriarch's death and the partition of the coparcenary among the surviving brothers. In Subphase B, the domestic group is moving from a nuclear toward an extended structure once again. Children of the household have experienced their Childhood (5–11) and are preparing to enter their "social apprenticeship" (Youth, 12–20) where the learning of adult roles commences in earnest.

On the basis of the foregoing, we may see that structural changes are not automatically indicated where families of a specific kind at any given point in time were observed. A certain number of nuclear families will be *normal* for the kind of kinship system described above. However, the value of determining the temporal characteristics of the kinship system is that it provides us with a basis for determining when events might occur which would fail to lead to a repetition of the normal developmental cycle. Such events would, of course, demand careful scrutiny as possible indicators of true structural change. With these thoughts in mind, then, let us now consider the domestic organization found among fifty *rickshawallas* whom I studied in 1959, and who reside and work in Lucknow, the capital of Uttar Pradesh, India.[8]

In 1959, Lucknow had a population of around 625,000. One of the chief means of transportation was the bicycle ricksha, a three-wheeled conveyance that is propelled and steered in the same fashion as a conventional bicycle. Two passengers are normally accommodated on the seat behind the driver, although, by overloading, more are sometimes carried. The Hindustani term *Rickshawalla* denotes one who operates one of these vehicles. There are in the vicinity of five thousand bicycle rickshas plying Lucknow's streets; driving these conveyances is obviously a purely menial occupation, and even casual observation reveals that most drivers are recent arrivals from rural areas, who have taken this job because they are qualified for little else.[9]

It was found that despite their living in a large city and practicing a modern occupation, the domestic groups of thirty-three *rickshawallas* fitted somewhere in the *normal* developmental cycle for North India, a cycle thought by many to be unmaintainable in an urban, modern occupational setting. These were a mingling of Plains Hindus, Nepalis, and Muslims, which suggests that the same kinship principles were operating equally for all. In Table I, the personnel of the domestic groups at each phase in the developmental cycle are given; these are subdivided by generation and kinship role from the standpoint of the *rickshawalla* as ego. Here we see that most domestic groups are going through those phases in which sheer numerical size and the pulls between conjugal and lineal ties are both at their maximum. That both are indeed subtly interrelated is suggested by the smaller number of *rickshawallas* whose domestic groups are in Phase IA, where numerical size averages about the same as for IB and II, but where the proportionate number of wives cohabiting with their husbands is less. Phase IIIA merely expresses the inevitable consequences of the process at work in the preceding phase. The domestic groups of ten *rickshawallas* have broken up into fifteen new units with an average personnel of less than four in each. Not all were the result of partitions among brothers, of course, because in some families there had been only a single son at the time of the father's death. However, all have in common the fact that they emerged as the end product of the natural series of temporal events which characterize the developmental cycle in North India. Most were nuclear, and the only exceptions were the presence of three widowed mothers entitled to maintenance for life in their deceased's husband's kin group. There were no indications that these groups would not repeat the normal cycle as they moved through time.

TABLE I

PERSONNEL OF RICKSHAWALLAS' DOMESTIC GROUPS IN DIFFERENT PHASES OF THE NORMAL NORTH INDIAN DEVELOPMENTAL CYCLE

Phase of the Developmental Cycle	No. of Domestic Groups	Average No. in Domestic Groups	Male *Agnates* Ego/ Fa Br So			Female *Agnates* Si Da		Wives of Male *Agnates* BrWi/ Mo Wi SoWi			Out-married *Females* Si Da		Total
IA	5	7.4	4	16	2	1	6	4	4	–	2	1	40
IB	8	7.3	8	17	15	–	2	5	11	–	5	1	64
II	9	7.4	–	23	10	1	6	4	12	1	1	4	62
IIIA	10(15)*	3.5	–	15	13	–	10	3	10	–	5	–	56
IIIB	1	7.0	–	1	2	–	3	–	1	–	–	–	6
Totals	33(38)	6.1	12	72	42	2	27	16	38	1	13	6	228

* Ten respondents' domestic groups had split into fifteen IIIA units.

Among these normally unfolding domestic groups, two basic residential themes prevailed—a dispersed residential pattern and a single-household pattern. Among the former many were rural-based, many were not. By rural-based is meant that the main body of kin are in a village while ego is in the city, either alone, or in company of his conjugal unit and/or some other male sibling, to earn a cash income which is seen as a contribution to the entire kin group's economic well-being. The main criterion of whether a group with a dispersed residential pattern is still definable as a domestic group is, of course, whether it continues to function as a coparcenary unit sharing economic resources. All of the urban-based domestic groups except one maintained a single household regardless of whether nuclear or compound, which indicates that even in the city the basic impulse to form complex corporate kin groups remains strong despite the supposedly atomizing effects of pecuniary standards, inflated costs, congested living, etc. The shift from traditional occupations and rural living to modern occupations and urban living does not necessarily destroy the corporate kin group. What actually occurs is that the emphasis of caste is shifted to what I have elsewhere [10] termed "adaptive functions," while concomitantly the emphasis of the corporate kin group is shifted from a narrower to a broader range of economic diversification. Put another way, the income structure of the domestic group is modified to accommodate the new economic environment in a fashion that preserves its corporate nature.

Corporateness undoubtedly remains a major value in the Indian kinship system because even in the contemporary urban society and social order it serves useful purposes. Menial occupations such as driving rickshas are very poorly reimbursed, which means that dependence upon other kin in an atmosphere of shared economic well-being inevitably has a powerful appeal. A low standard of living seems to impel the members of kin groups to tap all known sources of potential income and to pragmatically rearrange their occupational commitments in response to opportunities as they arise. The truth of this is apparent not only in the persistence of the normal developmental cycle among so many *rickshawallas*, but is equally apparent among many of the seventeen instances of domestic groups which failed to conform to the normal cycle. Among the latter, four general categories of aberrant structure could be differentiated, which are called: (1) the isolated individual, (2) arrested conjugality, (3) arrested lineality, and (4) true neolocalism. Each will be considered in turn.

In five cases, individuals were encountered who had simply broken off all ties with their kin groups and were leading an entirely isolated existence in Lucknow. It was clear that all, in one respect or another, were examples of severe social maladjustment. They were disturbed individuals who had found it impossible to make satisfactory adjustments to their domestic environment. One had abandoned his conjugal unit in the village and had fled to the city; the other four were either unmarried beyond the marriageable age, or else men who had lost their spouses and declined to remarry. One suffered from leucoderma, or "white leprosy," a highly stigmatic disease in India, and the other four showed distinct evidence of severe emotional disturbance. Driving a bicycle ricksha requires no special skills or education; it simply requires ordinary motor skills and reasonable physical stamina. It affords a variable, generally low income, to be sure, but subsistence can be at least minimally maintained through the occupation. It is an occupation that facilitates both spatial mobility and a measure of personal autonomy. The back seat of the ricksha, albeit with considerable discomfort, can be used as a bed at night if necessary, and I have seen it used in this fashion in innumerable instances; in addition, the owners of bicycle rickshas frequently have a shed or some other sheltered place where drivers may sleep and attend to other minimal needs. In short, features of the occupation have a ready appeal to certain classes of deviants and misfits, perhaps especially those suffering from strong feelings of alienation.

Another typical domestic situation, found to be characteristic of six subjects, was what may be called "arrested conjugality." In this pattern we have an illustration of how the desire to maintain the domestic group as a corporate body may lead to the almost complete suppression of conjugal ties in favor of solidarity based upon lineal ties alone. This occurs by the simple device of parents deciding to indefinitely defer the marriage of their children, particularly sons, so that the resultant domestic group remains a corporate body restricted to lineal kin. Under conditions of severe poverty and hardship, an attempt is made to achieve tight solidarity by foregoing the relationships on which temporal continuity of the kin group depends. This measure holds down the size of the domestic group while simultaneously obviating the necessity of coping with the potentially centrifugal conjugal and affinal relationships. I do not wish to imply that these are the reasons which respondents gave for establishing this type of domestic group, however. The usual explanation was that poverty made the arrangement of suitable marriages for children impossible. In reality, however, the cause has to be deeper, because it is easily shown that many domestic groups as bad or worse off than these nevertheless contracted marriages. It is perhaps a matter of not deliberately starting out in the direction of arrested conjugality, but of "discovering" at some point that "failure" to find "suitable" marriages for sons is beginning to pay dividends in that their single status renders a greater proportion of their income usable by the parents. One may draw this inference from much of the interview material.

Actually, there were two variations of the above pattern which merely reflected the different points in the developmental cycle where it was begun. Three were cases in which two or more brothers had remained joint (Phase II), while either themselves failing to marry or failing to arrange marriages for their offspring. The other three were cases of men who had established Phase IIIA of the cycle but had then arrested the process of development by neglecting to arrange marriages for their children. It must be realized, of course, that in both variations we are speaking of heads of domestic groups who range in age between Later Adulthood (36–50) and Old Age (50+), and who are either unwed themselves at this late point in life or who have children in Young (21–35) or Later Adulthood (36–50) who are unwed. It is only under these circumstances that we can meaningfully speak of an "arrested" pattern.

Perhaps the strongest proof that corporateness is a cherished value in itself in contemporary Indian domestic organization is contained in the characteristics of the type I have called "arrested lineality." This appears to be a pointed effort to enjoy all the functional advantages of the corporate kin group while at the same time overriding traditional unilineal considerations. What essentially occurred with four domestic groups fitting this category is that, strictly on the basis of economic expediency, three individuals and one entire conjugal unit had broken away from their lineal kin group and attached themselves to the domestic groups of persons who are normally residentially separate from ego. One person had adopted corporate residence with a mother's brother's domestic group in Lucknow, another with a father's sister's, and still another with a wife's brother's household. A fourth had affiliated with his father's younger brother, to be sure, but this had taken place long after the two had partitioned the original coparcenary and adopted separate domiciles in separate communities. Among the *rickshawallas*, only four subjects displayed arrested lineality; but evidence from other data to be published in the near future makes it plain that this represents an important functional adjustment to Indian urbanization and modernization, which must be taken into account by investigators. It bears repeating in this context that the principle of corporateness in the broad sense, which implies economic cooperation and the sharing of economic resources among a grouping of kinsmen, must be conceptually distinguished from a given formal kinship structure which, under given sets of conditions, has heretofore been the exclusive, recognized basis for determining the personnel of corporate kin groups. Variations in domestic organization that appear possible in Indian cities today suggest that a considerable latitude exists for compromise structures which both recombine established principles of kinship organization and at times override them completely—all of this being undertaken, of course, in the name of achieving corporate units bound together by kinship ties.

True neolocalism, in which a conjugal unit formally detaches itself from all other kin groups and assumes an entirely autonomous existence, was rare among *rickshawallas*. Only two cases were reported.

SUMMARY AND CONCLUSIONS

(1) Entry into modern urban occupations does not automatically imply the disintegration of the extended family and its replacement by the neolocal nuclear family. Assumptions that this invariably occurs arise from historical experiences with industrialization in the West on the one hand, and with failure to distinguish normal processes of transformation in domestic groups from genuine structural change, on the other. The case of the Lucknow *rickshawallas* indicates that in a country like India, at least, compound kin groups are retained with great frequency in the urban environment regardless of occupation. Nuclear families almost invariably appear to be merely phases in the developmental cycle, rather than genuinely new manifestations of kinship structure.

(2) Compound kin groups persist because corporate activities determined and validated by kinship ties continue to enjoy importance in the eyes of those whose life and work are situated in cities.

That corporateness is the principal end valued is attested by the variations that occur in domestic organization in order to achieve it. Both lineal and affinal considerations are at times overridden for the purpose of assuring the existence of a grouping of kinsmen who will contribute the fruits of an often wide diversity of occupations to the common lot.

NOTES

1. Radhakamal Mukerjee and Baljit Singh, *Social Profiles of a Metropolis* (Bombay: Asia Publishing House, 1962), p. 37.

2. Marc Bloch, *Feudal Society* (London: Routledge & Kegan Paul, 1961).

3. Meyer Fortes, "Introduction," in *The Developmental Cycle in Domestic Groups*, ed. Jack Goody ("Cambridge Papers in Social Anthropology," No. 1) (1959), p. 2.

4. D. F. Mulla, *Principles of Hindu Law* (Calcutta: Eastern Law House, 1952).

5. *Ibid.*

6. The Hindu Marriage Act of 1955 and the Hindu Succession Act of 1956 introduced fundamental changes in traditional systems of law like the Mitakshara. For example, female agnates now technically enjoy the same succession rights as male agnates in the coparcenary. In reality, however, most Indians are continuing to adhere to the old legal pattern. How long this will persist is difficult to judge at this juncture, but it probably depends in part on the rapidity with which females become familiar with their new legal rights and find ways of enforcing them.

7. The following categories are employed in making age differentiations among Indians I have studied:

INFANCY	0–4 years	Prelingual and dependent.
CHILDHOOD	5–11 "	Lingual, active but prepubescent.
YOUTH	12–20 "	Puberty, marriage, social apprenticeship.
YOUNG ADULTHOOD	21–35 "	Maximum physical contribution to family.
LATER ADULTHOOD	36–50 "	Maximum administrative contribution to family.
OLD AGE	50+ "	*De jure* status, rights to maintenance and "respect."

8. My work in India was made possible by three generous sources to whom I express my heartfelt thanks. From 1960 to 1962, support came in the form of concurrent postdoctoral fellowships from the National Institute of Mental Health. A postdoctoral fellowship from the National Science Foundation facilitated my work in 1959–1960. My first trip to India was in 1954–1955 as a Fulbright Student.

9. Basic data on the *rickshawalla* sample are contained in Tables II and III.

TABLE II

CASTE, ETHNIC AND NATIONAL COMPOSITION OF A SAMPLE OF FIFTY
RICKSHAWALLAS IN LUCKNOW, INDIA, 1959

Community, Nationality, Caste	Traditional Occupation	Current Caste Occupation	Number	
Plains Hindu				(27)
Brahman	Priest	Priest/Cultivator	4	
Thakur	Warrior/Ruler	Cultivator	4	
Ahir	Cowherd	Cowherd/Cultivator	1	
Gujar	Grazer	Cultivator	1	
Kurmi	Cultivator	Cultivator	1	
Murau	Veg. Cultivator	Cultivator	2	
Kumhar	Potter	Cultivator	1	
Kahar	Water Carrier	Variable occupations	4	
Kori	Weaver	Menial occupations	2	
Jaiswara	Scavenger/Tanner	Menial occupations	5	
Chamar	Scavenger/Tanner	Scavenger/Menial occupations	1	
Luniya	Grave digger	Menial occupations	1	
Nepali Hindu				(4)
Chetri	Warrior	Variable occupations	4	
Muslim	Non-Hindu	Variable occupations	19	(19)
Total			50	(50)

TABLE III

AGE, MARITAL STATUS AND RESIDENCE OF FIFTY BICYCLE
RICKSHAWALLAS IN LUCKNOW, INDIA, 1959

Age Category	Rural No.	Per Cent	Urban No.	Per Cent	Married No.	Per Cent	Unmarried No.	Per Cent	Total No.	Per Cent
Youth (12–20)	5	16	6	33	2	18	9	82	11	22
Young Adulthood (21–35)	20	63	12	67	17	53	15	47	32	64
Later Adulthood (36–50)	5	16	–	–	3	60	2	40	5	10
Old Age (above 50)	2	5	–	–	1	50	1	50	2	4
Totals	32	100	18	100	23	46	27	54	50	100

10. Harold A. Gould, "The Adaptive Functions of Caste in Contemporary Indian Society," *Asian Survey*, Vol. III (September 1963), pp. 427–438.

Religion as Resistance to Resignation

KARL H. POTTER

University of Minnesota

It is India's "spirituality," her constant attention to matters usually referred to as "religious," which Indian apologists regularly point to as that country's unique and outstanding contribution to world civilization. "Everything in India," they say, "is imbued with religion." But what exactly do these writers mean when they say such things? How are we, outside the fold, to assess the truth of such assertions, since we do not understand what Indians mean by "religion," and since in fact we understand only poorly our own concept of the word. Our Western dictionaries provide definitions of religion which ill fit the Indian context, if they fit at all. The purpose of this paper, therefore, is to see if a definition of "religion" in the Indian sense of the word can be found which will substantiate the above claims.

For this purpose we must avoid Western preconceptions and search Indian writings for clues. In this procedure I side with those who look to textual studies to illuminate Indian practice, and with traditional Indologists who emphasize the "big tradition" at the expense of little traditions. It is in the classical writings that are found the purest expression of India's aspirations. Emphasis on the texts, however, should not preclude the checking of our findings with contemporary village attitudes and practices. In recent years, some anthropologists have voiced suspicion of "literati" interpretations of Hinduism; it seems equally justifiable to suspect the reports of villagers, who are notoriously unclear as to the origins of their beliefs. The proper course is surely the interpretation of village lore as approximations to a norm identifiable by consulting authoritative scriptures.

Among the major texts of the great tradition of Hinduism, the *Bhagavadgītā* rightly deserves major attention. Western students of India are constantly frustrated when they try to gather from this poem the essence of Indian religion, and recently they have had a tendency to deplore Krishna's teaching as maverick and to find special explanations for its popularity. Yet it seems to me that Krishna's teaching provides a direct means of understanding the essence of Indian spirituality if we are not hampered by our preconceptions. Briefly I wish to set forth what I think is the heart of Krishna's philosophy and to suggest some of its implications and applications for the understanding of the Indian scene.

As is well-known, Krishna advises Arjuna to adopt an attitude of non-attachment to the fruits of his actions. Arjuna thinks he has to choose between action and inaction. If he acts and fights, he will destroy the most basic of all institutions, the family, for on the other side of the battle lines are ranged many of his kinsfolk. If he does not act, he will produce the same result in another way, for if he fails to fight, the Kauravas will probably win, and righteousness (that is, the inheritance of the kingdom by the Pandavas) will not prevail. Yet, at least if he does not fight, he cannot be held responsible for the actual destruction of traditional institutions, and so he lays down his arms.

Arjuna's dilemma has nothing to do with activism or pacifism. He does not propose to request or, by his example, to persuade everyone else to lay down his arms. The war will take place whether he takes part in it or not. The question is one of individual ethics, not the ethics of society. In Hindu thought, societies are not conceived of as making decisions. Instead, individuals make decisions, and their decisions are measured against the requirements of religiosity.

For an understanding of Arjuna's dilemma, one basic point must be kept in mind: namely, that Arjuna assumes that the traditional institutions must be maintained. Family, caste, society as they existed before this awful battle must be maintained if possible, but the apparent impossibility of maintaining them causes Arjuna to be afraid.[1] But why should it matter whether traditional institutions are maintained? Here the Western reader has difficulty in imagining the full pressure of Arjuna's dilemma. The maintenance of the family is not that important for us today, and as for caste distinctions the Westerner not only places little value in them, he believes they should be abolished. The difference between Western assumptions and Arjuna's assumptions on this point is, I believe, crucial. We tend to think of institutions (such as the family or caste) as agencies for obtaining goods for the collective membership, whereas Arjuna looks upon these institutions as organizations for protecting the potential for freedom of each participating member.

Here, if I am correct, is the key to the connection between the esoteric philosophy of the *Gītā* and the popular attitudes of ordinary Indians; the key is this conservative attitude toward institutions. Hitherto many writers have noted the strong role tradition plays in Indian society, but to my knowledge no one has suggested before that spirituality or religiosity in India consists precisely of this attitude of upholding tradition. It is my belief that this attitude constitutes a large part of the essence of religion in Hinduism.

If this assumption is correct what is the relevance of Krishna's instruction? Why should the attitude of non-attachment to the fruits of one's actions be regarded as deeply religious when religiosity is defined as the maintenance of institutions? For an answer to these queries we must first recall that the original philosophy of the Vedic peoples turned on the idea of sacrifice to gain power. Again, the Western scholar finds it difficult to dissociate the idea of power from that of goods-seeking; for him the powerful man is one who owns much land or money, or who wields much influence in securing advantages for himself and for those who serve him. But from the Indian point of view a person might hold such material wealth and exercise such influence and yet be a person of very little power in the special Indian sense of the term. In this latter sense a man who is at the mercy of "internal" limitations is a man of little power regardless of his wealth and political hegemony. Although in the Upaniṣads the sage Yajñavalkya is always asking for cattle as his prize for answering questions correctly, such an example may be misleading. The power that the Indian tradition venerates is that of the man with capacity for knowledgeable and discriminating action. Whatever enlarges a man's vision and capacity for incisive action is *dharma*; whatever blocks his vision and stultifies his capacity is *adharma*. Krishna's message is perfectly in consonance with this view; it is precisely his thesis that goal-seeking attitudes block one's vision and stultify one's capacity for discriminating activity.

By seeking goal-objects we make ourselves dependent upon their attainment, and in so doing we lose full control of ourselves. Being therefore unable to see situations fully and clearly, we can, as a result of our desires, be used by others for their devices. But if we refuse to allow desires to obscure our vision and limit our capacity for spontaneous action, we maintain power. Thus the adoption of an attitude of non-attachment to the fruits of actions is the logical advice for Krishna to give.

Insofar as we allow ourselves to become controlled by our desires for objects, we resign ourselves to dependence upon other objects and other people.[2] By resisting this resignation, we maintain our capacity to know and act intelligently. And this attitude of resistance to resignation, this "vigilance" as the *Gītā* puts it, is recognized by Indians at large as the essence of spirituality. Hinduism celebrates this attitude, and is undermined by anything which frustrates it.

This, then, is the message of Krishna, and, if I am right, the basis of Indian religion. As a philosophy, it has many conservative features. It postulates an original state of complete power (self-possession), and tells us that over the years men have fallen away from that state (*viz.* the well-known theory of the four "eras" [yuga]).[3] Moreover, this philosophy limits the proper function of institutions to a negative role, that of protecting the individuals from temptations to resignation. Arjuna, a product of orthodox Hindu thinking, presupposes that institutions must be maintained because institutions properly function to preserve what remains of the original power in men against the continual onslaught of evil desires and hatreds.

And yet it is by those very same institutions that power is destroyed. For institutions are two-faced: good men submit to them to preserve their power, but evil men use institutional affiliations to seek goals, and thus institutions breed resignation. Goal-seeking and surrender to desires by some people cause the religious zealot to stiffen his hold on tradition, an attitude which will brook no deviation from the procedure which enabled these institutions to maintain the power of each of their members to retain full control of himself.

What sort of institutions am I thinking of? The family and caste institutions come quickly to mind. These are natural institutions which grew out of the need to establish an individual's role among other people in such a way that he was provided with the minimum physical needs for survival while leaving him spiritually free to concentrate on self-improvement. With such objectives the village divided itself into units, each of which had different roles to perform. A village which functioned harmoniously was one which provided each of its individuals maximum opportunity to attain spiritual betterment. An individual grew up within institutions comprehensible to him and whose changes he could predict. By anticipating changes he could avoid threats to his welfare. Being thus provided with a minimal standard of living, he desired no more. Indeed, to desire more would be irreligious, since desires are symptomatic of resignation, that is, they represent relinquishment of control over oneself to external factors. This belief explains the critical attitude of the orthodox Hindu to the artificial institutions of contemporary society.

Despite this critical attitude, orthodox Hindus continue to form new institutions. New institutions are formed when individuals are threatened, and the orthodox Hindu today is very much threatened by democratic, welfare-seeking institutions. Just as the family existed to serve basic needs, so the rationale of the caste was to provide for minimal living. Today the Jan Sangh exists to protect Hinduism from erosion by modern social ideas.

If the heart of Indian religion be this resistance to resignation (to domination by other things or persons), then what may be said of the external manifestations of religion, the worship of gods, animals, and men? I think that two factors are involved in these manifestations. One is the idea of divinity, of pure power, manifesting itself in certain individuals or gods who thus deserve reverence and emulation. The other is the function of divinities as symbols to which to pray for succor. These two factors are of completely different orders. The expression of reverence for superior beings stems from the power philosophy which I have identified with Indian religion. The need for the projection of symbolic entities to which to pray stems from a quite different source which I would describe as "medical." I need not rehearse the well-known origins of such ideas in primitive superstitions, nor can I here review the data which anthropologists have collected on the folkways of primitive tribes in India, or the speculations of specialists concerning the growth of such beliefs through the years. Nevertheless, spectators of the Indian scene have regularly identified these two aspects of Indian religious practice as jointly generating "Hinduism." In part, as I have tried to suggest, the failure to distinguish between these two distinctly different concepts is due to the application to India of Western preconceptions. However, this is not the whole problem, for there are connections between the medical and the resistance-to-resignation conceptions of religion.

One connection stems from the willingness of the guardians of the resistance-to-resignation concept of religion—the Brahmans—to make use of any and all popular beliefs to help instill and reinforce religion among the common people. The Brahmans did not live on an ethereal plane far removed from the ordinary folk and their more or less primitive superstitions. Instead these clever, innovative priests quickly seized any movement arising among the common people and used it to illustrate their tenets of proper Hinduism. Rarely indeed did these priests allow an anti-Hindu movement to gain any momentum. Besides being expedient policy, this assimilation of rival views was dictated by the logic of the Brahmans' philosophy which was to avoid creating stress among individuals, for stress was likely to breed those goal-seeking attitudes which undermine the power of everyone involved. As a result of this assimilation, Hinduism to the external viewer appears to have differing forms from one age to the next. For instance, the Vedic sacrificial cult, the classical philosophy of *moksa* or *Nirvana,* and the *bhakti* cults of medieval times may seem, instead of different manifestations of a common spirit, the successive developments of differing local traditions. However, I hope to have suggested here that there is a common philosophy underlying these various manifestations, that the root attitude remains the same, even though the form under which the philosophy shows itself from age to age may differ.

It is important not to confuse these two types of religious manifestation, for worship in the primitive or "medical" sense may be inimical to the concept of resistance-to-resignation. The primitive man prays for succor in the same spirit with which he would go to a doctor if he knew one whom he could trust. His prayers are offered in situations which are beyond his control but in which he would take action if he possessed the requisite knowledge and capability.

As long as what is at stake is the means to minimal livelihood, religion as resistance to resignation has no objection, for this latter philosophy is put into practice only after a minimal standard of living has been attained. As soon as men start asking their gods for more than the minimum, however, the conceptions of religion as medicine and of religion as resistance to resignation diverge sharply. When one prays for more than one needs, one is confessing his desire for objects as well as his inability to attain these objects by means available to him. The concept of "minimum standards" varies from individual to individual and is dependent upon one's stage of spiritual advancement. However, the point is that the "medical" approach to religion is consonant with goal-seeking, while the attitude of resistance to resignation is opposed to goal-seeking. Confusion arises when the term "religion" is applied to embrace both of these types. Yet nearly everyone who has written in Western languages about Indian religion has made this mistake.

If we choose to distinguish between these two attitudes, then I think we would not say that "everything in India is imbued with religion." I have tried to suggest that an appeal to gods for material betterment beyond the requirements for survival would be antithetical to the true Indian conception of religiosity. As long as we continue to amalgamate the medical and resistance-to-resignation attitudes, our understanding of the true thrust of a particular Indian religious movement will remain unclear. This lack of clarity has enabled exponents of India's spiritual superiority to distort India's past by posing Hinduism in Western terms. As a result, Westerners who have not studied India carefully have become convinced that all Indian philosophy is mystical, that Indians at large spend more time in spiritual exercises than other peoples, that the general Indian attitude is "other-worldly" or "world-negating," and so forth. But each of these beliefs is even less than a half-truth, applicable only to a small proportion of Indians past or present.

NOTES

1. See *Bhagavadgītā*, I, 28 ff.
2. The special sense of "resignation" understood here is discussed in more detail in my book, *Presuppositions of India's Philosophies* (Englewood Cliffs, N. J.: Prentice-Hall, 1963), pp. 15–19.

3. According to one version of this bit of Indian mythology, each cycle of creation, lasting for millions of years, follows a pattern wherein men begin with their *dharma* perfected, and proceed gradually to lose their *dharma* until eventually they arrive at the fourth age, our age, in which men have only one quarter of their original *dharma* left. See, e.g., Heinrich Zimmer, *Myths and Symbols in Indian Art and Civilization*, ed. Joseph Campbell (Pantheon Books: Bollingen Press, 1946), pp. 13–14. There are many versions of this myth, some widely different from this one.

Saṁsāra Revalued

WINSTON L. KING

Vanderbilt University

Almost from time immemorial Saṁsāra—the Hindu-Buddhist name for the mode of ever-changing or becoming, space-time, birth-death existence in which all sentient beings participate—has been devalued by both Hinduism and Buddhism. For the Theravāda Buddhist, indeed, Saṁsāra is the best possible synonym for all that is fundamentally evil in the universe. Signifying "continued passing on into new existences" it is that quality of existence which calls most insistently for salvation from it. Nor does it matter greatly that at some levels in the thirty-one planes of existence[1]—say the Brahma-lokas of immaterial and almost infinitely long duration— existence is *relatively* more pleasant than in one of the deeper, hotter hells. In the final analysis *all* individuated existence is indelibly marked by the three signs: *anicca* (impermanence), *dukkha* (dis-ease or suffering), and *anattā* (insubstantiality or no-souledness). Life, or existence, is a malady to be remedied; a torment-house of infinite frustration to be escaped.

To be sure, not all Buddhists give the appearance of suffering from an incurable alienation from life, least of all Burmese Buddhists. For just as the average Christian is able to make out fairly well with at least a few minor joys in this vale of tears, so the average Buddhist is able to adapt emotionally to the prospect of a few thousand more existences or so in Saṁsāra. The majority indeed have no stomach for Nibbāna, immediately and forthwith at least. Nevertheless, the Buddhist pessimism with regard to the worth of Saṁsāra, and the proposed remedy of complete detachment from saṁsāric goods and evils, hopes and fears, have pervasively affected Buddhist cultures. Not only is there a certain paradoxical insouciance, so to speak, about the fate of the world—for should it achieve perdition, how greatly different would this be from its present condition? But, more fundamentally and Buddhistically, who can *do* anything about

Saṁsāra? Saṁsāra is incurably incurable; the only way to improve upon it is to be individually rid of it.

Yet, unexpectedly, in these latter days Theravāda Buddhism is revaluing Saṁsāra. Not all thirty-one planes of it equally to be sure, but most particularly the human plane. This is not only in keeping with the obviously greater availability of this latter realm for consideration and possible action, but is in keeping with the unique nature of human-level existence as compared to other existence-levels. For, says Buddhism, only on the human plane can Saṁsāra be remedied even by escape from it. Yet in somewhat *non*-Buddhist fashion it is today proposed that some improvement may be, and possibly ought to be, wrought in Saṁsāra itself. But one must hasten to add that such improvement as is now proposed is proposed under cover of the impossibility of such improvement, and thus becomes an intricate exercise in both having and not having the orthodox pleasures of other-worldliness.

We may begin by observing that this process of sub rosa, almost unconscious, change of saṁsāric substance is accompanied by staunch affirmations and reaffirmations of the traditional devaluation of Saṁsāra. How can such things be? Obviously, the very fervor of the contemporary affirmation of orthodoxy is an indication of the strong pressure under which that orthodoxy labors today in seeking to maintain continuity of its tradition in a changing world; of the magnitude of the change actually taking place in Buddhism; and is witness to a deep and largely subconscious guilt with regard to the progress of that alteration of orthodoxy.

We shall, therefore, not expect to find direct evidences of the positive revaluation of Saṁsāra in the form of any explicit announcement of change, nor in the glorification of religious modernity, nor even in any hypocritical double-faced presentations of differing orthodoxies to different groups. It is both more simple and subtle than this. *What is occurring is the recommendation of orthodoxy (in all good faith) as unchanging, but with this the unconscious employment of the terms and values of the "opposition,"* i.e. non-Buddhist secularism. For the Buddhist preacher today in Burma speaks approvingly of saṁsāric involvement as often as of nibbānic detachment; and of the twentieth-century Christian-secular values in Buddhism as eagerly as first-century Buddhist-monastic virtues.

There is, for instance, the immense vogue of the words "science" and "scientific." Now for the Buddhist East science represents (1) the primary and outstanding accomplishment of Western-Christian intellectual genius, and (2) the twentieth-century technological revolution with all its products. And here is a prime instance of ambivalent cake-eating and cake-having. For superficially, at least, the East discounts and distrusts scientific development *in toto* as evidence of the West's unspiritual, decadently-religious materialism. And it points to the encroachments of Western commercialism and industrialism, to the West's engendering of personal and international strife, as the essence of enshrined greed. Yet on the other hand, and with equal vigor, Buddhist apologetic goes out of its way to prove that Buddhism not only has nothing to fear from the advancement of scientific thought, but is in fact itself the essence of the scientific spirit. Thus:

(1) The Buddha might have devoted himself to science, and could have made all of the modern scientific discoveries some 2,500 years ago had he so desired; but he deliberately turned to the more important realm of the mind, yet in a truly scientific, self-validating manner proceeded to analyze the inner life of man and to set forth as experimentally confirmed truth the way to salvation.

(2) However, when, in the course of discussions concerning salvation, the Buddha *did* make reference to physical matters, his words were infallibly true, and indicate a knowledge of which science has only now become aware. For example: his description of grain-of-dust smallness is clearly anticipatory of the atom; his doctrine of a causally ordered flux comprising all that exists (perpetual change governed by dharmic order) is only now being discovered by physics; the fluxing nature of human consciousness and so-called selfhood, long known to the Buddhist meditator, is only now hailed as a new discovery by Western psychologists; parapsychology, it is held, is confirming the doctrine of rebirth; a doctor affirms that the Buddha described stages of the human foetus as yet imperceptible by microscope; a layman writing to a newspaper asserts that when once men land on the moon they will discover the Buddha's measurement of it was more accurate than any of the guesses astronomers have made.[2] And no less a person than the Honorable U Nu, then premier of Burma, in a speech in New York in 1955, invited ten selected, scientifically-minded individuals who truly wished to prove for themselves the absolute

truth of Buddhist teaching, to be guests of the Burmese government at a meditation center.[3]

How shall we evaluate this? It is, of course, legitimate, from the Buddhist point of view, to suit the truth to the individual and his age; indeed, how can he otherwise apprehend it? Hence the only way to prove the truth of Buddhism to prospective converts in a scientifically indoctrinated age is to demonstrate its *scientific* truth. Yet one gains the impression that many Buddhists themselves would like to be assured on these matters.

Cosmologically, of course, there is considerable room and fluidity for harmonious adjustment, because Buddhism is the inheritor of the Indian religious-philosophical imagination which in fine careless raptures could speak as easily of a billion years as we speak of a fortnight, and speak of ten thousand times ten million universes as readily as we speak of Main Street. Yet inevitably there must still be a major overhaul of ideas even here. There is for instance the matter of Mount Meru,[4] the central earth-mountain, and its spatially related planes of existence. There is also the thought-world of *nat*- (earth, air, water-spirit)[5] worship, so real to the average Burmese Buddhist, so much a part of traditional Buddhist vocabulary. Much of this will disappear with the full advent of science. But, since planes of existence are also integrally tied to meditational states, they can perhaps be symbolized into acceptable contemporary forms. And the infinite framework of ever-changing universes, so fundamental to Buddhist thought in general, renders thought-forms about *particular* universes relatively unimportant in the long run. How flexible literalistic Theravāda Buddhism can be in such matters remains to be seen, however.

There is a second area of sub rosa transformation—the new stress on practical-social values. Of course Nibbāna is still officially the supreme good for all Buddhists. But the words of the critics of Buddhism, including some home-grown communists, to the effect that Buddhism is good *only* for world-denial, are in turn stoutly denied. This comes out in several ways:

(1) The scriptures are searched for instances of the Buddha's practical prescriptions for the life of the layman and these are hailed as complete blueprints for world peace.

(2) Buddhism is declared to be democratic in its view of human nature. Buddha is portrayed as an ardent campaigner against caste

in his day, and karma is interpreted to mean the right of each individual to be himself.

(3) Social service and welfare motivations begin to appear in Buddhist writings, and to be incorporated limitedly even in some programs of the Sangha (order of monks), who by definition are dedicated solely to Nibbāna-seeking.

(4) There is hope on the part of some that the monks can be more broadly educated than at present, and be made more directly useful to society by a strengthening of their traditional role as teachers of the young.

(5) It has been declared several times that socialism and Buddhism are consonant with each other. In his 1960–1962 term as prime minister, indeed, U Nu sought to achieve a Buddhist socialism and was supported by most members of the Sangha. His rationale of the harmony of Buddhism with socialism was stated by him in his 1959–1960 campaign speeches in the following description of the proposed Buddhist-socialist State:

> So under the new society people can spare their surplus money to set up a common pool for the establishment of a Socialist State. This is true Dāna (charity). I believe the Socialist Society has these four virtues: (a) Right view with regard to property; (b) the main emphasis can be put on the achievement of Liberation (i.e., Nibbāna); (c) Sīla, Samādhi and Paññā may become dominant principles in daily life; (d) communal charity becomes possible, and the practice of Dāna (alms-giving) leads to Nibbāna.[6]

To be sure, this plan aborted due to many factors. And the socialism of Ne Win's government is quite different in several important respects from U Nu's Buddhist socialism. Yet even Ne Win's socialism, secular though it may be, is being backed by the Sangha. A recent statement from a senior monks' conclave indicates the lines along which social, political, nationalistic, and religious interests can be made to support each other harmoniously. Quoting from the newspaper account of one monk's speech:

> The Revolutionary Government, he said, stood for the emancipation of the people from the economic strangulation. If the people became prosperous the *Sasana* [i.e., Buddha-teaching] would be well supported. . . .
> When the people became prosperous, evils would lessen, and more

and more would take the path of the *Dhamma*, [for] as the saying [has it] *Sila* [morality] can be kept only on a full stomach.

He also pointed out these further benefits of the attempt of the Revolutionary Government to achieve Burmese socialism:

> This goal, the Sayadaw stated, envisaged a classless society, freedom from want, economic well-being for the entire people, ending exploitation of man by man.
>
> Our Lord, the Sayadaw stated, had also striven for a classless society, and had preached against inordinate greed in making one's livelihood as one of the ways to the blessed goal of Nibbāna.[7]

And with this urging the two hundred monks present unanimously passed a resolution approving the Government's banning of all political parties because they were opposing the march to socialism —including the fragmented Union Party of U Nu, who presently still remains in protective custody.

It should be added that this is the furthest limit of "political" activity encouraged or allowed by the present government for the monks. Ne Win has repeatedly pointed out that:

> The Revolutionary council . . . desires the purity of religion, especially of Buddhism, the religion of the majority of the people of the country, and believes that this task of keeping the Buddha sasana pure should be borne solely by the sanghas.
>
> For this purpose of keeping the Buddha sasana pure, the Revolutionary Council said, the sanghas' sanctity is besmirched by dabbling with the mundane affair of politics.[8]

He further went on to promise the Sangha all possible aid against those who might seek to use it for other than religious purposes. It is of course quite obvious that resurgent nationalism has played, and continues to play, a considerable part in this adaptation of Buddhism to the modern situation. Burmans take great pride in the fact of the large (85 per cent), devout, and traditional Buddhist following in Burma. To be Burman is essentially to be Buddhist; the two can almost be equated—though there has been no persecution of non-Buddhists, by and large, even in these post-British days. Nonetheless the promotion of the welfare of Buddhism is also the promotion of the welfare of Burma, and vice versa, in most Burmese minds.

One more aspect of this adaptation of Buddhism to the contemporary world scene and of its yielding to worldly pressures is to be found in the reinterpretation of its basic imagery and religious vocabulary. Again, and especially here, it is to be noted that the *fact* of adaptation is flatly denied as the rule. If there seems to be change, it is maintained that the one who believes there *is* change is simply mistaken as to the true and traditional meaning of the Buddhist doctrine and practice. But to the outside observer it seems there has been a considerable shift in emphasis from other-worldly-oriented passivity to this-worldly-oriented activity of a hopefully dynamic sort. Since I have dealt with this at length elsewhere[9] I shall here only briefly list some half-dozen manifestations of this new emphasis:

(1) There is the recent emphasis, for a decade or two now, upon the meditating *layman*. Not only does this raise the layman's religious status, so to speak, making him in part at least a co-traveler on the road to Nibbāna with the monk, but has importantly modified the context and connotation of meditation itself, the central discipline of the Buddhist way of life. Meditation becomes useful *both* for this world and for Nibbāna. For, it is held, by the meditational practice of concentration of mind, one becomes capable of greater dispassionateness, objectivity, and concentration in *everything* that he does—while at the same time only by meditation can Nibbāna itself be reached. Therapeutic byproducts, both mental and physical, are also claimed for meditation.

(2) Karma, which has stood for centuries as the primary Buddhist rationale of one's unfortunate lot and the unhappy status quo, and whose connotative flavor has been that of fatedness, is consistently being interpreted as the capacity to *change* one's future self and destiny, here and now, on the spot, and is praised as promoting self-reliance in general.

(3) The Bodhisattva ideal,[10] so central to Mahāyāna Buddhism, is being given an increasing hearing in Theravāda Buddhism. One is sometimes told that there are many instances of self-sacrifice for others in the Buddhist tradition; that it may be better in this world-age to have many more who will deliberately become public servants rather than pursue the career of a Nibbāna-questing monk; and that there is an increasing disposition on the part of some to make Buddha-vows, i.e., turn away from the narrower ideal of achieving Nibbāna as soon as possible for oneself, to the ideal of countless lives of holy, service-filled endeavor to achieve Buddhahood and its

salvation-bringing power in the end. When I once inquired why this then was not indeed the better way, I was given only a prudential reason: The longer way is open to many more possibilities of failure and retrogression.

(4) Equanimity or detachment, the hall-mark of the Nibbāna-farer, is often expressly stated to mean, not neutrality or indifference to things worldly, but on the contrary, a disinterestedness which can meaningfully inform the most active sort of life. One is struck here by the fact that traditionally inaccessible Nibbāna and its values are now being brought nearer to the practical world, indeed ·being quite specifically and definitely related to it. Nor in this same connection can it be viewed as an accident that today much is said about the possibility of achieving nibbānic peace, right here and now in one's daily busy life.

Such then is the general quality of the contemporary Buddhist revaluation of Saṁsāra. The particular forms that this revaluation may take in the future, the nature of its practical applications, and the success of such applications, will depend in part upon the course of future political events in Burma. But unless—and it must be admitted that both of these "unlesses" are not beyond possibility— there is a Communist take-over, or a thoroughgoing secularization of the total cultural life under Burmese Socialism, Theravāda Buddhism in Burma will increasingly seek to remake Saṁsāra nearer heart's desire, even though that heart's desire be Buddhist-ically oriented, and though it be done under the form of the impermanence and utter unworth of that "same" Saṁsāra that is being redone.

NOTES

1. The thirty-one planes of existence represent four nether planes of subhuman existence (hells, disembodied spirits, animals, Titan-like spirits), the human plane, and some twenty-six superhuman planes in which live gods (devas) i.e. men-become-gods through their good deeds. Life in these is progressively longer as one rises in the scale, and is progressively disembodied. In general it is delightful in nature—though still short of Nibbāna, and not leading to it.

2. See author's *A Thousand Lives Away* (Harvard: Harvard University Press, 1965), chapter entitled "Theravada Buddhism Encounters Science."

3. Pamphlet "What is Buddhism?" An address by the Honorable U Nu, Prime Minister of Burma, delivered under sponsorship of New York University, July 6, 1955.

4. Mount Meru, as the central earth-mountain, is an archetype of all universes, according to Buddhist cosmology. Ringing Meru are seven concentric seas each ringed in turn by a circular mountain chain. In the seventh sea are the earth islands; and beyond the seventh sea is the edge of the universe, marked by a mighty circular iron-mountain range. On the slopes and above Meru is the hierarchy of the twenty-six superhuman planes of existence.

5. Nats are demoted devas (from Indian Hinduism), Burmese spirits, ogres, and spirits of departed persons. Their power is over the physical environment of man and they are often prayed to for personal and material success, but never petitioned for salvation in Nibbāna since they too stand in need of such salvation.

6. Quoted, in Winston L. King, *The Hope of Nibbana* (Open Court, 1964), p. 267. (*Nibbāna* is the Pali form of the more widely-known Sanskrit *Nirvana*.) Materials in numbered items from Part II of same volume. *Sīla* means ordinary morality; *Samādhi* means the power of mental concentration gained in meditation, necessary to achieve *Paññā* or wisdom, which in turn is necessary for achieving Nibbāna.

7. *The Guardian*, April 6, 1964. *Dhamma* here means, rather narrowly, the Buddha's teaching about the way of salvation. *Sayadaw* means senior teacher-monk.

8. *The Guardian*, April 19, 1964.

9. King, *In the Hope of Nibbana*, Part II.

10. The Bodhisattva, or Enlightenment Being, is a future Buddha who by his almost endless lives of meritorious deeds will win Buddhahood and Nibbāna, but who will in the end remain one step short of his own Nibbāna to be reincarnated over and over again in Saṁsāra for the salvation of others. This is the chosen ideal of the Mahāyāna Buddhism of China and Japan.